PUBLICATIONS
OF THE
ARMY RECORDS SOCIETY
VOL. 11

LETTERS OF A VICTORIAN ARMY OFFICER
EDWARD WELLESLEY
1840–1854

The Army Records Society was founded in 1984 in order to publish original records describing the development, organisation, administration and activities of the British Army from early times.

Any person wishing to become a Member of the Society is requested to apply to the Hon. Secretary, c/o the National Army Museum, Royal Hospital Road, London, SW3 4HT. The annual subscription entitles the member to receive a copy of each volume issued by the Society in that year, and to purchase back volumes at reduced prices. Current subscription details, whether for individuals living within the British Isles, for individuals living overseas, or for institutions, will be furnished on request.

The Council of the Army Records Society wish it to be clearly understood that they are not answerable for opinions or observations that may appear in the Society's publications. For these the responsibility rests entirely with the Editors of the several works.

Lieutenant-General Sir George Cathcart and his staff on the Orange River Expedition December 1852.
Left to Right: Lt.-Gen. Sir G. Cathcart, Colonel A.J. Cloëté, Lt.-Col. C.Seymour, Capt. E. Wellesley (in light
coat), Capt. Hon. M. Curzon, Lt. A.G. Greville, Capt. Hon. G. Elliot, Lt. Gough. Behind the latter, Capts Knight
and Goderich, Cape Mounted Rifles. (Note 1.)

LETTERS OF A VICTORIAN ARMY OFFICER EDWARD WELLESLEY

Major, 73rd Regiment of Foot
1840–1854

Edited by
MICHAEL CARVER
Field Marshal
his great-grandson

Published by
ALAN SUTTON PUBLISHING LIMITED
for the
ARMY RECORDS SOCIETY
1995

First published in the United Kingdom in 1995
Alan Sutton Publishing Ltd · Phoenix Mill · Far Thrupp · Stroud ·
Gloucestershire

British Library Cataloguing in Publication Data

A catalogue record for this book is available from the British Library

ISBN 0 7509 1079 8

Typeset in Ehrhardt
Typesetting and origination by
Alan Sutton Publishing Limited.
Printed in Great Britain by
Hartnolls, Bodmin, Cornwall.

Contents

Maps

Acknowledgements

The Society is grateful to the following for permission to reproduce maps:

Map 1. *The Eastern Frontier of Cape Colony*: to Random House UK Ltd, from *Remember You Are An Englishman* by Joseph Lehmann.

Map 2. *The Action at Berea*: to The Earl Cathcart, from his copy of *Correspondence of Lieutenant-General The Hon. Sir George Cathcart KCB relative to his Military Operations in Kaffraria until the Termination of the Kafir War and to His Measures for the Future Maintenance of Peace on that Frontier and the Protection and Welfare of The People of South Africa*.

Map 3. *Turkey and the Crimea*: to Arms and Armour Press, from *Raglan* by John Sweetman.

Introduction

Edward John Wellesley was the father of my mother's father, Courtenay Wellesley. He was the second son of Richard Wellesley, the eldest son of Richard, 2nd Earl of Mornington, created Marquess Wellesley in the Irish peerage and Baron Wellesley in that of England. The Marquess was Governor-General of India from 1798 to 1805, Ambassador to the Spanish Junta in 1809, Foreign Secretary 1810–12 and Viceroy of Ireland from 1821-8 and 1833–5. He had four brothers and a sister. The first was William, who changed his name to Wellesley-Pole on inheriting a legacy, and was created Lord Maryborough in 1821 towards the end of a rather undistinguished political career; the second was Arthur, the famous Duke of Wellington; the third Gerald, who took holy orders and finished his clerical career as Prebendary of Durham; and the fourth Henry, later Lord Cowley, who was Private Secretary to his eldest brother in India and Spain, succeeding him there as Ambassador until 1822, when he was transferred to Vienna until 1835, serving in the same post in Paris 1841–6. The sister, Anne, married first The Honourable Henry Fitzroy, and, after his early death, Mr Charles Culling Smith. Many of their descendants are mentioned in the correspondence.

When visiting Paris in 1786, while Arthur was at the French Royal Cavalry School at Angers, Lord Wellesley met and fell in love with Hyacinthe Gabrielle, a beautiful and lively young lady 'on the stage', who used the surname of her mother's husband, Monsieur Rolland, although her real father is believed to have been an Irishman, who called himself the Chevalier Fagan and served as a cavalry officer in the prerevolutionary French army. Wellesley brought her over to England as his mistress and had five children by her before he married her in 1794. She did not accompany him to India and, on his return, they quarrelled, separating in 1809. She died in 1816. In 1825 Wellesley married an American widow, Marianne Paterson, by whom he had no children. He died in 1842. Lord Wellesley's children were therefore illegitimate, and his titles passed on his death to Lord Maryborough, who himself died in 1845, when they descended to his son, another William, a disreputable character,[2] whose only son died unmarried in 1863, when the titles passed to descendants of the Duke of Wellington. The Marquess's children were Richard, Edward's father; Anne, who ran away from her first husband, Sir William Abdy, with Lord Charles Bentinck, whom she later married; Hyacinthe, who married Lord Hatherton;[3] Gerald, who served as a district officer in India, where he died unmarried, but leaving three daughters by his Indian mistress; and Henry, who became Dean of Windsor. Richard did not live up to his father's ambitions for him. Having worked for his father in Spain, he entered Parliament as Member for Queensborough in 1810, switching to East Grinstead in 1812, and then to Yarmouth in the Isle of Wight until 1817. He was greatly affected by his mother's death and thereafter was on bad terms with his father. Having twice attempted suicide, he died in 1831. His wife was Jane Chambers, daughter of George Chambers, son of the famous architect Sir William Chambers, her mother being a daughter of Admiral Lord Rodney. They had five children. The eldest, Richard, to whom most of these letters were written, was born in 1821, entered the Foreign Office as a Clerk in 1839, and married Mary Drummond, by whom he had no children. The second son, born in 1823, was Edward, author of these letters, of whom more below. The third, born in 1826, was Hyacinthe, who at the time of these letters was unmarried and living with her widowed mother. Later she married Sir Victor Houlton who, from 1855 to 1883, was Chief Secretary to the Government of Malta. She died in 1897, having had no children. The fourth, born in 1827, was Gerald, who appears to have started life in the navy, but in 1854 seems to have suffered some sort of nervous breakdown. In 1849 he married Emma Boys. The youngest, born in 1831, was Augustus, whom Edward accuses of lack of ambition [39]. He married Clare Ashmore in 1854, when he worked in the Ordnance Department. They had six children, whose descendants are the only ones of the Marquess still to bear the name of Wellesley.

Edward, straight from Eton at the age of 16, obtained a commission in the 25th Regiment, no doubt through the influence of its commanding officer, his uncle Lieutenant-Colonel Courtenay Chambers. He went with them to South Africa in 1840 [1] and was probably not with them when they went on to India in 1842. Prospects of promotion to captain in that regiment appearing slow, he obtained a transfer to the 73rd Regiment in 1844. This appears to have been through the influence of Lord Fitzroy Somerset,[4] who was Military Secretary to the Commander-in-Chief at the Horse Guards, then, for the second time, Edward's great-uncle, the Duke of Wellington, whose first commission had been in that regiment [49]. Lord Fitzroy was also a relation, having married Emily, second of Lord Maryborough's three daughters. The regiment was in Ireland when Edward joined them, gaining a captaincy in 1848, when he was adjutant of their depôt, to which he was appointed in 1846 [5] when it was at Clare Castle. In May 1849, at Fermoy, Co. Cork, he married Hannah, known as Annot, Morse, daughter of Sarah and John Morse, about whom nothing is known, except that on their marriage certificate he is described as Merchant. It would appear from some of the correspondence that she was not previously well known to his family. Their first child, my grandfather Courtenay Edward, was born in 1850. When they set sail for South Africa in March 1851, she appears to have come directly from Ireland to Holyhead, before embarking at Southampton [7].

On arrival at Cape Town at the end of April, he went up country to join his regiment, leaving his wife, now pregnant, and son in the Castle barracks at the Cape. After commanding a company in action, he was, in July, appointed to the staff of the Governor and Commander-in-Chief, Lieutenant-General Sir Harry Smith,[5] as Deputy Assistant Adjutant-General. The Governor's headquarters, from which he was directing operations in the Amatola Mountains, was at King William's Town. Edward Wellesley wrote frequently to his wife and approximately monthly to his brother Richard, occasionally to Richard's wife, Mary, and to his mother. Their second child, christened Hyacinthe, was born at Cape Town on 5 October 1851.

No letters to his wife in South Africa after 9 December 1851 have survived, and there is no indication in his letters to his brother as to whether he ever got down to Cape Town to see her and the children.

In April 1852 Sir Harry Smith was replaced by Lieutenant-General Sir George Cathcart,[6] who, in December 1852, led the Orange River expedition against the Basuto, in which Edward was slightly wounded in the action at Berea [53]. Soon after this, the Kaffir War (the 7th) came to an end, and in August 1853 brevet promotions were announced, rewarding the participants, including Edward's to the rank of major. As his post was established in the rank of captain, and there was no vacancy for a major with his regiment, he was posted home, he and his family travelling back to England by sailing ship, the voyage lasting from 31 December 1853 to 10 March 1854, his wife apparently suffering a miscarriage about two weeks before they landed [65].

Very shortly after his arrival, he was appointed to the staff of Lord

Raglan (as Lord Fitzroy Somerset had become) as Assistant Quartermaster-General, and set off on 10 April with him for Turkey, travelling by Paris, where they were fêted by Napoleon III, Marseilles and Malta. His wife Annot, having initially stayed with his brother Richard, later joined his mother and sister Hyacinthe. Lord Raglan's headquarters was first established at Scutari, on the opposite shore of the Bosphorus to Istanbul (or Constantinople as it was usually called then), moving to Varna in Bulgaria in June 1854. There are no letters to Annot after that. His last letter to his brother [107] was written on board ship as he sailed from Varna to the Crimea, where Edward died of cholera on the day of the Battle of The Alma, 20 September 1854, at the age of 31. His widow was granted a Grace and Favour apartment in Hampton Court Palace from 1859 until her death in 1878, a year before that of her mother-in-law.

These letters were left to me, together with a large number of private papers of Lord Wellesley's and some of his son Richard's, by my uncle Richard Wellesley, who had no children. His father, Courtenay, had inherited them from Hyacinthe, Lady Houlton. I kept these letters back, when I gave all the others to the Hartley Library of Southampton University in 1987, after they had been used by Iris Butler in her biography of the Marquess.[7] They have never been published before. Edward's letters to his wife, with some exceptions [81, 83, 87, 92] were transcribed and typed by my mother before she married my father in 1911; the originals have not survived; the others are original holographs which I have transcribed and typed. All of them will join the other papers in the Hartley Library.

I have reproduced the letters exactly as they were written whatever the idiosyncracies of the spelling and punctuation. The principal one of the former is Edward's spelling of 'Kaffir' as 'Kafir', in his earlier letters even 'Cafir'. He uses the term generally to refer to the Bantu Xhosa tribes against whom the British were fighting, but sometimes to mean any African native. His punctuation is sparse, often using commas or semi-colons where a full stop would be more normal. In the ones my mother typed, she has clearly corrected these idiosyncracies, as comparison with his other letters, written at the same time, show.

Figures in square brackets refer to one of the letters.

I
South Africa 1840–1853

Britain acquired the Dutch colony of the Cape of Good Hope during the Napoleonic wars, when Holland was forced into the French camp, and managed to hold on to it in the Treaty of Vienna which concluded them. Its purpose, in British eyes, was strategic: as a staging post on the route to India. Having acquired it, the British government found itself saddled with the security problems of the Dutch colonists, especially of the farmers (Boers) who were widely scattered over a huge area, extending hundreds of miles northeastwards from the Cape itself. While they had been establishing their presence, the aboriginal African inhabitants, generally referred to as Hottentots, were in the process of being forced out of their ancestral grazing grounds by a Bantu people, making their way south, the various tribes of which were described as Xhosa. Their culture, like that of the Hottentots, was based on cattle grazing. The result was a direct clash between them and the Dutch farmers.

The British government immediately faced a classic colonial problem. Its sole interest was strategic. It had no desire to expend money and men on protecting Boer farmers; but, under political pressure from its Liberal opponents, backed by religious and anti-slavery groups, it could not let the Boers deal with the problem by the brutal methods they had hitherto employed. The solution found, which would also help to alleviate agricultural depression and unemployment among ex-soldiers at home, was to encourage Britons to emigrate, given free grants of land, who would combine farming with the provision of a local security force, thus avoiding the need to provide a military force at the Treasury's expense.

This policy was adopted, at a cost of £50,000, in 1820, and was not a success. Few of the settlers knew anything about farming and the land they were allotted was in many cases unsuitable [50]. It only added to the security problem. At that time the Fish river had been declared as the boundary between 'settled' and 'Kaffir' land, the area beyond it, up to the Keiskamma river, being declared 'ceded' or 'neutral', but the settlers, Boer and British, took little notice of this.

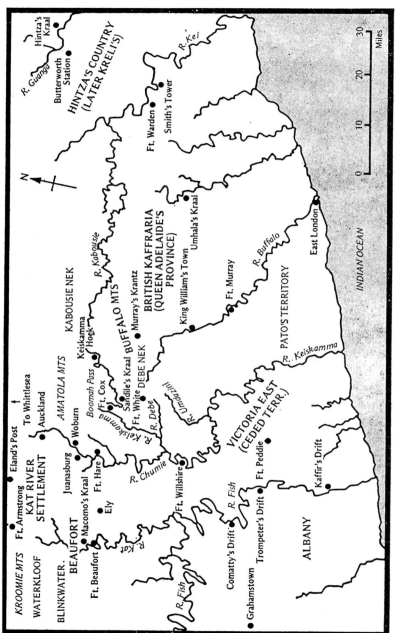

The Eastern Frontier of Cape Colony.

Matters came to a head at Christmas 1834, a year after the appointment of Lieutenant-General Sir Benjamin d'Urban[8] as Governor, when 15,000 Xhosa, led by Macomo, Chief of the Gaika tribe, swept over the frontier, plundering, burning and killing, forcing many of the settlers to abandon their farms and take refuge in Grahamstown. D'Urban appointed Colonel Harry Smith, his Deputy Quartermaster-General, as commander of the regular and burgher[9] troops and his deputy. Smith immediately rode on a succession of horses to Grahamstown, covering the 600 (some say 700) miles in six days. There were only 800 regular troops, under the command of Lieutenant-Colonel Somerset,[10] scattered about in fortified posts in the frontier area. Recruiting burghers as reinforcements, Smith crossed the Fish river in February 1835, cleared the area up to the Keiskamma and on beyond it to the Kei. There he began negotiations with the powerful Chief Hintza, who was supposed to exert some sort of control over Macomo and other Xhosa Chiefs. An agreement was reached by which Hintza was to deliver a large number of cattle, said to have been stolen from the settlers. When Smith, with a small body of Hottentot troops, was accompanying Hintza to supervise their collection, the latter tried to escape and was killed. His son, Kreli, accepted Smith's terms, and further negotiations with the other Chiefs brought the fighting to an end by the end of the year, d'Urban announcing that the whole area between the Fish and the Kei rivers was annexed and to be called Queen Adelaide Province, of which Smith was appointed Lieutenant-Governor.

While he was being acclaimed by the burghers as their saviour and was presiding over a ceremony at which the Xhosa Chiefs were forced to kiss his feet and accept him as their *Inkosi Inkulu* or Super-Chief, a very different view was being taken in London. In April 1835 Lord Melbourne succeeded Sir Robert Peel as Prime Minister and appointed Lord Glenelg[11] as Secretary for War and Colonies, when pressure for the abolition of the slave trade was at its height. He instituted a Court of Inquiry into the circumstances of the death of Hintza and, on 26 December, sent a 150-page despatch to d'Urban, which arrived at the Cape in March 1836. In it he said that 'the Kaffirs had ample justification for the war'; expressed his displeasure that they had been referred to by d'Urban as 'irreclaimable savages'; and that the 'wanton and indiscriminate manner' in which Smith's troops 'destroyed the dwellings and food of these virtually defenceless people' showed that they were 'motivated by feelings of revenge' and that their conduct had been 'unbecoming of soldiers wearing His Majesty's uniform'. Rejecting

Smith's version of Hintza's death, he concluded by stating that 'the original justice is on the side of the conquered, not the victorious party', and demanded that the newly acquired province should be abandoned and all troops withdrawn from it by the end of the year. Smith was to be replaced as Lieutenant-Governor of the Eastern Province by Andries Stockenström, a Swede brought up in the colony. Smith resumed his post of DQMG until he left for India in 1840, shortly after Edward Wellesley's first arrival at the Cape [1], d'Urban having been replaced by Lieutenant-General Sir George Napier[12] in January 1838.

Glenelg's policy stemmed from pressure exerted by the evangelist James Stephen of the Clapham Sect, fed with critical reports from Dr John Philip of the London Missionary Society at the Cape, and supported by Thomas Fowell Buxton, chairman of the Parliamentary Select Committee which investigated the treatment of indigenous people in the colonies. Its application led to a massive exodus of Boers, seeking a new life where they were not subject to such pressure and could provide their own security by their own methods. Thousands trekked north across the Orange river or northeast to Natal. The British government was not prepared to see that area converted into a Boer republic, and, after an armed clash with the Boers, led by Andries Pretorius, it was formally annexed in August 1843, provoking another Boer exodus to the north. At the end of the year Sir George Napier was replaced by another Peninsular War veteran, the 68-year-old Lieutenant-General Sir Peregrine Maitland.[13]

Glenelg's policy did not remove the grievances of the Xhosa nor the temptation provided by the presence of the settler's herds, while the exodus of Boers made security more difficult to provide. In March 1846 an incident at Fort Beaufort sparked off major trouble with the Gaikas, led by Sandile, Macomo's half-brother. Colonel John Hare, who had succeeded Stockenström as Lieutenant-Governor of the Eastern Province, and the commander of the troops, Colonel Somerset, were slow to move. It took a month to assemble 2,000 regulars[14] and 1,500 Hottentot irregulars, accompanied by 125 ox-drawn wagons, to advance upon Sandile's kraal, which they found deserted. Pursuing him into the Amatola mountains, they were ambushed, losing 15 men killed and 14 wounded, and being forced to withdraw, leaving behind 61 wagons and 800 oxen.

This disaster led to a major crisis, settlers grouping themselves for mutual defence, their plight made worse by a severe drought. Tribes, which before had sided with the government against the Gaika, now joined with the latter in plunder and pillage. In spite of his age, Maitland took the field in person, having been reinforced by the 90th Regiment, which was on its way to Colombo. After suffering a further setback in an ambush near Fort Peddie, the tide began to turn and, by the end of the year, the area to the Keiskamma river had been cleared and a line of posts established along the Buffalo river from the sea through King William's Town to the Buffalo mountains. Sandile however had not complied with a demand for the return of stolen cattle and was still lurking in the Amatolas. Nevertheless Maitland considered the war to be over, and accepted that the 90th should proceed on their way to Colombo; but in January 1847 he was replaced by Sir Henry Pottinger,[15] with Lieutenant-General Sir George Berkeley[16] as Commander of the Troops.

Pottinger was determined to deal with Sandile and cancelled the release of the 90th. After methodical preparations, Berkeley invaded the Amatolas and, after five weeks, succeeded in forcing Sandile to surrender. He then moved on to deal with Kreli and Pato, advancing to the Kei. Pato surrendered in December and Kreli took refuge east of the river. By then Pottinger and Berkeley had been moved on to Madras, and Harry Smith, now Lieutenant-General Sir Harry, who had covered himself with glory in the recent Sikh War, arrived to replace them, enthusiastically received by the settlers.

His head swollen by this and by the hero's welcome he had received in England, he made the mistake of assuming that his reputation and charisma were enough both to keep the natives quiet and the European population behind him. Within a few weeks of his arrival, he held a great meeting of Chiefs at King William's Town, having released Sandile, and then announced the reversal of Glenelg's policy. The area between the Fish and Keiskamma rivers was to be included in Cape Colony, the territory of which would also be extended northwards to the Orange river. The area between the Keiskamma and the Kei was also annexed as a new colony, called British Kaffraria. He then visited the area north of the Orange river to try and bring about a reconciliation with the Boers who had moved there, but were still regarded by the Cape government as British subjects, as were the half-caste Griquas in the same area, and to settle disputes between them and the powerful Basuto. While there, he announced that the area between the Orange and the Vaal rivers was annexed as the Orange River Sovereignty, and he left Major Henry Warden[17] there as his representative, with only 60 men of the Cape Mounted Rifles as a security force.

Although Smith intended this as an act of generosity towards the

Boers, Pretorius took a different view and moved a body of armed men from beyond the Vaal to challenge it. Smith immediately took the field in person and led 600 men of the 45th and 91st Regiments to face him. They met at Boomplatz on 28 August, the Boers being routed, and Smith rode in triumph to Bloemfontein and Winburg, leaving a garrison of three infantry companies and a troop of artillery at the former. At the latter he met Moshesh, Chief of the Basuto, both expressing admiration and friendship for each other.

Harry Smith's confidence that his combination of charisma and firmness was enough to secure peace seemed to have been justified. His principal concern in 1849 was not with the Kaffirs but with the Europeans, whose indignation at the proposal of Lord Grey,[18] now Secretary for War and the Colonies, to export convicts to the colony added fuel to the fire of their desire for a constitution which would give them a larger share in the Cape government. Smith's vacillation over the issue began to undermine Grey's confidence in him. The ship carrying them, having been at sea for four months and held at Simonstown for another five, was eventually sent on to Tasmania in February 1850. Shortly before that, Smith had assured Grey that his policy in Kaffraria had succeeded 'beyond his wildest expectations'. Grey's response was to demand troop reductions, and Smith agreed to send home the 1st Battalion of The Rifle Brigade, leaving him with only 1,700 regulars, two-thirds of whom were tied down manning widely scattered frontier posts.

Harry Smith had spoken too soon. An extremely severe drought coincided with prophecies by a witch-doctor called Mlanjeni, directed against the Whites. Sandile resented the loss of his power as a result of the appointment of British officials in the administration of Kaffraria. Tension grew during the winter months and Kaffir servants began to desert their settler masters. In October Smith summoned the Chiefs to meet him at Grahamstown and, when Sandile failed to attend, he deposed him. Cattle thefts increased, an ominous sign being the involvement of Hottentots as well as Gaikas. The situation deteriorated further when swarms of locusts destroyed what greenery had survived the drought.

On 9 December Smith, bringing with him the recently arrived 73rd Regiment, went to King William's Town and summoned the Gaika Chiefs to meet him at Fort Cox. Again Sandile and Macomo failed to attend. Smith decided to move against them. The force available consisted of the 6th, 45th, 73rd and 91st Regiments, the Cape Mounted

Rifles and some 400 Kaffraria native police; but all the battalions were weak and more than half of the 45th and many of the CMR were in the Orange River Sovereignty and Natal, leaving only some 2,000 men available for the expedition. Smith wished to avoid war, and intended the move to be a demonstration of force to bring Sandile to heel. While Lieutenant-Colonel Eyre,[19] with the 73rd, moved northeast to Kabousie Nek in order to prevent Kreli from coming to Sandile's help, Lieutenant-Colonel Mackinnon[20] was sent to Keiskamma Hoek to deal with Sandile himself. In the hope of reaching a peaceful solution, Mackinnon was ordered not to fire unless fired on, and his men's guns were unloaded. They were ambushed in the Boomah Pass, suffering 18 casualties, whose arms were taken together with six cases of ammunition. Smith withdrew both Mackinnon's and Eyre's troops, while the Gaikas swarmed round the isolated frontier forts, joined by deserters from the CMR and the Kaffraria police, and by the Hottentots of the Kat River Settlement under Hermanus.[21]

Smith himself was shut up in Fort Cox, but managed to escape with an escort of CMR, in whose uniform he was disguised, and to reach King William's Town. There he promoted Somerset to the rank of major-general and empowered him to raise local levies, with which, reinforced by regulars, he was to drive the Gaikas out of the Amatolas and expel them for ever from British Kaffraria. Lord Grey, although pointing out that it was Smith's duty 'as an officer representing a Civilized and Christian Power to endeavour not to exterminate but to reclaim and civilize these fierce barbarians', nevertheless agreed, on the Duke of Wellington's advice, to send out the 74th Highlanders. Smith established two lines of defence, one following the Buffalo river, the other from Port Elizabeth through Grahamstown to Fort Beaufort. Having established these, garrisoning which absorbed 1,700 men, he moved against Hermanus, who was ravaging the area round Fort Beaufort. Somerset was in command, and, by March 1851, Hermanus had been killed and the Hottentot rebellion defeated, William Uithaalder, a former soldier of the CMR, having taken the place of Hermanus.

Shaken by the desertions from the CMR and the police, Smith was further depressed by the reluctance of the burghers to answer his call for volunteers. Their place was partly taken by various rough-riding volunteer bodies, notable among which was that of the 22-year-old Stephen Lakeman, most of whose recruits were unemployed seamen or had been released from prison at the Cape [46]. Smith considered raising a force of 3,000 Zulus, but was dissuaded by Theophilus Shepstone,[22] who was responsible for native affairs in Natal.

By May 1851, when Edward Wellesley joined his regiment, the 73rd, at King William's Town, Smith had 9,000 men available, and, having dealt with another Hottentot revolt, embarked on his major effort to clear the area of the Fish river and the upper reaches of the Buffalo at the end of June, extending operations into the Amatolas and the Blinkwater and Waterkloof areas of the Kroome mountains, described by Edward Wellesley in his letters from Smith's headquarters.

These operations continued throughout the year, a further threat developing from the north, where Henry Warden was in difficulties, the Basutos being truculent and the Boers uncooperative; but Smith could spare no troops for him. Just when the operations appeared to be bearing fruit, Sandile having made overtures for peace in August, they flared up again, and criticism grew, both locally and in England, that, although substantial reinforcements had been sent, no successful end to the war was in sight. Lord Grey became increasingly disillusioned with Sir Harry, being fed with critical reports by one of the Assistant Commissioners he had sent out, Major Hogge [27]. After hopes of a peace had been dashed in January 1852, Smith renewed his assault on the Amatola and Kroome mountains, and by the end of March appeared to have succeeded.

Just as victory seemed assured, he received the unwelcome news that he was to be replaced by Lieutenant-General Sir George Cathcart, who took over on 8 April [42]. The latter announced that he would make no change to the policy that Smith had pursued. Now that the Gaikas had been cleared out of the mountains, he felt free to deal with Moshesh and Kreli, who, although professing neutrality, had been helping the Gaika, particularly by secreting stolen cattle.

In November Cathcart moved north to the Orange River Sovereignty to meet Moshesh on the Caledon river. Having failed to secure a satisfactory assurance about the return of cattle, he crossed the river and advanced in three separate columns to Moshesh's kraal at Thaba Bosigo, behind the plateau of Berea. There the column which he accompanied, consisting only of three companies of the 43rd Regiment, detachments of the 12th Lancers and the Cape Mounted Rifles, with three 12-pounder field guns, was attacked by 6,000 Basuto horsemen [53]. It was lucky to hold out successfully on its own for three hours, its casualties being seven wounded, one of whom was Edward Wellesley. They were then joined by the centre column under Colonel Eyre, which had captured 1,500 cattle at a cost of six men, including one officer, killed and 14 wounded. The eastern column, of 114 12th Lancers and 109 Cape Mounted Riflemen, suffered a reverse in a defile, still known as Lancers' Gap, five men being wounded and 28 killed, 23 from the 12th Lancers, whose lances proved ineffective and unwieldy and whose tight overall trousers immobilized them when dismounted. The fighting had, however, inflicted heavy casualties on the Basuto and Moshesh prudently made peace. This action at Berea, together with a sortie across the Kei to bring Kreli to heel, brought the 7th Kaffir War to an end.

It had been an exacting one for the troops involved. Captain William King of the 74th wrote:

> Nothing more difficult and trying can be imagined than our laborious progress through this all but impracticable forest, studded throughout with enormous masses of detached rock, overgrown with wild vines, twining asparagus trees, endless monkey ropes and other creepers, so strong and thickly interlaced as almost to put a stop to our advance; covered, moreover, with dense thorny underwood, concealing dangerous clefts and crevices, and strewn with fallen trees in every stage of decay, while the hooked thorns of the 'wait-a-bit' clinging to our arms and legs, snatching the caps off our heads and tearing clothes and flesh, impeded us at every step.[23]

The weather varied from extreme heat in summer to bitter cold and rain in the mountains in winter. Supply was always a problem, as Wellesley points out [27], relying heavily on ox-drawn wagons moving at a snail's pace over rough tracks. Some of the soldiers were fortunate to carry the new Minié rifle instead of the old musket, a few of them having been issued experimentally for the first time in 1852 [48]. Most officers provided themselves with rifles which they also used to shoot game [10]. The soldiers found it a trial that, in Captain King's words, 'nowhere could they feel assured, that naked savages, unencumbered except by their arms, and at home in crag and thicket, were not lying in wait for them, savages who could move swiftly and noiselessly and were so cunning at self-concealment that, at a pinch, they would sink themselves, like a hunted deer, in the water, with nothing above the surface to betray them'. Their successors over the next century and a half, in many parts of the world, would have the same experience.

With the 25th Regiment in South Africa

Edward Wellesley to his mother, Mrs Richard (Jane) Wellesley

Cape Town,
Cape of Good Hope
Sunday 15th March [1840]

My dear Mama

Here we are at last having been 76 [?] days at sea. I suppose you heard from the Colonel[24] from Teneriffe. We stopped there 3 days and then sailed. We anchored in Table Bay on Thursday the 12 of March and marched in on Friday morning at 6 o'clock. I then commanded a Company marching in, the Captain of my company remaining on board and the Senior Subalterns carrying the colours. I considered myself rather an important character on the occasion. Nothing but sand here. The Second Ship has not arrived yet. I shall begin drilling soon. I hope you are settled by this time in your new house and that you like it. There are a great variety of people here. Dutch. Hottentots. Malays. Indians every variety of Colour. If when you write address me 25th Regiment Cape Town Cape of Good Hope. On looking over my diary I see that I have nothing interesting to tell you we saw very few Monsters of the Deep and the Voyage was as dull as most voyages are. Cape Town is much dearer than it used to be since the War. There is not much duty here the 72 Highlanders whom we relieve have been here 13 years and some of the officers say they are not exactly anxious to go, they embark Thursday week. A Ship sails to-morrow. this goes by it. This month is the beginning of Autumn here it is hot but not unpleasantly so. I hope Richard and all of you are quite well give my love to all.

If you have any inclination for a Lion's Leopard's or any other kind of Skin to adorn any Room say so when you write they are to be had here Cheap my Funds are in a very flourishing condition

good bye
your affectionate son
E Wellesley

2

To his mother

Cape Town
Wednesday 1st of Apr 1840

My dear Mama
The Colonel is making up a Despatch so I write though I have not much to say. Today I have seen the first <u>African</u> rain. They have not had rain here for an immense time – I attended the General's Levée on Monday Sir G Napier has only one arm its rather a curious thing, I believe there are four brothers and 3 of them have only 3 arms between them.[25] The people are very religious here they have turned the Theatre into a Methodist Chapel which is rather a bore as I and a rather theatrical mad officer had an Idea of getting up private theatricals here. Tell Richard to pen an occasional letter about theatrical news. We are rather behindhand in news here the latest papers we have are of the 3rd of January. I was sorry to see the death of Lady Emily Wellesley[26] in a paper of that date. We are unsettled rather still as the 72nd whom we relieve are not yet gone. There is a capital public library here the Military have a free admission. This is certainly a beautiful climate I always sleep with my window open. Cape Town is in a complete valley surrounded by mountains on one side with the Bay on the other & Table Mountain rises at the back of the Town also a hill

which they say has a resemblance to a Lion some part is named the Lion's head and its <u>Antipodes</u> lies (you may imagine what) I have no more news to tell you

love to all
your affect Son
E Wellesley

3

To his mother

Cape Town
September 4th 1840

My dear Mamma

I received your letter announcing the receipt of mine some days ago. I have been very busy lately getting up <u>Hamlet</u>. On the 31st of August it was acted together with a Farce (I enclose you a Bill). It went off very well. All the people say they were enchanted with my personification of the Prince of Denmark which I am vain enough to believe. The gay season at Cape Town is going out. we have sundry Balls &c. This night, one of our Major's nieces gives a concert, in which I am to figure. I am glad to hear you like your new residence so much.

I have to inform you that putting <u>the Coffee in the same drawer with the other things did not spoil it or them</u>. I never tasted better coffee.

Believe me ever
your very affect Son
E Wellesley

4

To his mother

Cape Town
Dec 10th 1841

My dear Mama

I received your letter of the 28th Sept together with papers. I have received lots of papers from you at different times the enclosures

12

from Richard together with his letters to me were very amusing. I am glad to hear you all go on well and I cannot understand Lord R's [?] motive in saying that writerships[27] got for R & me, it seems to have been merely a wilful misstatement or in other words falsehood. With regard to the Artillery it is a much better service than the line & if Gerald [then aged 14] wants to be in the Army, I should think the best for him. in the first place they do not go abroad so much as the line, in the second they are better paid & they are alternately in the horse Brigade & in the foot, the Horse Artillery is acknowledged to be a very splendid branch of the service & their dress is very fine which Gerald I should think would like. I hope Lord W. will live till Augustus [then 10] is old enough to get a writership but I am afraid he & the Duke are missing us all together

Give my love to Hyacinthe [then aged 15] & tell her I hope she will attend to Lady W's[28] [illegible] & keep herself as much out of sight as possible, till the time comes when she is to burst forth upon the astonished world like the sun from behind a cloud. (This I am afraid is not poetical enough) but you are aware that

your affect Son

E Wellesley

is no poet.

Love to Montague[29] & all the family

With the 73rd Regiment in Ireland

5

Addressed to his mother at Poste Restante Basle, forwarded from there to Mayence and Spa

Cork
16th August 1845

My dear Mama

I received your letter from Basle this morning. I have not written much lately, my last letter went by Ostend to Brussels. I am sorry there is any delay or anxiety about the house; as it is important that every thing should be well arranged about the letting, if you have any doubt, I should <u>strongly</u> advise you returning & seeing to it all yourself, if not now too late, things are never done so well by agents as by oneself, and I don't see how it is possible for Philips or any one else to manage, if there is no one on the spot to direct him, beside this who is to prevent a wholesale robbery on the part of any one who may choose to take anything, I cannot say more than repeating the idea that if you wish to have things advantageously arranged, you had much better return & see to them yourself. I as I mentioned in another letter I cannot go to London the Adjutant-General here having said that he would not give any one leave except in a matter of life & death, only one officer has got leave & that arose from his father writing a pathetic letter saying he was eighty-two & never expected to see his son again after he embarked.

A day or two ago the Colonel[30] asked me if I would like to have the Depot Adjutancy, as it would probably be vacant on account of some steps going. I said yes and he then was very complimentary saying he knew of no one better fitted for it & so forth, and promised it to me, & also that if the Depot Paymastership fell vacant first I might have that, these are the only two appointments in the Depot which Subalterns can hold on the Regimental Staff, all this was very flattering as I have here mentioned that I wished to remain at home, on account of my belonging to a Company which always goes abroad & which I should not think of leaving if the Regiment was going to any place but the Cape where I have been before, so now I am pretty secure of remaining at home, if I get the Adjutancy, for two years after the Regiment embarks, and have only to wait until some promotion takes place, which we expect any day, which will make the man who now holds the appointment a Captain, this is also another reason for my not being able to get away at present as it would not do to ask a man who has behaved so very kindly & thoughtfully to me for leave just after he has offered me an appointment which others are anxious to get & also recommended my attending to get myself au fait at the Regimental business, which I do since daily; if there is any chance of an emeute in Switzerland the sooner you are out of the country the better.

Edward Wellesley
I don't write often as there is chance of miscarriage

6

To Mrs Richard (Jane) Wellesley from [? Colonel] C. Chambers

February 22 [1846]

My dear Jane

You will have perceived that Sir Harry Smith whom Edward knew very well at the Cape where he was D.Adjutant General has gained a victory with his Division. It is those dastardly French Officers in their service that enable the Seiks to fight so well – that is do so much execution with their Cannon. It is a pity the 25th is at the other extremity of [illegible] from which Cause it has lost participating in the Glory that has been and is yet to be achieved. Every Day we are expecting to hear of our Army having crossed the Suttlej River and fought another Battle. There can be no doubt of our success but not probably without great loss again – Poor Lord and Lady Fitzroy Somerset must be in Great Distress[31] I have been writing so much that I can hardly feel the Pen so Believe me

affectionately yours
C. Chambers

Love H.

Return to South Africa

7

Edward Wellesley to his brother Richard Wellesley

Oxford
March 14 1851

My dear Richard

In case the Duke will not do anything for me I must [be] free to go and ask [illegible] for me to find my own passage to the Cape & to be excused from embarking with the Draft at Southampton which they will do on Monday. My reasons for asking for his indulgence are which you can tell him (or the Adjutant General)[32] that Lieutenant Harison who is at the Cape will be gazetted to be Captain immediately; that the next Lieutenant – Burne will then succeed Captain O'Connell's Company who is going to sell out immediately the former [illegible] goes & that Lieutenant Burne is with the Draft & will be gazetted a Captain on his passage; that Captain Rennie is understood to have joined at the Cape from Mauritius; that Captain Bicknell is then on the strength of the Regiment at the Cape; and that therefore I should be the ninth[33] Captain of the Regiment whereas their proper strength is only six; under the circumstances & as I have suddenly returned from a detachment in Ireland & have not had time to make any preparations for the voyage I request the indulgence of being allowed to find my own passage to the Cape by the next steamer, you can say this or read the reasons to the Adjutant General or the Duke & if they will give an order for me to be left behind You had better take charge of it yourself and send it by a special messenger by the first train so as I arrive there as soon as possibly at

Southampton <u>on Saturday</u> for there is not a minute to be lost or I shall have to embark on Monday. I shall see Henry Wellesley[34] tonight & if he is a good sort of fellow make him go up to London by an early train & communicate with you and see the Duke or A.G. too that his consent be depended upon. My wife meets me at Southampton where I have sent her by Holyhead L C. You must see the Authorities as early as possibly on Saturday, <u>speed</u> is the word.

Yours affectionately
Edward Wellesley

8

To his brother Richard

On Board [illegible] Singapore
off Lymington
Monday Night

My dear Richard

We are at anchor here for the night & I take the opportunity of sending this by a stout party a Sister of the Captain who is going on shore to-morrow morning. We left at [illegible] & Annot was only just in time. She took a glass of Sea Water soon after coming on board & is now rather annoyed at having done so as we are to remain at anchor to night. The accomodation is really very good & she is the only Lady on board & has the whole Saloon to herself & Mine. The letters of introduction &c must be sent by the first Steamer from Plymouth on the 15th of next month unless there is an opportunity by steamer before – We are a party of twenty on board & the Captain says he will do his passage in 23 days. We touch at Sierra Leone and Teneriffe from which place I will write.

Good night
All's Well
Edward Wellesley

9

To his brother Richard

Cape Town
April 27 1851

My dear Richard
We arrived here on the morning of the 25th after a slow passage from Sierra Leone altogether the ship did not behave as well as was expected as we were to reach here only twenty-five days whereas we have been forty, the Governor at Sierra Leone was very kind & civil to us & we spent a day with him & his wife, he is a nephew of the old Adjutant-General Macdonnell[35] & has been there twenty-seven years which speaks very much in favour of the place so much [illegible] in England, as far as the scenery is concerned it is charming but the heat is certainly intense I remain here until the 30th when I go on to the Frontier where my Regiment is at present in Camp, I leave Annot here in the Castle where I have got rooms for her & where she will remain until the war is over this is only six days from where I shall be so that we can easily communicate & steamers are continually running between here and the mouth of the Buffalo river which is the port where I shall disembark & from where I have to march two days to find my Regiment. The accounts from the Frontier are not very cheering as a large number of the Cape Corps which is composed of Hottentots & officered by English officers have deserted from their Regiment taking their horses & now infest the country robbing and murdering all whom they meet Soldiers, & others. Sir Harry Smith who is with the Division of the Army to which my Regiment belongs has for the present it would seem suspended more active operations & will probably not advance again until he receives re-inforcements & will be delighted when he gets the regiments now on their way to the Cape & which should have arrived here about this time but which have not yet come in. I have been very busy since I came getting a Servt & other things for the Frontier. I leave everything here except the barest necessities required in Camp. I have sent the order from [?] June £550 [illegible] Spanish [illegible] free in India. I shall keep this open until I leave Cape Town in case I have anything more to tell you.

April 28 1851

I close my letter as I am to start early to-morrow morning in the Ace Steamer for the mouth of the Buffalo river where we expect to arrive in 3 days & then march to King Williamstown 3 days march – I have settled Annot in the Castle Barracks here and to-day she called upon Lady Smith[36] the Governor's wife who no doubt will be kind to her. Annot will write to Hyacinthe when she has time and spirits which latter are not very high as you may imagine at the prospect of my leaving her. We heard yesterday of the death of our Adjutant,[37] who was killed in a skirmish with the Cafirs he was formerly a Non-Commissioned Officer of the Guards promoted for his good conduct & has left a wife & children quite destitute. Give my love to Mary & anyone else &

Believe me
Yours affectionately
Edward Wellesley
The boy is not very well but will improve with the fine climate

10

To his wife, Mrs Edward (Annot) Wellesley

King William's Town
May 31.1851.

My dearest Annot
We returned yesterday at 3 o'clock from Patrol, having been seven days out. The first day we went to Fort White, a small fort into which we left provisions and also took Mrs Mansergh to her husband. The second day we went to Fort Cox a fort most beautifully situated at the entrance of what is called the Amatola Basin a deep valley in the Amatola Mountains, and where we also left supplies, most acceptable to the officers and soldiers stationed there, as they cannot stir from their post and never hear any news or receive any provisions except what is taken to them from this place. The river Keiskamma runs at the foot of the hill on which this Fort is placed and is the purest water in the Colony. At Fort Cox the force we had which consisted of a part of my Regiment,

some of the 6th Cape Corps and Levies was divided, part going under Colonel Mackinnon along the ridge of the mountain and the other under Colonel Eyre to penetrate into the Amatola Basin into which British Troops had only once been before and which enjoys a great reputation among the Kafirs for security. We marched from Fort Cox at 5 in the morning and after passing through a dense bush at last emerged into a place where a deep gully crossed the road and where the bush became less thick and as the Levies passed this the Kafirs commenced firing upon us from the Bush. Our Companies were extended and the firing continued on both sides for about three hours and until we had gained an open space in the centre of the valley where we halted for breakfast. We relieved each other in the skirmishing and burned several Kraals which are the native villages as we passed along; we breakfasted in the valley surrounded by splendid hills and the scenery altogether beautiful. After breakfast we ascended one of the hills and as we again got into more bushy country and intersected with ravines the Kafirs again attacked us and we fought all the way up the hill on reaching the top of which the firing ceased and after resting the men we proceeded to ascend the top of the range and passing through a dense forest of larger trees than are generally seen in this country we reached a spot a short distance below the Amatola Peak which is the highest of all the Amatola Mountains where we found old Mackinnon and halted together for the night. On the 27th we marched at daylight and retraced our steps to the hill where we ascended the day before and descended for the second time into the Amatola Basin and halted in the valley where we breakfasted. While at this meal the hills were covered with Kafirs who commenced singing their War songs which had a fine effect echoing through the hills; after breakfast we commenced ascending a steep hill on the opposite side of the valley to the one we had descended. The Kafirs as we left the valley rapidly crossed from the other side and attacked our rear and fought us the whole way up the hill which we were one hour and twenty minutes ascending. My Company was in front this time and I did not get much of the fighting. We then descended the hill and as the ground was quite open and the Kafirs had the advantage of firing from the top of the hill we again were attacked, my company being this time the last to descend had all the fighting and the lads [balls?] fell very thickly about us; we had no casualties however and reached at last a rocky spot where we halted and at a short distance we halted altogether for the night, Colonel Mackinnon with the other part of the troops having joined us. The valley we halted in is called the Valley of the Wolf and is very beautiful. On the 28th we all marched together and ascending the hill we had so much fighting the day before descended for the third time into the Amatola Basin. This time we were not molested at all, the Kafirs seeming to be cowed by our thus penetrating for the third time into their greatest stronghold and from which they had said that no one would ever get out alive; we crossed the valley and again ascended the hill which we had descended twice before and then descended into the Chumie Valley a lovely spot, the Cavalry having been sent on in advance succeeded in capturing 250 head of cattle and killed some Kafirs in the plain. We halted here for breakfast and then marched to the Yellow Woods where a small stream gave us water and where we halted for the night. On the 29th we marched at 8 to Fort White having breakfasted on our way at Fort Cox and taken the waggons which we had left behind when entering the Amatola Basin; we did not see one Kafir to-day. On the 30th we marched at 6 and passing through a pass called the Debeneck celebrated for several disastrous affairs with the Kafirs but where we did not have a shot fired at us we reached this place at 3. The efforts [?effects] of this Patrol have been 250 head of cattle, taking a number of Kafirs killed and all the Kraals in the Amatola Basin and anywhere we passed burned to the ground. The Kafirs skirmish very well and have all the advantage over the regular troops which a dense bush, light or [illegible] clothing and a complete knowledge of the ground may be supposed to give; you seldom see them, as that being the first intimation you have of their vicinity and you cannot tell what number you have killed as the bush hides them; they never attack you in front but always in rear and as we are generally going on to some place or halt for the night we have the disadvantage of fighting and retreating at the same time. Our men are perfection in every way and quite au fait at all the different duties of this sort of campaigning, a very complimentary order was issued by the Officer Commanding the Regiment on the actions of the 26 and 27th in which he praised all the men, and named the four Captains who were out including myself, thanking them for their gallantry and the way in which they led their Companies. I enjoyed very good health while out not feeling the cold at all which I had heard several complain of, Pinckney[38] and I lived together. I had my two horses, one I rode, the other carried tent and cooking things &c. Every one rides except when we are skirmishing when you dismount and gun in hand fight on foot. I bought a gun here and on the 27th in descending the hill where my Company was engaged had several shots at the Kafirs who were dodging from stone to stone and firing upon us as hard as they could. The country we have been through has been most beautiful . . .

[rest of letter missing]

11

To his wife

King William's Town,
British Kaffraria
June 3.1851.

My dearest Annot

Since I wrote nothing has occurred here; the Mail from Graham's Town was due yesterday but has not since arrived and I am afraid has again been cut off by the Kafirs and consequently I have not heard again as I had hoped from you. I lead a monotonous and regular life enough while in Camp here. At 8½ we breakfast and then have Parade. We are supposed to lunch at 1½ and at 4 we ride that is Price King, Campbell[39] and I. We cannot go much more than a mile from the Camp and then only in places where there is no English. All the people here lead a similar life – the Governor's white hat is seen galloping forth on horseback attended by his Staff punctually as the clock strikes four or rather as it would if there was one but there is not. On Sundays the whole garrison attend church in a school room set apart for it. There is a Chaplain of the Army here who officiates. The whole of this part of the Country is under Martial Law, Justice being administered when necessary by Court Martial. There is however little or no crime with the exception of cattle stealing, a vice inherent in the Kafir. We have heard that we killed numbers of these savages in our last affair and that a [illegible] of Sandili a great Chief of the Gaika Tribes and the principal cause of this war was hit but not seriously. Some day I will give you an account of these Tribes and the causes of this and other Wars with them but at present I am not well acquainted with their history myself. There seems however here to be but one feeling with regard to the missionaries who are scattered amongst the Kafirs which is that they are frequently the cause of these attacks and that they even supply them with guns and ammunition and that this is done through their instrumentality. While I am writing in my tent I hear the riders with the post and hope to hear from you. The letters are carried by Kafirs through the enemy's country and then escorted by armed men on the latter part of the journey. It is now 6½ and I have just returned from seeing a race on the race course which there is here and I am now going to dine so I shall wish you a good dinner also and finish this to-morrow. Our great want here are vegetables and if you have an opportunity and they are cheap you can send me as many potatoes as you like.

June 4.
    You can give Mrs Aichron [Dickson?] 10 shillings her husband's wages for May. He cannot send her any more money this month but on the 1st of next he will get all his pay which will then be sent to her monthly by the Paymaster in the same manner as the rest of the men who have wives at Cape Town. On thinking over what you told me with regard to Mrs Campbell, you can do what you choose, cut her and insult her if you please but I think the higher way is to take no notice of her at all. I am friends here with Campbell but if you wish I would cut him on this account to-morrow but of course he knows nothing of his wife's proceedings and I think no notice should be taken of low conduct from anyone. If you have an opportunity send me a pair of thin black trousers

with a regimental red stripe which you will find somewhere; the mail has not yet come in neither has Mrs Cockram[40] with my Box, he by the bye was a sergeant major of some regiment and was given his promotion and subsequently became a Paymaster. He has a house here which consists of one room and a kitchen.

Goodbye always yours
Most affectionately
Edward Wellesley

12

To his wife

King William's Town,
British Kaffraria
June 5. 1851.

My dearest Annot

As we are going out on Patrol to-morrow morning I write to you to-day which I shall leave to go by the Post on Saturday as I shall be then out and also on the following Thursday most probably. Nothing has occurred here since I last wrote. A Patrol went out this morning and I believe we are to meet it to-morrow. The weather here is very beautiful and I hope you have the same at Cape Town. This is the day for the Mail but none has as yet arrived. This is the second post now due which is most annoying. Mrs Cockram has arrived and I suppose has my Boots but I have not seen her yet. I do not know what the object of this Patrol is but I shall let you know all about it on my return as usual.

Good-bye always yours
Most affectionately
Edward Wellesley

I have just received your welcome letters of the 24th 25th and 26th with your delightful present of Books, [illegible] which is beautiful, hat, potatoes, jacket, newspapers, boots and letter from Richard, two others and one from Mamma. You are a most prompt agent and the Potatoes have come just in time to take out on Patrol and will be a most welcome luxury. Alas I am afraid the letters from Lord Fitzroy &c have miscarried as they have not arrived and Richard in his letter refers to one he had sent before and which I have not received. Mama also refers to them. Richard says that Mary is recommended best to travel by railway which looks suspicious. She was going to write to you. I would send you his letter which is very short but it fills up the post too much in these days of War and I therefore also do not return Mama's. If you like to write to her some day giving her a plain statement of our adventures you can but this is just as you like. Many thanks for all the things you have sent. I must now say adieu again as I have a good deal to do this evening, it is now 5 and we start on Patrol to-morrow morning at 8. You ask how I like my Camp life and I must say that I prefer being on Patrol to this place. Mrs Cockram was delighted with the boy and I am glad to hear that he is so good.

Yours affectionately
Edward Wellesley

13

To his wife

King William's Town
June 13. 1851.

My dearest Annot

We returned from Patrol yesterday at 11 having been seven days out. We marched on the first day to Fort White nothing of interest occurring on that day – the force consisting of about 1,500 men under Colonel Mackinnon. On the second day we marched and encamped on a small river called the Iquili where we remained that night. The third day we left the Camp standing and marched to the banks of the river Keiskamma the scenery being very beautiful, wooded hills and grassy plains sloping to the river, which is the largest I have yet seen in this part of Africa and the water is very pure. The country seemed quite deserted and we did not see a solitary Kafir the whole day, now and then we started a buck the only seeming tenants of this lonely country; we burned numerous Kraals or Kafir huts on our return to the Camp where we arrived at 4. On the fourth day we again proceeded from the Camp to another part of the river Keiskamma which we crossed at a ford near to Fort Willshire now deserted but which was built at enormous expense to contain a Regiment of Infantry and a squadron of Cavalry and was afterwards given up to the Kafirs on the withdrawing of Sir Benjamin D'Urban from the Government of the Cape in 1837 when the Government at home rescinded all his Colonial Policy and restored to the Kafirs a large country which had been taken from them and which we have now re-occupied.

We returned to our Camp after breakfasting at the Fort and a part of our force had a short affair with the enemy after capturing some cattle and had an officer wounded. We however did not see a single being. On the fifth day we broke up our Camp and passing Fort White encamped on a hill over a small river called the [illegible ?Umdegine] where we halted for the night. On the sixth day we marched at 5 in the morning and went through a very intricate but fine country belonging to a chief called Seydo, one of the most pugnacious of the whole. We rather surprised the Kafirs to-day, captured 280 head of cattle, some horses and goats and killed some of the enemy who were to be seen running away pursued by the Cavalry. We returned to the camp and just at the dusk of the evening on passing through a densely wooded height were fired upon, the firing was returned on our part and we soon overpowered their firing and reached the Camp at 6½ having been thirteen hours out. The seventh day we returned here having had fine weather the whole time with the exception of a few hours rain on one day. The Kafirs seem now disinclined to fight as with the exception of the affairs in the Amatola of which I gave you an account the last four Patrols which have been out have had no fighting; the cattle all seem to have been driven from this part of the country some people say into the Fish river bush which is in the Colony and some beyond the river Kei far into the interior; all these rumours however I discredited as I believe no one knows anything about the movements of these savages. There are reports also that some of the Chiefs are inclined to come to terms with Sir Harry who they say would not be disinclined to make a peace on any terms, these are reports, but I know nothing of their truth and neither believe, or disbelieve. On my return here I find happily your letter of the 31st May or rather June 1st and also the papers of the 25th and the other which you sent and one from Mamma. I received some from her before at the same time that I received your parcel. The hat which you sent fits very well as do my boots. You have sent some very nice books some of which I shall have an opportunity of returning to you by an officer of the 75th who is going to Cape Town on his way to join the Depot in Ireland a Subaltern whose name is Barnes. The Ace Steamer and the Hermes I hear are both going to leave Table Bay for this place soon and therefore if you have anything to send you could send it by them. I don't think of anything else which I want as we have written for provisions for the three mess[es] which will be divided amongst us. In the supplement to the Graham's Town Journal of June 3 is the whole account of our former Patrol into the Amatolas. I suppose it will be copied into the Cape Town Mail and as my name is mentioned you will like to see it and can then send the paper direct to Richard or Mary or Mama without sending it here, if it is not in the Cape Town try and procure a Graham's Town Journal of the date I mentioned and perhaps had better send it to Mama first. The Mail came in this morning but brought no letter from you. I find that the [illegible] left England on the 5th of April and has not yet arrived having made a very long passage as Richard said in the letter I received that he had written on the 1st and that the other letters were sent. No doubt she will bring them out and they are not lost. If you get them it is safer to send them by the Ace or Hermes than by the regular post to Graham's Town.

I will finish this to-morrow the day of the post in case I have any more news to tell you.

June 14.

I have just seen Mrs Cockram who has described to me the situation of the rooms she had in the latter [Castle?] and as I now remember them you can if you like change to them as there are four and you have only three and I enclose a note which you can send to Hall if you do so, if not you can burn it.

A Patrol came in to-day which have been out under Major Wilmot[41] having captured 80 head of cattle.

Good-bye and recollect you are not to fret at all which from something which Mrs Cockram said I expect you have been doing.
Always yours most affectionately
Edward Wellesley

14

To his brother Richard Wellesley

Camp King Williams Town
British Kaffraria
June 14 1851

My dear Richard

On the 24th of last month I went on my first Patrol as they are called an account of which I send you enclosed. We were out eight days & as you will see had some fierce fighting on two of them. We penetrated into the Amatola Mountains where European Soldiers had only been once before, and then in time of peace & also into a valley called "the Wolf" where we none had ever been & from which the Kafirs had said that none of us would return. On the two first days we took supplies to two of the frontier posts, the unhappy occupants of which cannot stir out and never hear any news except when we take them supplies from here which takes place about once in six weeks, one of the posts called Fort Cox is most beautifully situated on a hill at the entrance of a gorge in the Amatolas, the river Keiskamma flowing at its base one of the finest rivers in Kafirland. On the third day my Regiment a few Cavalry and some of the Levies who are a mixture of all the Mongrel breeds in the Colony consisting of Hottentots & others marched into what is called the Amatola basin a fine valley surrounded by steep and high hills on all sides, we crossed at the entrance of the valley a deep ravine & the men lay down, the Levies in rear & as they crossed the Kafirs opened their fire upon them which the Levies returned firing as they always do in every direction, into the air & occasionally into us, the men were then formed and rushed with a cheer into the Bush & from this time for three hours until we reached a spot more open than the rest & where we halted for breakfast the skirmishing continued the Companies relieving each other, there were four men wounded in the affair & one Levy killed. After breakfast we continued up the valley & then ascended a hill the Kafirs were soon upon us again & skirmished with us all the way up, we then proceeded on & joined the other part of our force under the Amatola Peak where we halted for the night. The other part had also been engaged for a short time in passing a wood in which a Kafir who was sitting in a tree & firing down was shot like a rook by two officers who later fired at him & brought him down. On the fourth day we were again ordered to retrace our steps into the Amatola Basin & rejoin another part of the force which had to be sent in another direction the whole to unite in the Valley of the Wolf. We descended again therefore & halted in the Basin for breakfast & while eating it a large body of Kafirs assembled on the hills & commenced singing their War Songs, this had a very fine & dramatic effect as the songs echoed through the hills; we then commenced the ascent of a very steep & rugged hill & the Kafirs in an inconceivably short space of time descended, ran across the valley & filling the wooded ravines on each side of the hill were ascending & using every bush or stone as a [illegible] commenced firing upon the rear of our column my Company as you will see by the paper was one of the first to ascend & I therefore had nothing to do on its occupation but the rear was very hardly pressed & had several men wounded they at last reached the top having been engaged for one hour and a half; we then commenced descending again towards the valley of the Wolf, here I was in rear of the whole with my Company extended covering the Column & we had to retire across an open plain while the Kafirs had the advantage of the tops of the trees & some large rocks as a cover, they took every advantage of these & the firing was very warm & continued until we gained the bottom of the valley when the Kafirs ceased as the ground was more open, fortunately I had no men wounded one only being touched in the eye & another hit by a spent ball which however did not penetrate through his clothes. We united our force here with the other & the whole the next day went over the same ground as we had been the day before & on this day had no fighting; our Cavalry however took 280 head of cattle & killed the Kafirs who were driving them these unhappy wretches being completely blown by the time the horse came upon them themselves blown & more than that. On the next day we returned for our Wagons which had been left at Fort Cox & here to King Williams Town. We remained here for seven days & then another patrol was ordered & on the 6th of this month we marched to a place called Fort White where we proceeded to a hill on a small river called the [illegible ?Umdegine] where a Camp was formed & from which we went in Light Marching order to the river Keiskamma & on the first day saw no Kafirs or Cattle, the scenery which we passed through was however very beautiful wooded heights & sloping plains to the river & all as formed by nature, not the least sign of habitation, or one of a human being, a solitary buck which we put up accidentally being the only sign of life in the solitude. On the second day we proceeded to another part of the same river which we crossed, on this day a part of our force had an affair with the enemy in which one officer was wounded, our men had however nothing to do. On the . . .

[rest of letter missing]

15

To his wife

King William's Town
June 17. 1851.

My dearest Annot
Yesterday I received your two letters of the 6th and 9th of June and also two papers. I received the book you sent as a letter the other day. I enclose you a letter from [for?] Richard which you must post to go by the Steamer of the end of this month in it I have put one of the papers I mentioned to you and when you therefore get your own account you can send it to Mama if you wish. The bill which you sent is correct and I return it and you can pay it. You can also pay for my boots which fit very well and I shall not want any more at present. You can also pay for the hat. I am sorry to hear that you have the petty annoyance you mention of the child which however you cannot prevent as children who are

badly brought up must say what they choose; if however we are attempted to do what he says I hope the servant would give him a good beating. I recollect Mrs and the Misses Schmidt who are good people enough he told me that his wife was in a dying state. Mrs Maydwell is the wife of Captain Maydwell[42] who is Military Secretary to Sir Harry Smith. His real name was Smith and he is the nephew of the Governor. He changed his name for a fortune which however I believe he never got. I have made his acquaintance here and bought a very good horse from him. I think you had better change your rooms as I mentioned in a former note to Mrs Cockram if you think them better and that they will do when I return. Don't pay attention to stories you hear of any one or enter into it as I hate the tattle of a party of Barrack people. One cannot avoid <u>hearing</u> but <u>replying</u> is not necessary.

I understand that a large Force is to go out either the end of this week or beginning of the next and that we are to have a standing Camp somewhere in the Amatola Mountains and that General Somerset is to continue with us. It is also reported that Col. Mackinnon has said that this is to be the end of the War. These reports I never believe but give them to you as I hear them. I hope you will take a subscription to the Library if you wish it as it is one of the best in any Colony and books are indispensable. Those which you sent me are very good and amusing. You can tell Mrs Dixon that her husband is quite well. He cannot write but tells me that he has procured a literary substitute to do so for him.

I don't think of anything I want at present as we are getting some things amongst us here from Cape Town. To-morrow is the anniversary of the Battle of Waterloo on which occasion Sir Harry gives a dinner party. It is also the post day and I shall conclude this to-morrow. We have been to-day playing at Cricket which is an acquisition at this place – we played a game in which I beat them all off my own bat so you can imagine they are not very good players.

June 18.
I have no more news to–day, but that I am always
Yours most affectionately
Edward Wellesley

16

To his wife

King William's Town
July 4. 1851.

My dearest Annot

You will be very glad to hear that Sir Harry Smith has given me a Staff Appointment having made me Deputy Assistant Adjutant General which attaches me to the Head Quarters of the Army with himself and (which you will like more than anything else, I think, by your last note) prevents me from going on Patrol unless he goes out himself. He communicated this morning to me himself yesterday having ridden out to meet us all returning. He came and spoke to me and sent his Aide de Camp and told me he was going to give it to me. He then said that Colonel Eyre who was riding with him had said he was very sorry to lose me which was the greatest compliment he could pay me and concluded by saying "Your great uncle gave me my first Staff situation and I don't see why I should not give his grand nephew one." This day I began my duties and was in the office writing for four or five hours. My immediate superior is Colonel Cloete[43] the Deputy Quarter Master General a very nice person and whom I knew when I was previously at the Cape. My addition to our income will be something like £200 a year and I have forage for three horses.

We returned from Patrol yesterday having been ten days out and having taken 1,500 head of cattle the most that has been taken this war. We had fine weather and went through some beautiful country and up some of the highest points of the Amatola Mountains. The Kafirs fought us on two days but we had only one man wounded. I had your three letters the last dated No 4 of June 26. I am glad to hear that you had decided to move and hope you will be quite comfortable in your new house if not let me know at once. This day Saturday 5th I called upon Sir Harry to thank him for my appointment again, he was exceedingly kind and said that he had allowed me to go on two or three Patrols to see as he said himself "What sort of fellow I was," that he was very glad to have me near him and that every one had spoken so well of me. I gave him Mama's letter in which she I see repeated Lady Smith's friendship for you if Sir Harry writes to her she will most probably call upon you and you may be prepared to see her.

Sir Harry said a great many other complimentary things one of which was that I owed my appointment to nothing but to my own merits and ended by asking me to dinner to-morrow. To-day I have been writing all day and have therefore only time to say a little before the post. I have written to a man in Cape Town to buy me a good horse as one is not to be got here. I shall tell him to take it and shew it to you before he sends it here. I want a good looking handsome horse and the man I have written to I understand can fully be trusted but I like your taste to judge. You will only have to look at it and no other trouble. My under garments are so very bad that you must really buy me a dozen and a half of good <u>Linen</u> ones. You can give one of my linen ones as a pattern of the size I left one or two behind and I enclose a pattern for the collar. Be particular in having neat pearl buttons on them and well made in all respects. Those that Mama sent have dropped to pieces from extreme old age. I find that I shall not be able to write by this post about my horse so must put it off to the next. Any parcels you can send me address

On her Majesty's Service
Captain Wellesley
73rd Regiment
Deputy Assist. Adjt. General
Good-bye I have no time to write any more always
Yours most affectionately
Edward Wellesley

17

From Major-General Sir Harry Smith to Mrs Richard (Jane) Wellesley

British Kaffraria
7th July 1851

My dear Mrs Wellesley
It is very friendly of you to treat me as an old acquaintance for most deeply was indebted to your brother poor Col Chambers for his care of my nephew. I contemplated placing your son upon the Staff of the Army upon his arrival under my command <u>provided</u> I found him what his name made me anticipate a very [illegible] Soldier in the Bush upon Patrol, he was out upon a true very long [illegible] and his gallant Comdg Officer Col Eyre being highly satisfied – I at once gladly availed Myself of his Services on the Staff – after the appointment he gave me your Letter – I mention that to show that he owed his appointment to <u>himself</u> alone – Lord Fitzroy Somerset introduced him to me well knowing from his connection with the Dear Duke if [two illegible words] Mentioned officer he would in My sight receive Attention. I have written to Lady Smith – who is 800 miles off to show Mrs Wellesley any attention she may be able –

Believe me
My Dear
Mrs Wellesley
faithfully
H. Smith

18

From Edward Wellesley to his wife

King William's Town
July 12. 1851.

My dearest Annot
The Frontier Mail has not yet arrived and I therefore have no news from you. I dined with Sir Harry last night and dine with

him again to-night and played Whist which is the usual after dinner practice. I shall soon become a good player. I am to go on a short Patrol on Tuesday for three days Colonel Eyre having applied for my assistance and Sir Harry wishing me to go as he says it may be of use to me. We are only going about ten miles from here. I have succeeded in getting a room in the Town with a Stable attached which will be better than a tent and I have consequently sold the one I bought at Cape Town as I never keep anything I do not use. Your oranges were very delightful and quite a novelty in this part of the world and your Plum Pudding also and also the Sugar Candy and the Potatoes were very good. Now however you need not trouble yourself to send any more of the latter as I now dine at the Mess of the 6th when not at the Governor's. I hope you are now settled in your new abode, you must go out if it is possible daily and get anything you want to make your house pleasant to live in. I keep this open until the last moment in case I have to acknowledge the receipt of any of yours.

July 12. The Mail has not arrived and I dine with Sir Harry again to-night.

Good-bye in haste
Always my dearest Annot
Yours most affectionately
Edward Wellesley

19

To his brother Richard

King Williams Town,
British Kaffraria
July 12. 1851

My dear Richard

You will be glad to hear that Sir Harry Smith has given me a Staff Appointment having made me Deputy Assistant Adjutant General and attached me to the Head Quarters of the Army here. When Lord Fitzroy's letter arrived I sent it to him & dined with him the same night. he however did not once allude to it, two days afterwards we went on Patrol an account of which I will give you and we remained out for ten days in the Field, the longest Patrol which has taken place since the War commenced. Sir Harry met the Force on its return & rode up to me saying "Well Wellesley Are you quite well how do you like the Bush work" he then went on to the front of the Column & in about five minutes sent his Aide de Camp for me he was then riding with Colonel Eyre the Officer who Commands the 73rd Regiment; he then said "I intend to place you on the Staff, since my name would be enough to make me grateful to any one holding it, but independently of this your own merits on Patrol would incline me to give it to you. Colonel Eyre says that he will be most sorry to lose you which is the greatest compliment which he could pay you" he then ended by saying "Your Great Uncle gave me my first Staff Appointment & I don't see why I should not give his Grand Nephew one." A day afterwards I called again to thank him when he kindly said that nothing but my own merits had induced him to appoint me that he had allowed me to go on two or three Patrols to see as he said "What sort of a fellow I was" & that he had written to Lord Fitzroy to tell him so & he also said that he had written to Mama Whose letter I on this occasion took him, to the same effect.

Since then I have frequently dined with him & seen him & nothing can exceed his kindness to me. I commenced my duties the day after we returned from Patrol. I am generally at my office from 9 am sometimes earlier for everybody begins very early here & remain to 3 or 4 as there may happen to be work or not. My immediate superior is Colonel Cloete a very nice gentlemanly man who is Deputy Q Master General & has also charge of the Adjutant General's Department. He has worked hard enough before [illegible] appointed as we have no Clerks up here in the Field the work being done by the Officers themselves & I find my training as Adjutant of the greatest service being quite au fait at the details of the officers in Ireland & England & the system of carrying on the service. As I told you we were out on Patrol for ten days & had a most successful foray having captured 1500 head of cattle in one day. We had some fighting on two days but only one man of the 73rd wounded which occurred in getting the Cattle up a steep wooded hill & through a dense Bush. On this occasion the Kafirs came on in some force & I send you a rough or <u>very rough</u> sketch of our skirmishing done or rather <u>underdone</u> by the Adjutant[44] I have been obliged to add some Letter press to it to aid you in making it out. I have your note of the 14th of May & also Annot received a letter from Mary. I have got a room in the town here which I succeeded in with great difficulty as the whole place is full. Annot is at Cape Town in the Castle Barracks there as also the Boy. One leads here a very regular life an example set by the General who breakfasts at 8 o/c with all his Staff breaking theirs & then rides still accompanied by all his personal Staff, at 6½ he dines all the Staff always dining there with him, he then plays at Whist; no stakes being allowed, & retires at about 9½ or 10. I have had some very interesting conversations with him his anecdotes of Military & other great people being very good & his reverence & affection for the Duke very fine & I have seen him quite affected when talking about some Kindness which he had shown him & says he is the kindest-hearted man in the world but no [?spoon]. Pray make a point of calling upon Lord Fitzroy & thanking him for the letter he sent & for which I am indebted for Sir Harry's appointment on my part.

Yours affectionately
Edward Wellesley

Remember me affectionately to Mary

20

To his wife

King Williams Town
July 30th, 1851.

My dearest Annot

I received yours of 20th and 24th and by the latter was glad to see that you had returned to the Castle but you must take the greatest care of your health as these fainting fits will never do. I am very glad that you put a decided veto on Muter buying one of Campbell's horses as I meant to tell him on no account to buy me one that had been in harness but fought; as the Hermes sailed so suddenly after yours of the 24th, I am afraid he could not send the horse if he had got it by now and he must therefore take the first opportunity by some other steamer of which there be plenty with the new troops and if he goes to Carruthers and asks him I dare say he will get his passage for the horse to East London if there is any difficulty.

Pray do not be fretting as you seem to do. I am sorry you were out when Lady Smith called but hope you will make her acquaintance soon. The De Schmidts have been very civil to you but you were quite right to refuse their offer of the house.

With regard to your superstition about rooms I should think as I have often told you that there is hardly a house or room in the world in which some one has not died. The 12th Lancers and two other Infantry Regiments are daily expected and of course every one is in high spirits at the reinforcement.[45]

I have no doubt that my appointment is permanent but you can easily imagine that I could not ask any one who would be the only person to know whether it is or not, matters of delicacy which you will appreciate would prevent me and with respect to my remaining here when the War is over and so on which you say some one has mentioned to you be sure no one not even Sir Harry himself has yet settled any plan of what is to happen when the War finishes. The first thing being to end it. I hope the boy is going on well plenty of cold water I know will be used with him. Any furniture you want you may get as it would be useful anywhere but only the <u>best</u> and handsomest if you buy any. I said in a former note about you going into a boarding house but think now you are much safer where you are and had better remain there.

Adieu I have been writing all day and it is now near the post time. I dine with Sir H to-night and wish it was with you. Give up thoughts of coming here it is only a place for men but not for ladies at present.

Always yours

Most fondly

Edward Wellesley

We have no English letters yet except the Governor's Despatches but suppose we shall get them to-morrow. Keep all the papers if there are any for your own amusement.

21
To his wife

King Williams Town
August 1 1851

My dearest Annot

This is not a day of much work so I begin my 1st weekly communication.

I dined with Sir Harry on Wednesday night who enquired after you and said that Lady Smith had been or was going to call upon you. I wish you would send me by any opportunity Van de Sandts Cape of Good Hope Almanac and Register for 1851 which you can buy at Robertsons I think. No mail from the Colony has arrived although yesterday was the day. Messrs Borrodaile and Co are the agents in Cape Town for the 73rd Regt. and you can send and ask them when you have anything to send whether they are sending to East London if not you can send any parcel to Segt. Carede who I dare say will see it forwarded by any one of the Queen's Steamers which is going and put O.H.M.S. which will ensure its quick passage. On letters however which go by the regular post you must not do this as I should thereby defraud the Government. I hope you are well and pray do not excite or fret yourself. We must take all our moments as matters of course and provided for us for the best. We are obliged to be separated now. No horse by the 'Hermes' so I hope Mater [Muter?] will send him by the first steamer which happens to go.

August 2nd

I received your parcel yesterday by Segt. Penny the things quite safe and very pretty the opal glass which Richard was so fond of is exceedingly pretty and the Prayer Book exactly what I wanted. I had no letter from you by the Mail and hope you are not ill. I also expected some English letters but only a very few came. I dined with the Governor last night. We have now a Patrol out which is expected back to-day. I got your note in the parcel dated July 16. The under garments not as yet tried because I wrote what I wanted you to do.

Good bye
Always yours most fondly and affectionately
Edward Wellesley

I gave Dickson the parcel. I paid the little bill which you sent to the Quarter Master here sometime ago when the things arrived.

Keep me au fait about your money matters when you are running out.

22

To his wife

King William's Town
August 6. 1851.

My dearest Annot

I have been writing so much all day that I have only time before the post to say how much I felt the intelligence in your note of the 28th and only trust in God that the poor boy is now recovering as children are so subject as I know to illnesses of all descriptions, and I feel the more deeply for you as I know your kind heart which suffers more than the person can themselves.

I have every confidence in Bickersteth[46] who is very clever and hope he has been enabled to turn the current of the disease. Pray do not fret yourself in your present state too much.

Adieu my one darling and note Annot I have only time to say
Edward Wellesley

23

To his wife

King William's Town
August 8. 1851.

My dearest Annot

I received yours with the welcome intelligence that the boy had got over the fever, this evening – the Mail having been late as usual as it should have arrived yesterday. You can imagine how glad I was and as much on your account as his, as I know what a dreadful state of mind you must have been in. I hope he will now get quite well again and we are greatly indebted to Bickersteth who I am sure is very clever. Here we go on the same as usual – there is no Patrol out. We have not had any rain here and the country is quite dried up. I trust you do not feel the storms in your rooms and am glad that you like them. Next month I fancy is the first of summer. I shall close this to-morrow Saturday. I received your papers and numbers of Illustrated from England which I will send you. When the subscription is up of the Cape Town Mail which it is the end of next month I shall give it up as it is infernally radical, and you can take a Quarter's Subscription of the "Cape Monitor" from the 1st August – it being a very good Colonial paper and its tone far above any other in the Cape. Your servant's husband has given me £6 which you can therefore pay to her. I have not seen the individual but he gave the money to Dickson who gave it to me. He belongs to some Volunteer Corps here of whom we have all sorts and descriptions and whose appearance is the most amusing in the world and I often wish that I could draw to send home a sketch of some of the figures of people who do the duty of soldiers here. Sir Harry has not been well lately in fact I do not think he is very strong and the unpleasant duties he has had since the day he arrived in the Colony from [words missing] Kafirs' Wars and convict questions have been more than any governor of the Cape ever had to contend with.

Adieu my own beloved Annot I hope your next will contain as favourable accounts of the boy as your last.

Always yours most
Fondly and affectionately
Edward Wellesley

24

To his brother Richard

King Williams Town
British Kaffraria
August 14.1851.

My dear Richard

Since my last letter to you this War has been languishing and all the spirit and daring which distinguished the Kafirs at the commencement have disappeared they now seldom if ever fight the regular troops, they seem entirely to have deserted their great strongholds the Amatola Mountains and have broken into the Colony in small parties of mixed Kafirs and Hottentots where they burn the Farm houses carry off the Cattle and sheep, and commit every harm and devastation on the unfortunate Border Farmers, these latter were warned at the beginning of the War that they should embody themselves for their own protection as the regular Army had to carry on offensive operations in Kaffraria, very few of them have responded to the appeal from the Governor, and they have suffered in consequence. I have only been out on Patrol once since I wrote when we took some Cattle and two Women Prisoners who were released although our Black Allies the Fingoes would have been most happy to cut their throats had they not been narrowly watched, Women have been frequently taken Prisoners during the last month and they all say that the Kafirs have migrated across the Kei river taking their Cattle with them. In the meantime Sir Harry has sent out from here Patrol after Patrol in quick succession who have taken much Cattle destroyed every "Kraal" they could and harassed the Kafirs in every way – these frequent successes have had the effect of bringing the Chiefs who were professedly neutral at the beginning of the War but who there is no doubt assisted the Chiefs in actual rebellion, to wish to ingratiate with the Governor which they have done and one of them "Umkala" [?] who occupies country near this came in the other day bringing with him some Cattle (which he stated had been driven into his country by some of the Gaikas) as a peace offering. Cows are the pivot on which all turns here and the sight of a herd when out on Patrol sets a whole Column of troops wild with excitement their capture being in fact the only proof one has to give of a successful foray. We are in daily expectation of the reinforcements of troops from England which should have been sent here on the first outbreak & thereby prevented half the expense, and enabled Sir Harry to finish the War at once, but the reverse was the policy at home and cost the Country no more here than they do there, the Governor was obliged to raise Hottentot Levies here who are twice as expensive as the regular Soldier, all unfit and useless for duty for some time after they join and the whole of whose families have to be supported by the Government while they are in the Field at an enormous cost. The country in the vicinity is quite parched and dried up as the rain having failed; our days pass here with great regularity. I am generally employed until three or four o'clock from nine in the morning. I dine frequently with Sir Harry who finishes the night with successive rubbers of Whist his invariable partners being Colonel Mackinnon who is Commandant of British Kaffraria and Commander of the 2nd Division of the Army and who I see has been sufficiently abused in some of the English papers for a disastrous affair he had at the beginning of the War when he went to take a great Chief Sandili with unloaded Muskets, he is an old guardsman to which of course all his misfortunes are attributed by men in the Line. We have some Cricket which is an acquisition as you cannot ride a hack very far here now without the chance of being shot by a stray Kafir, a few days ago one of the Levy here had an Assegai (which is a short spear or rather dart) thrown through his leg by a Kafir on the banks of the river one mile from the town, in the open plains you are safe, but the Bush is to be avoided.

One of the regiments expected has just arrived, and the whole country is being scoured to purchase Horses for the 12th Lancers. A few Kafirs here come in giving up their guns and Assegais and reports that a great meeting has been held in the Amatolas to concert what measures to take, the people being perishing with hunger, were it not for their allies the Hottentots the Kafirs would perhaps give in, the former however may not yet have given up their idea of a "Hottentot Republic" (nearer the mark) which scheme was discussed the other day in some papers taken from their Camps, and driving the White Man into the sea; in the meantime the London Missionary Society at home as seen by their last adopted report encourage and foment rebellion, murder, and anarchy, by their abusive and disgusting details imputing Kafir rights and the injustice of their rulers and such like humbug and the Missionaries here have been by all that I have heard totally different people, are if not the <u>sole</u> cause of the present outbreak of the coloured people against the European, and still more, are strongly suspected of carrying on an infamous trade in Arms &

gunpowder with the savage, to enable him to fire upon the Queen's troops, or massacre the peaceful inhabitants of villages as has been perpetrated on the unoffending people of Auckland and Woburn two villages in Kaffraria at the commencement of the War. This description of [illegible] should be hunted from the world and in fact I don't think their Funds are so flourishing as they were in Sir F. Buxton's time, so we may hope for their gradual extinction.

Annot is at the Castle at Cape Town, our boy has been ill with a fever which was prevalent there, but is now happily getting rapidly well again. I have received no end of Illustrateds interesting enough from the views of the Exhibition in which FM <u>the Duke</u> is invariably introduced. I hope they will keep it open for some years and then perhaps Colonial parties of which I am now one may have a chance of seeing it. Lord Grey has approved all Sir H. Smith's acts which is of course flattering enough as we have no chance if the Minister at home does not support you and I believe he would have sent the whole British Army here if required, he has just sent some additional Instructions which have been published and which have authorized the Governor to carry on his Government with only five Members if necessary & which is a death blow to all the democrats who have refused to sit in the Council thereby depriving the Cape of any Government at all for two years as more Members were necessary to form a quorum.

Give my kindest love to Mary and believe me
Yours affectionately
Edward Wellesley

25

To his wife

King William's Town
August 26th 1851.

My dearest love
I received yours of the 18th yesterday. Our Mail still adhering to its good character and being in time. I sent you a cheque in a former note, and recollect in future always let me know in time

when you want money as the post is seven days to me, and seven days back, which makes half a month and you should therefore always let me know <u>that time</u> before you actually want it as you are quite right not to owe money in Cape Town at present. Your nurse's husband although I have not seen him very recently told Dickson that if he did not send her the money he would spend it probably himself; with regard to Dickson he was in debt in his company upwards of 30th [£30?] when he came here in which position his wife probably assisted to place him, therefore he has done very well in clearing this and also putting in the Bank £2 in three months since he has been here. I shall also make him put something in every month in future; I have no idea of any one annoying you by crying &c but common people do little else, and I also know some one else who is fond of it and whom I shall scold one day very much if I hear the one does anything of the sort, spoiling her eyes and complexion. I did not understand what you mean by the three rooms off your own, because you told me before that you had four rooms. Let me therefore know when you next write, as you say you wish to have one which I could no doubt write and get you.

You are right to give up the Cape Town Mail and take a subscription to the "Monitor" as I told you before, when I was formerly at the Cape the Mail was a good paper but since has become radical and abusive.

You may rely upon it no Troops will leave this Frontier and positions until the War is completely finished and least of all the 73 Regiment, although I think privately that they will go to Cape Town as they have been engaged more in it than any other; their movements however as you know will not affect mine in any way.

Do not associate the name of an office with the usual idea of gloom and darkness, mine is a sunny little room with three tables occupied by Col Cloete the Deputy Qr. Mr. General Col Mackinnon the Commandant of Kaffraria and myself. The windows open to the ground and on to a grass plot where one can go out and sun and air oneself at any moment, and I have rendered the business into a methodical arrangement as you may easily imagine from me and considerably reduced it thereby.

Send me with the maps I asked you to get my "Regulations for the Dress of the Army" a red book which you will find in my bookcase.

The "Birkenhead" people have not yet arrived the weather has been tempestuous and I shall leave this open to tell you to-morrow whether they have or not. I hear the Reverend Dacre[47] is very unreverend indeed, scandal again you see on my side.

Pray do not nurse that heavy boy whom I am happy to hear is so well take great care of yourself and don't cut any one you know on account of No 17.

It is now nine o'clock at which hour I generally retire as I dare say you do. I breakfast at eight punctually, the mornings are fresh and lovely, no fear of any summer until November and December.

Good night dearest Annot
Yours most fondly and truly
Edward Wellesley

27th

I have just received your note and book from Birkenhead all safe and the other have arrived and this place is quite alive to-day with people and a number of Rebel Hottentots who have been brought prisoners from Fort Hare.

26

To his wife

King William's Town
September 12. 1851.

My dearest love

No English Mail, and no other from you and I am beginning to be afraid that you have not become well. The packet by the Steamer has not yet arrived, the bar at the Buffalo being we understand not practicable.

I have been riding to-day my new horse whom I like very much. Sir Harry enquired very kindly of you on the last time I dined there, and in his usual manner asked me rather a home question

47

which I could not <u>positively</u> answer. There has been much fighting lately in the Fish River Bush where there have been several Patrols out. The Drafts for Regiments here have arrived by the Cyclops and I supposed touched on their way at Table Bay. I hope and trust you are quite well but as I received no letter in the Bag last post I am anxious about you. I shall leave this open until tomorrow Saturday hoping that the mail may come in and I may have a letter from you.

Saturday 13.

I received yours of the 4th last night. I cannot imagine why the parcel I gave the man of the 6th did not arrive. However there was no letter in it so I do not much care for the other things merely books and newspapers. Recollect never put a letter in a parcel at present. I am glad to hear that the boy is going on well.

Having weather here which will give some pasturage for the unhappy cattle who are very much starved.

No parcel as yet from the Cyclops.

Yours very truly and
Affectionately
Edward Wellesley

Don't use black Wax any more

27

To his brother Richard

King Williams Town
British Kaffraria
September 14. 1851.

My dear Richard

This Kafir War has now completed its ninth month of pregnancy but as yet no signs of a deliverance have appeared. The curious and mysterious causes which have united the Kafir and Hottentot races, before the hottest enemies, the former having driven the latter out of this country, against the English, are still in existence, and both still continue to fight with the greatest bravery and in fact the War seems just at this moment to have commenced again as we have just had accounts of two actions in both of which the loss on our side has been immense both in killed and wounded. In the first the 74th Regiment were engaged, they had ascended a steep summit called the Wolf's head in a range of what is called the Kroome Forest, and were here attacked on an open plain by 2000 Kafirs and Hottentots led by Macomo and Gaika Chiefs, these they beat off, and drove back into the Bush, in descending a narrow pass where only two or three Soldiers could march abreast, this small force of only 600 men were again attacked and the Fingoes[48] our black allies became panic stricken, rushed down the hill shrieking and firing off their guns in all directions, and so crowded upon the 74th Highlanders that the latter could not use their arms and the Kafirs seeing their advantage, rushed in upon them shooting and stabbing with their assegais all within their reach. In the second affair in which the 2nd Division of the Army have been engaged & are still out, an equally unfortunate affair for us has taken place, a small party of the 2nd Regiment who were detached from the Main body with a portion of Levies seem to have got into a pass or defile where they were surrounded by the enemy on three sides and shot down by numbers, their officer killed, and the guides, and but for the lucky appearance of another part of the force who arrived the whole of them would have been massacred, as it was those who escaped threw themselves over a precipice and all the dead with their Arms, Ammunition &c fell into the hands of the enemy, this took place in what is called the Fish River Bush a most dense and impenetrable forest of small wood which has lately been occupied by Kafirs & Hottentots in great force & which the 2nd Division from hence has been occupied in clearing and is now engaged there, consequently we have no authentic accounts of this affair but the Kafir reports from which I take the above are always astonishingly correct. Unfortunately the Regiment which has suffered so severely has only just arrived in this country and so cunning and wily is the Kafir that he no doubt took advantage of this inexperience in Bush fighting to inflict so severe a loss, the Officer who was killed was married only before he left England and I am told always had a

presentiment of his fate, a not unusual occurrence. The Troops
sent out from England and one Regiment which has arrived from
Mauritius will increase the Army materially but nothing can be
more disgraceful to a country like England with such a Navy and
Steam fleet than the manner in which they have been sent out,
fancy the miserable economy which makes the Admiralty order a
Master of a Steam Vessel taking out Troops to an Army in active
operations in the field, not to use his Steam but to sail whenever
he can, that he may save a few shillings worth of coals, when the
Farms are being devastated and the poor people driven out of their
homes penniless, which the presence of these very troops might &
would have prevented; or can you imagine anything more
blameable than the state in which the Steam navy is kept when <u>no
Steam</u> can be found capable of conveying a Regiment of a few 600
men to the Cape, but three break down in their trial before starting
and the Government in the 19th Century are obliged to hire <u>two
sailing vessels from private owners</u> to perform this duty which of
course take three or four months in the passage, & have not arrived
yet. The French do these things better, they build Steam vessels
expressly for the conveyance of Troops, and which no doubt we
ought to they should be capable of containing 1000 men and the
Troops thus provided for would land in a far more efficient state
than as at present where they are crowded into a transport never
intended to carry human beings but possibly pigs or sugar, &
where disease is contracted & where nothing but great discomfort
can be experienced by the poor Soldiers. I think the Government
should have five of this description of Vessel, one or two built to
carry Cavalry, for it is certainly not too much for England to be
able to throw five thousand men on any point which might be
desired suddenly, and without the aid of private persons. The
country has suffered severely lately for want of rain and in
consequence the horses and Cattle are in wretched condition
which influence the movements of the troops very materially, all
the supplies for the Army are carried in Wagons drawn by oxen
which when in bad condition travel very slowly, sometimes not
more than seven miles in twelve hours, attached to the 2nd
Division there are Mule Wagons drawn by spans of six mules and

the superiority of the mule over the ox both in endurance and speed is very great, they also keep their condition much better and on less food. I have often thought that the introduction of the Camel and Elephant into this country would be of the greatest utility in connection with an Army in the field; in India they are both used, can carry large burdens and are (the former especially) tractable and easily managed, the Cape seems naturally suited to the Camel, the soil is similar to that of Asia, the shrubs and bushes they could well feed upon, and the want of water so prevalent here and from which the other animals suffer so much, would be less felt by the Camel accustomed to travel miles without it; the advantage to troops operating in the country would be very great, now when in the field for any length of time, supplies must be carried for their sustenance and also corn for the horses of the Cavalry in Wagons, these travel very slowly, are always an impediment from oxen falling from fatigue & other causes, are also an object of attack by Kafirs, and can only be taken on certain roads and when in Camp require a large guard thus taking part of the force which might otherwise be used in active movements; the Camel on the other hand is the most hardy of animals, he can also travel wherever a horse can go, and could consequently always accompany the troops, and their supplies would thus always be with them and not as is the case sometimes with Wagons, miles in their rear nothing is so hopeless a task as convoying a long train of Wagons of which the first is perhaps five miles from the last, to guard them effectively requires a large force which if you have not they are lost, as was the case in the last War when the 7th Dragoon Guards had sixty captured from them by the Kafirs when they lost their plate and everything belonging to themselves and their Mess and had an Officer and several men killed and wounded. I observed in my last letter to you the Missionaries of whom I retain the same hard opinion, one of them is even now living in the midst of hostile Kafirs who are fighting against us and it is absurd to suppose that his holy character prevents him from having his throat cut, although probably his trade in gunpowder & Arms has that effect; when Savages have been civilised to some extent then Clergymen, true Ministers, are of the most incalculable benefit, but when to obtain popularity with their half savage congregation they preach the equal rights of man and the wrongs of the Black, they abuse their Mission, and create discontent and misery in place of peace; a course which most of those here have followed and which has ended in rebellion of a large portion of the coloured population against the white.

To assist Sir Harry Smith in settling the affairs between the Kafirs & ourselves Lord Grey has lately dispatched here two Assistant Commissioners who arrived and are now living here, their Commission is for two years & they receive each £1000 per annum and allowances for as many horses & servants as they choose to keep, one of them Major Hogg or as since he became a Commissioner he writes himself Hogge,[49] was very much known here in the last War when he organized a Hottentot Levy and brought them to a much better state of discipline, & more useful as Soldiers than ever done before, or have been since, whether he will be as successful in his present office remains to be proved; the other man was an Officer in the Kafir police, a body of men raised by Sir Henry Pottinger during the short time he was Governor here and who were trained & disciplined as Soldiers, taught to shoot &c, and who on the breaking out of the War, first led a detachment of Troops into a decoy where they were shot down & assegaied by dozens and lost all their ammunition, and the next day all deserted to the enemy taking their horses, arms & ammunition, and have since been exercising the skill he taught them in shooting and maneuvring, on the Queen's Troops; Mr Owen this ex-Kafir Police Officer whose duties consisted in tracing thieves who had stolen Cattle & other Bow street duties, finds himself suddenly transformed into a Commissioner for "settling the affairs of the Kafir tribes" &c by Lord Grey, one of whose reasons for choosing him, as he states in his despatch, being his knowledge of the Kafir language, of which I am told he knows a little more than I do, my knowledge being confined to one word; how great our Ministers are in finding out the exact man suited for a crisis.

In addition to the War now going on in this part of the Cape, we have lately become embroiled with another tribe of Kafirs called Basutos who occupy a country near the Orange River, to protect another friendly tribe called Baralongs the British Force came into contact with the Basutos and but for the great courage of some Artillerymen, and a portion of the 45th Regiment, would have lost their guns and suffered themselves severely, the Baralongs who had in a former part of the day gained some advantage over the Basutos, were so elated with their success that a number of them got intoxicated not with joy, but with Beer and spirits which they obtained in some manner, and while in this state were set upon by the Basutos who tumbled them all over a precipice killing 150 of them.

To reinforce the Force of English Troops at Bloem Fontein, where these occurrences took place, a party of the 45th Regiment has been sent to the place from Natal, which is commanded by an old Eton Man Parish[50] whom I dare say you will remember, this party is accompanied by a body of a tribe called Zoolahs who inhabit the country adjacent to Natal, and who have thus volunteered to send some of their fighting men to aid the Government, as yet this aid has always been refused, and justly, as the employing one savage tribe against another is to be avoided, all control over them being at once lost when hostilities commence; now their assistance has been taken and the results remain to be seen. These Zoolahs are a very large and most powerful tribe of Kafirs, it is said they can bring innumerable warriors into the Field. Their Chief Chaka who raised them seems to have been an African Napoleon, he first formed these savages into regular Battalions, distinguished by the colors of their shields, his orders were that whenever any of their Chief Captains returned unsuccessful he was to be put to death, victory of course was the result of this order, as a man could only die once, and knowing that if he failed he would be put to death, was careless how he exposed himself to attain victory; Chaka was at last stabbed in the back & killed by his Mother. We have not yet come into contact with these people, and they possess neither guns or Horses, which other Kafirs do, consequently are not so dangerous, but when they obtain these, which they eventually will, and when we come into contact with them which will assuredly be the case some day, they will be the most hardy and valiant foe we have had to contend with in Southern Africa. The Fingoes are the result of Chaka's wars, having been driven out of their country and eventually been taken under the protection of the Government, they fight well on our side in open country, but in the Bush are hardly equal to the Kafir. I wish you would get and send me the best and latest Map published by either Wild or Arrowsmith of the Frontier of the Cape. I want more particularly the country of the Orange River Sovereignty, so perhaps two, one of this and the other of the Eastern Frontier, would be the best plan. I do not want British Kaffraria as I have a good map of that part, consult Wild or Arrowsmith as I understand that there are maps in preparation from very recent surveys. I wish you would also get me a Book called "Fifteen decisive Battles of the World" from Marathon to Waterloo, which I see advertised for publication, it is by Creasy whom you will recollect as gaining the Newcastle at Eton, and who has written a very good book on that College which if you have not seen I advise you to read.

Annot is well at Cape Town and the Boy. Give my best love to Mary and believe me

Yours affectionately
Edward Wellesley

The English Mail which left England on the 15th of July has not arrived and it is feared has met with some accident.

28

To his brother Richard

King Williams Town
British Kaffraria
September 23. 1851

My dear Richard
I wrote you so long a letter on other day all about Kafirland that I will not inflict another upon you, but merely acknowledge the receipt of your note from Broadstairs of the 29th of June and hope that Mary and yourself benefitted from the sea air which after a season in London is very delightful if you could see the costume of some of the Natives here you would at first exhibit I think a

succession of Broad stares. There is nothing new from here since I wrote. The English Mail has not yet arrived and the August one is also now due, and I am afraid that Sir Robert Peel must have met with some severe accident or been entirely lost.

Annot tells me that she heard from Mary from Broadstairs. Give my love to the latter & believe me

Yours affectionately
Edward Wellesley

Let me know if you received my cheque for yourself on Easter.

29

To his wife

King William's Town
October 3. 1851.

My dearest love

I received your letter of the 25th and all the newspapers and the mail from the Retribution also arrived from East London to-day and I got your note of the 13th and Cape Monitor and Muter's receipt. I got and acknowledged previously all your numerous letters and parcels &c. I enclose a cheque on the commissariat for £35 which I hope will reach you safely. The people from the Retribution have not yet arrived as the bar at the Buffalo mouth has been impracticable for landing so Reeve with your parcel has not yet made his appearance. How lazy they are in England not to write even one line. I however never make many friends even in my own family. We have a lull here at present, no fighting, but unsatisfactory accounts of the feelings of the Tribes not actually at War with us. The appearance of the Troops from the Retribution will have a good moral effect. We had some rain yesterday and the country looks beautiful.

Good bye God bless you
Always yours most affectionately
Edward Wellesley

You ought to have kept all the papers for yourself as I told you before.

30

To his wife

King William's Town
October 15. 1851.

My dearest love

I received Doctor Bickersteth's very welcome note which I have replied to and enclose, and hope that you and the little girl are going on well, by this time.[51] If you recover as rapidly as you did before you will be out again, ten days I think saw you out before. I hope Bickersteth was attentive and have thanked him for his attention when the boy was ill in my note. With regard to a nurse for the child you must do as you like best yourself, whatever you like I shall also, but I am afraid you will be too delicate to nurse her as you mentioned, and if so pray do not attempt it. The girl must eventually be named Hyacinthe a family name with us.

Have a carriage as often as you like and take plenty of air, I shall write to Richard by the next post and send him an announcement to be put in the Times. I am very happy that you are so far well and you must have had great courage to write to me on the 2nd as Bickersteth says you were very ill on the 3rd.

Good bye
and God bless you
Always yours most affectionately and fondly
Edward Wellesley

31

To his brother Richard

King Williams Town
British Kaffraria
October 16. 1851.

My dear Richard

I received your limited note of the 14 August from which I perceive you are again in London, I am much obliged to you for paying the small bill I sent you & must also trouble you to pay the enclosed by Post Office order and send me the receipt by an opportunity which will leave £9-7-6 of mine with you

There has not been much going on here but since I last wrote to you, the Kafirs and Hottentots are principally located in the Fish River Bush and Kroome Forest range where they subsist on the Cattle and Sheep stolen from the unhappy Colonists, in the former we have had a stationary Force latterly, endeavouring with shot and shell to drive them out, the latter we have as yet not been able to attack from the paucity of our numbers & the vast extent of forest to be cleared, where Macomo a Chief of the Gaikas is located a clever and influential man with some two or three thousand followers and Major General Somerset is about to attack him having been strongly reinforced from here, if he succeeds well it may have an important effect on the termination of the War. All the Troops expected from England have arrived and there would be occupation enough for six thousand more if they could be sent out, as our enemies seem to increase instead of diminish and some of the neutral Chiefs, particularly Kreili who occupies the country on the other bank of the Kei River which is forty miles from here, have become pugnacious & impertinent, and as all the cattle of the Gaikas is known to have been driven into Kreili's country for safety, in the end we shall most probably take some signal measures upon him for his duplicity and treachery.

We have had very little rain here and the country is parched in consequence, the summer is also commencing and the heat increasing; in this month the Kafirs sow, the operation performed by the Women, who with a child generally slung to their backs may be seen digging & planting in their gardens, if for <u>sow</u> we could read <u>sew</u> the work would be more feminine. Annot was safely confined of a daughter on the 5th instant & they are both going on very well, I shall call this child Hyacinthe being a family name. I send you a paper which perhaps you will be so good as to send to the Times for insertion.

Give my kindest love to Mary

believe me

Yours affectionately

Edward Wellesley

32

To his wife

King William's Town
October 21. 1851.

My dearest love

I received Bickersteth's third note – a reply to which I enclose. He tells me that you were very anxious to write yourself but I hope you will not exert yourself too soon, and he also said that you and the baby were going on very well, although you had had a slight fever. I saw Mrs Maydwell also the other day who gave me a very favorable account of you and the Baby whom she said was very fat and well. She is a matter of fact woman and talks enough for ten. She told me that you had a very good nurse and praised Bickersteth who it seems attended her for something or other.

Major General Somerset has had some hard fighting in the Kroome range where Macomo a cunning and influential Chief of the Gaikas is located. There had been fighting for two days and Somerset would go on until he effectually clears this difficult country from all the enemy who infest it. The Kafirs and Hottentots have been fighting very well and we have lost many men. If Somerset completely effects this duty it may have more influence on the termination of the War, and I confess I should very much like him to be successful having a great partiality for all Somersets to whom we are connected.

There is another force from here the 6oth Rifles being out for the first time. The Lancers are not as yet mounted so they are not of any use at present.

We had some rain here the day before yesterday and the weather has been delightful. We have our post regularly now that I hope to hear from you or about you to-morrow before the mail leaves and this open to acknowledge it.

October 22.

No other news as yet,

Always yours
Most fondly, and truly,
Edward Wellesley

33

To his wife

King William's Town
October 30th 1851.

My dearest Annot,

The rain came on last night and still continues and being heavy and no wind we shall have plenty of grass eventually. No Mail has yet arrived and we have no news from General Somerset.

31.

The Mail arrived last night and I was very glad to see by your handwriting of the 24th that you were evidently gaining strength. What a concatenation of illnesses you have had to endure with the boy's and your own, so unfortunate all happening together. I am happy however that you all seem to be getting better. Bickersteth must have enough to do. I laughed at Ingleby's note.[52] You see how right I was when I told you what a bore it is to live in a Barrack particularly when ill. I don't wish you to carry your acquaintance any further with the Colonel in fact I don't see what right he had to write to you. I suppose however he is an Irishman. I am happy to hear that the little girl is so fat and well and had such pretty black eyes. I do not much like the idea of your making a nurse of yourself, but I do not either like to prohibit it, but I am afraid you will not be strong enough, and if feasible the baby might from its infancy be brought up by the hand which I fancy is often done.

I do not wish you to accept Mrs Eyre's offer, but pray hire a carriage from Kannemeyer whenever you can go out. I dislike her and her husband most particularly.[53]

A very good report from Somerset has arrived – he seems to have driven Macomo and his band from the Blinkwater country and will probably follow them to the Amatolas and there will very likely be a co-operating party sent from here to assist him. A Patrol of the Rifles who had joined him have come in. Sir Harry made them a flattering speech on their arrival and we then went out riding. I will ask him to stand godfather to the little girl and Lady Smith godmother, and the other must be Hyacinthe or Mary whichever was not before. He has however had so much to do the last few days that I have not spoken to him and there is no hurry until you are perfectly well again. I think one name quite sufficient for any one and in fact never myself use my second, but perhaps if Lady Smith stands as godmother it would be complimentary to let her name be the second, Hyacinthe being the first, of which I will write you more hereafter.

I enclose a cheque for £15 which perhaps you may want. Bickersteth should get £15-20 or £25 which should it be, if you can decide without referring to me pray do and pay him when you like, if not let me know, but whatever you do will I am sure be right only more generous than the reverse, and after you have once paid him if he calls professionally give him always his £1, and insist upon his taking it. I will write to him again some day as he seems to have been most kind and attentive. We still expect the Styx with English Mail.

Most people whose opinions are of any value seem to think that our successes under Somerset may have the greatest influence on the War, and these have made some of the neutral but wavering chiefs become all at once very abject. They all however differ so much as to what has the most influence in causing the Kafirs to wish for peace, whether taking their cattle or fighting and killing themselves, that for one who like myself has not been sufficiently long here to form my own opinion, it is difficult to decide which is right and which wrong. Macomo has however so much influence and sagacity that I think if he is thoroughly beaten into submission the other chiefs will follow.

In the meantime the women we hear have sown all their gardens in the Amatolas while the men have been fighting, who shall say whether they will also reap.

I fret for you very much with all your illnesses and to be alone, why do people marry soldiers – a farmer's wife jogs on from day to day never having her beloved object out of her sight for perhaps one day in three score years and ten. Perhaps they get tired of one another, although of course you on reading this, in fact I see you, blush and say not if they love each other I think the Duke in the Peninsula did not see his wife and children for six or seven years.

I am getting sadly prosy so good-bye,
                                    Ever yours most affectionately
                                            Edward Wellesley

November 1. No more news.

34

To his wife

[First page(s) missing]

                                            [November 2. 1851]
the reason that Mary's and Richard's letters arrive in so mysterious a manner is some deep laid plan of economy on the former's part to save the shilling which you say you have not to pay, she will spoil Richard and I shall tell him that the effect of their plan is that we never receive their letters until a month after everyone else and sometimes not at all.

Pray change your rooms if you like and can get others which you prefer. Mrs Maydwell told me that you had made some acquaintances and I am glad that they call upon you. You are right in saying Mrs Eyre is sensible too much so or else she would I think have cut her husband long ago. You will have seen by my last letter that I intended to ask Sir Harry and Lady Smith to stand for the little girl, but I will think over what you say about Lord Hatherton and let you know by the next post.

If the girl is fair and has also black eyes she will be very pretty and notwithstanding your sage remarks about women and beauty I say (as I forgot who said before) give me beauty and I will make a child good. Lord Chesterfield shewed a deep insight into human nature when he said what a passport into ones good opinion it was and how it prepossessed people in the possessor of its favour, and I think Satan should be painted as a beautiful woman and not as a devil black and with a tail, as in the former case one might be induced to obey the dictates, in the latter one is only delighted [?disgusted].

We have had a violent thunder-storm with lightning rain and hail to-day which latter have refreshed our parched earth. Mr Dacre preached in the morning and not badly his text being the parable of the people who were first invited to the Wedding whom he explained to mean the Jews &c, so you see I remember my text. The room where the service is held is very small and hot. I dine and live more in my room as I found the Mess a long journey in wet weather living at an opposite end of the town. Don't however think of sending me any things which I know will be your first thoughts as I now can get anything I want even to potatoes here.

I send the Monitor to Richard, it is a good paper for the Colony and I have no doubt has been of some service in counteracting the tendency to ultra-democratism which the Cape Colonists seem lately to have been imbued with. The bitter animosity however between it and another paper are highly amusing, so perfectly provident and little, and so exactly like what Dickens describes in the Eatanswill Gazette and Independent in Pickwick.

Remember at the Cape all the Cloetes a most numerous clan, the Rivers &c are all connected in some way or other and be careful, this is the bore of a small community and you may be abusing a person's intimate relation by mistake as I have often done, not that we should care for anything of the sort on account of our family peculiarity of disliking our own, but other people are more amiable, or unamiable shall I say.

I send this by the Styx which will sail from East London to-morrow Monday the 3rd whereas the regular Mail does not leave until Wednesday.

There is no Military news of any description, the Assistant Commissioners Hogge and Owen leave this place on Tuesday with some Troops going on Patrol. They go to the Orange River Sovereignty where our officers have arrived at a complicated state which they are to, or attempt to, settle. Somerset is still indefatigably fighting in the Blinkwater. Most people here are sufficiently sanguine to anticipate an approaching term to the War; for my part I say nothing but that I am ever

Yours most affectionately,

and truly,

Edward Wellesley

The Boy must be put on a course of porter if he is too sensitive. Always put the address of a place you write to last thus

Captain Wellesley

Dep.Assist.Adjt.General

King William's Town.

I sent you yesterday a cheque for £15.

35

To his brother Richard

King Williams Town

December 2 1851

My dear Richard

As the Vulcan which is daily expected will probably return to England immediately I send this to Cape Town to await its departure. I received your letter of the beginning of October with the news of Lady Charles transfer and am only sorry that she did not send for you to entrust you both with all her fortune which from her uncertain temperament I always considered highly probable however what she did was unusually generous although it is possible that we might have had this money in the first instance but for her and it is merely an act of restitution due on her part. The discovery of the £200 was curious and I certainly think we must bring an action against Montagu who may be made to discover some more dormant hundreds lying in the Bank unclaimed.[54]

Since I wrote to you the operations of General Somerset against Macomo in the Waterkloof and Blinkwater (an extensive Forest of large trees unusual in this country and broken up into a succession of deep ravines and heights) were continued for upwards of six Weeks and all the troops from here having been engaged as well as those of the Major General's own Division, he had three more British Regiments employed than were ever brought to bear on one point in any former Kafir War, and more than the Duke had in some of his first and great battles in India, and yet the result has not been completely satisfactory and the loss on our side most severe both in Officers and Men, whilst we have not the satisfaction of knowing how many of the Enemy have been killed from the nature of the ground but it was hoped it was considerable. After this had gone on for about seven Weeks, the Troops were all withdrawn, and have now all marched across the Kei where a large Force has been assembled under Somerset the object being to capture the whole of the Cattle belonging to the Gaika Chiefs and people, and to inflict a punishment on Kreili the Chief whose territory has thus been invaded, for his permitting the property of our enemies to be sheltered there, and for allowing his men to fight against us which it is well known has been the case although he was nominally at peace and we have had a Resident with him until the last moment; to save himself the following are I hear his terms, to deliver up all the Gaika Cattle, to deliver up all Colonial captured Cattle, and a fine upon himself of 10,000 head for his treachery and these terms would seem hard, but they sufficiently show one point, namely that Cows are as usual principal accessories in peace and War in this part of the world, and in fact this expedition has been long urged on Sir Harry, it being the opinion of many people who ought to be well experienced in Kafir Wars that to take your enemies Cattle is the only and sure way to end hostilities, and if such is the case the movement must be considered the most important of the whole War and is watched with great interest. As the Troops only concentrate on this day the results I cannot tell you by this; but before the regular Mail leaves it will be known whether we have been successful or not. The country in which the men are now operating is totally different from this part, being perfectly open and in which there will be I fancy no fighting, but hard galloping for the Cavalry of whom are assembled nearly one thousand a large number for this country.

I had hoped that Sir Harry himself would have taken the Field on this occasion, or before, but he has not done so, which personally I regret very much indeed, I suppose he is obliged now to be stationary as a long pending question of a Constitution for the Colony is now about to be settled the draft Ordinances for that purpose having arrived from Lord Grey.

We have had some Cricket here during the last month and impromptu horse racing has taken place nearly every day, the poor brutes who get very little forage occasionally fall down dead on arriving at the winning post. The 12th Lancers who have lately arrived create a great sensation amongst the natives who never saw a Lance before in their lives, it is however a weapon perfectly useless against Kafirs in this warfare; in case of another Boer rebellion it may be useful, and the spectacle of a very fat Boer with a lance through his back would be amusing enough.

A son of Greville[55] the Duke's Secretary in the 60th Rifles has been made an Aide de Camp to Sir Harry he tells me he knows you, I also met a Messmate of Gerald's here one Sterling, son of Sir James; all descriptions of people arrive here to see service and then disappear again. Men from Oxford with plenty of Latin & Greek are transformed into Officers of Native Hottentot Levies of whose language and habits they are profoundly ignorant. The man who was shut up in a cage by the Chinese came out patrolled [?paroled], a ponderous Indian perpetually smoking Cheroots and imbibing what they call brandy pawnee, his servant taught the sturdy British Private how to concoct the original Bengal curry out of nothing at all. A midshipman of the Navy volunteers, and during a night movement when the strictest silence is to be observed shoots by mistake an innocent Levy man on his own side, he gives him secretly money, and is never heard of. Annot is at Cape Town where the little girl and herself are going on very well. I asked Mary to be its Godmother with Sir Harry & Lady Smith. Apply the £47 as you proposed.

Give my love to Mary and

believe me
Yours affectionately
Edward J. Wellesley

36

To his wife

King William's Town
December 9. 1851.

My dearest Annot,

I received your letter of the 30th with the enclosures from Mary and Hyacinthe which I return and the pens for which I am much obliged. I am glad all your things have arrived. I expected besides the things which I have heard of a hat and cap &c from Moore. Did they arrive? If not I suppose he will send them by the next steamer or perhaps they are in a deck's box as I think I ordered them to be sent so. The patterns of your things which I also return seem all [old?] fashioned and dowdy enough. However one cannot tell except when they are together so I daresay they are pretty enough. I should not give Mary much credit for good taste as all that family seem old fashioned and seedy and she is too much afraid of spending money. Hyacinthe has taste. You need not be afraid of what they cost as Richard has £56 of mine in his hands which I told him in my last letter to apply for that purpose. I am not certain on reading your letter whether the patterns are for my approval or whether they are the same as the things you have got and will therefore keep them until you tell me. I read Mary's "dear" letter, the reason they were not altogether at the Isle of Wight was because the house was small as I see Hyacinthe says that it was the smallest cottage in the world and anything in that part of the world is so delightful. They none of them mention anything of Augustus even Richard in the letter I sent you. I hope he has not become very wild but if he has it will only be like the others of his games [friends?], who all do something which they had better avoid. I am certain there is some mystery as I asked Richard to write to me about him and it is so like him to avoid mentioning anything unpleasant. I see thay have not let Moulsey[56] yet and are evidently heartily tired of it. There is no news from here and nothing from beyond the Kei — a Kafir report says there has been some fighting, and I fancy we shall have an express from Somerset in a few days. I have received no English paper with my appointment or I would send it to you.

66

We have rain and consequently cool weather here at present. I am sorry to hear that the rats pay you so many visits. I should invite a cat to have the pleasure of meeting them as they are clean animals I believe. I gave Dixon your message in your last letter and he says that he has written to his wife; he cooks quite well enough for me as I am not particular when in Camp.

Good bye
Always yours affectionately
Edward.

[This is the last of the letters to his wife in South Africa to survive, although she remained at Cape Town and he up country, until they left in December 1853]

37

To his brother Richard

King Williams Town
British Kaffraria
December 19. 1851.

My dear Richard

The Vulcan having only arrived at East London two days ago the letter which I sent you by her will probably only arrive with this one, we have however not much Military news. Somerset on the other bank of the Kei has taken a few Cattle but the rain has been so incessant that his operations have been impeded. Eyre who marched on Butterworth a Mission Station, the inhabitants of which must have been in hourly expectation of being murdered until he arrived, was opposed on crossing the Kei but his guide having found another ford at which a portion of his troops crossed, the enemy were taken in the rear whilst fighting in front and lost 30 killed, some Cattle has also been captured it is reported by this Column but the Kei had risen so much that it is impassable and we consequently have no authentic intelligence. The Colony in the meanwhile is quiet; a strong line of defence having been formed along its borders pending these distant movements, and to prevent a rush similar to the one which took place after we had driven the

Kafirs from the Amatolas in July, and which caused such dreadful losses to the border farmers. No signs of submission are however apparent in any of the Chiefs and the War seems as far from its termination as at the commencement of hostilities. Independently of this War there are elements of confusion and anarchy in this Colony which will eventually require a firmer and more talented Governor than is required to manage the Kafir Wars. There is a strong and overpowering spirit of democracy here which has been for years gaining ground. The Government have given these people a Constitution liberal enough in its tone, but they no sooner are certain of obtaining it than they are not satisfied and ask for more. The Civil List which fixes the Salaries of all the public Servants in the Colony cannot be altered except by the Sovereign, the people here wish to give the power to the parliament which is hereafter to assemble, and there is no doubt that if they had the power they would effectually prune the salary of any obnoxious Governor or other official who might happen to offend them. All young countries pass through this ordeal of mob tendency before they attain to good order and respect for good government, it is the same with all our Colonies Canada, the Australias and others, they all have an intense desire to govern themselves and manage their own affairs, America perhaps was only the fore runner of many others who all exhibit the same growing antipathy to home Government as she did, they feel no assistance is required from the Mother Country they say, we can dispense with your troops and arm ourselves for our own protection, we do not want your Navy we are rich enough to build our own ships sufficient for the defence of our own shores, we will no longer submit to be plunged into incessant wars by the mismanagement of rulers you send us, we will not pay enormous salaries to officials who by their incapacity have reduced the country to that state that our farmers are daily murdered and their wives and children turned out from houses burned and destroyed by savage foes, made so by your ignorance, we are no longer content to be ruled by a Minister who daily exposes his ignorance of our Country in detailing to a little more ignorant Parliament his notions of Colonial policy which excite our ridicule and contempt, you England [English?] have tried and failed in ruling us we will now follow the example of our sister America and govern ourselves and perhaps become as great a country. We find in the only case which will bear any comparison with England in her vast empire of Colonies that of Spain, that Colonies have the tendency after they have become full grown to separate from their parent, South America now divided into innumerable petty republics was once the Colony of Spain in territory so great that Cortés the Conqueror of Mexico said to Charles the Fifth "I have given you more kingdoms than you had towns before" and yet not one now remains, and although an Englishman at once attributes this to the mismanagement of Spain in her Colonies, yet if you believe the Colonists of England they are as much mismanaged and show this feeling by, in Canada mobbing the Governor whenever he appears, in Australia by refusing to vote one shilling to pay their own Government unless they are allowed totally unrestricted legislature, and at the Cape by the same proceeding as in Australia, at the same time telling England that they could finish a War which is costing her millions of money and the blood of some of her best Soldiers, in three weeks if permitted to manage it in their own way.

When you walk in Pall Mall will you be so good as to pay the enclosed as I think you have some money of mine and send me this and any other receipts you have of mine as you know I am methodical on this point. Wilkinson a clever man will make you a suit of chain armour should you be going to act the part of Brian de Bois Guilbert, or anything else in the cut and thrust department.

26th.

We have an express from Somerset who has taken 2000 head of Cattle, the rain has been incessant and he describes himself as living on the top of a tree an amusing position for a General Commanding a force.

Annot is well at Cape Town as well as the little girl who was christened on Wednesday last. Give my love to Mary.

Yours affectionately
Edward J. Wellesley

38

To his brother Richard

King Williams Town
January 20 1852

My dear Richard

The expedition across the river Kei has been entirely successful not only in the large capture of Cattle, 30000 head, but also in its effects on the other Chiefs who have all sued now for peace and say they will fight no more, I have been myself twice on Patrol since I last wrote once to Fort Cox with the 43rd Regiment escorting supplies for that Fort and another, and once to the Banks of the Kei as [?] Indentured to accompany a Force sent from here to cover the return passage over the Kei was the most curious I ever [witnessed?]; the river Kei is muddy and rapid not very broad with precipitous banks rising abruptly from the stream and on the occasion of the passage was high enough being at the ford above my knees when I rode across and I was on a tolerably big horse and being there could not leave it without crossing; the Wagons, Cavalry and Cattle crossed at the Ford, the Fingoes at a point higher up the stream, and we had a pontoon bridge at a deeper spot conveying across the Infantry, the Women and Children of the Fingoes were to have been brought across on the pontoon but our humanity was thrown away as some of the men having found a place where they thought they could pass convoyed the others over and the scene was curious enough, they were all perfectly naked for although the Fingo Women habitually wear a leather tunic which reaches below the knees and a ceinture of beads underneath, on entering the water these were thrown aside and they all proceeded as they had previously come into Fingo existence, there were upwards of three hundred sometimes in the water at one time the men supporting the women and carrying the children on their heads and the old people tottering along barely able to breast the stream, some were blind and had to be led over. At the same time the Wagons and Cavalry were crossing at the Regular Ford, the former could hardly be pulled through by their Bullocks and the unhappy Missionaries with their Wives and families who travelled in these the only conveyances in their country had the prospect at one time of passing the night in the middle of the river or if perchance it rose, not an infrequent occurrence with South African rivers, of being carried out to sea Wagons and all to preach to the winds who would possibly understand and adopt their rules about as much as the Kafirs, their former flocks. The 12th Lancers who crossed at the same place were very unfortunate every second Trooper being submerged and in some cases if it had not been for the Fingoes who swam about and picked them up would have been drowned, a Dragoon always remains with his Horse until the last moment a dangerous practice when the Horse goes down as the sooner you get away from him the better a Kick on the head under water being a complete finisher to you, being bumped against the rocky bottom of a river with a steed on top of you being equally unpleasant and fatal. The Cape Corps understanding the thing better had none dismounted. The Infantry crossed very rapidly on the pontoon which is a boarded stage laid upon Cylinders of India Rubber blown out and thus buoyant, in this case a rope being carried and fixed to a rock on the opposite Bank forty men were ferried across in about five minutes for each trip without any difficulty. You can perhaps imagine the picturesque effect of all these various passages going on at the same moment, also the immense confusion and row, the Soldiers on the heights covering the passage of the Main force, the Cavalry in the Water tumbling and splashing, Wagons breaking down, Wagon drivers shouting and urging their unwilling beasts, Fingoes shrieking and driving Cattle over, Goats, Pigs, Mules floating down the stream ten thousand Cows bellowing in concert, the woods on one bank accidentally on fire and burning fiercely, the multitude of black figures in the water striving to get over with an intensely hot sun and a breeze as if from a furnace. The scenery on the banks is bold and precipitous, very few Kafirs were seen and we destroyed all the huts and our native Levies robbed all the gardens during our stay, an inglorious part of the war but unavoidable. A force will penetrate into the Amatola Mountains in a few days for the purpose of destroying all the cultivation of the Kafirs, the men are to take sickles, swords &c for this purpose and this will possibly be the closing movement of the War – as the Chiefs have all sued for peace but as yet are not so humbled as to surrender themselves unconditionally, which are the Governor's terms, and which the next movement in which all the troops are engaged may effect. By this mail the only truly encouraging despatches since the commencement go to Lord Grey, Sir Harry is consequently in high spirits.

I write in haste as this is my last day and Annot tells me my last letter to you was late for the Steamer, she is quite well at Cape Town. Give my best love to Mary and believe
me yours affectionately
Edward J. Wellesley
I have received numerous Illustrateds.

39

To his brother Richard

King Williams Town
British Kaffraria
February 15. 1852.

My dear Richard

After returning from the Kei expedition the troops remained in their cantonments for two days, but on the 27th of last month again moved on the Amatola Mountains in four separate Divisions while a fifth marched into the country of the Chief Segolo [?] (who has been one of our most active opponents although not a Gaika) the whole having orders to burn, cut down, and destroy all the huts, fences and Corn fields of the Kafirs (the latter – corn not Kafirs – being in the point of reaping) and thus destroying all their means of sustenance; for this purpose all the men were provided with reaping hooks, sickles and Dragoon Swords, and have been committing the greatest devastation which you can imagine when you consider that to reap an acre is a very small day's work for a man at home, that about four thousand men were employed, and also how much food and for what numbers of people one acre of corn will yield particularly to the Kafirs who live principally on milk and consequently do not sow in any great abundance. The Indian Corn has a stalk of the thickness of a cabbage stalk or thicker and the other species called Kafir Corn which is a kind of millet, the same, although the grain in the latter case is more similar to oats; the people crush it between two stones and when in a pulp bake it in cakes.

The Chiefs having sued for peace but not having complied with the terms of unconditional surrender which were imposed by the Governor these operations of destruction have been going on until the 10th of this month, and on that day Sir Harry issued a proclamation ordering out all Burghers and announcing his intention of taking the Command of all the united forces Regular and Irregulars from the 8th of March next to expel the enemy from all the points he still holds and drive them across the Kei,

The Chiefs hearing of this begged a suspension of hostilities to meet and "talk" about what they were to do, hostilities were consequently suspended, and three days were given them to decide whether they would all unconditionally surrender themselves or leave the country and remove themselves and their followers beyond the Kei once and for ever, they All met and their answer was evasive and Kafiresque "We are your Children, we have offended you, and have been punished, why should you punish your children any more? children will sometimes commit faults". On receipt of this, orders were immediately despatched to recommence operations with the greatest vigour and on Monday 14th a combined movement will take place on a small mountain stream the Lenya where Sandili the paramount Chief of the Gaikas has been secreted during the whole War, and by the same night I think he will find himself in the same predicament that an Irishman would be if you dug up surreptitiously all his potatoes, that is without any food for the coming season, and fortunately enough the day before hostilities ceased Eyre with the 74th Regiment had captured 500 of his own Cattle, so he will be completely destitute.

During the whole of these operations scarcely any opposition has been met with, which attests in a powerful manner the sway the Chiefs have over their people, they fought, were killed and wounded without any sympathy with the cause of quarrel (for they were much happier under our rule) When ordered by the Chiefs to do so, although knowing that if they won the day the result would be to return to the old oppression where a Chief could seize his subject's Cattle and impoverish him without a hope of redress; but when ordered not to fight, they will sit patiently and see their huts destroyed their women and children turned out into the open plain, and the whole of their means of subsistence suddenly and irreparably deprived of them, and starvation coming on, without shewing any sign of opposition; you seldom see, or read of in civilized countries such implicit obedience as this; a dog will not allow you to take his food from him.

To be obliged to resort to such modes of warfare is, and has to be confessed by the Governor in his orders, sufficiently revolting, but no alternative was left. There have been so many wars ended here by hollow truces, that the Chiefs even yet do not believe that the English are in earnest when they press such hard terms on them, to such a state of feeling has the miserable so called Glenelg policy, and the humbug of the Aborigines Protection Society system reduced English faith, we have taken their country from them, and then given it back to them, imposed fines on them, and carried this on for so long a period, some thirty years, that now they do not believe a word you say and think that if one Governor imposes one thing on them at any rate the next will cancel it; and they are also cunning enough to know our horror of expense, for Macomo one of the Chiefs and brother of Sandili told the Chiefs to "hold out for we should never be able to bear the expense of the War much longer" he could not have been better informed if he had read the "Times" habitually.

In allowing the Chiefs a truce to accept the alternative of submission or banishment no one can accuse the Governor of undue severity in fact most people would say after the losses we have sustained that they should have been allowed no cessation of war, but he can be generous, and having allowed them this interval for reflection and decision, no one can now accuse him of severity if he brings into force all the power he can to utterly quell them, and their partners in rebellion the Hottentots.

I imagine we shall all leave this place on the 3rd or 4th of March, and Sir Harry will in the first instance establish his Head Quarters at Fort Hare, thirty miles from here, or at Fort Beaufort, the first object being to completely clear out the Kroome range, comprising what is called the Blinkwater; it was in these fastnesses, which are described to be forest ranges of some twenty miles circumference in the whole, and mixed with rocks, precipices, ravines, and other naturally strong positions for defence and offence, that we lost in October and November last, as I then described to you, so many men amongst them being Fordyce[57] whom I never saw but who was a most gallant Soldier beloved by his 74th Highlanders, and by all accounts kind and humane as he was brave. Somerset commanded in these attacks which we have since ascertained were not so successful as then reported, in fact the combined Kafirs and Hottentots under Macomo, a most wily savage, are in as great force there as they were in the former months, if not in greater numbers. I fancy the whole of the troops will move on this place, and it is to be hoped that the Burghers will be inclined to assemble and cooperate with the Queen's Troops now that the Governor will command in person, although they have hitherto refused to do so and we shall then no doubt effectually turn all the rebels out of the country. I cannot say what will be the next movement as so much will depend on circumstances which may arise between this time and the date of assembly, but Sir Harry will no doubt remain in the field until he brings the war to a successful termination.

I received your letter of the 14 December by the last Mail, there will soon be many opportunities of communicating with the Cape as I see the contract for the Australian line has been accepted and the Cape is a point of re-[loading?].

Annot is well at Cape Town, give my love to Mary.

yours affectionately

Edward Wellesley

I sent a bad minute at the hand of Augustus in the shape of a letter endeavouring to persuade him to accept the Indian profession as I heard it was still available. Why don't you speak to him? Who with any true feeling of ambition would not rather be a Clive or Warren Hastings than all the Handel's and Rossinis whom God ever created.

Pray send him to Hanwell [?] and I will support you.

40

To Mrs Richard (Mary) Wellesley

Fort Beaufort
March 8. 1852.

My dear Mary

I received your letter which contained the intelligence of Sir Harry's recall, a most impolitic measure at the present crisis and which may lead to a continuance of the war for an indefinite period at the moment it was being brought to a satisfactory conclusion, as the Kafirs will naturally suppose that the appointment of a new Governor will lead to a change of measures and they will now probably not submit – but fight on until his arrival. This is the second time Lord Grey has recalled the Governor from the Cape at the moment of a War being brought to an end from motives of mere caprice, a fear of Parliament, and unnecessarily insulting and degrading old [all?] General Officers whose worth he was not aware of.

We left King Williams Town on the 5th and arrived here yesterday after a two days march, the Kroome range which is seven miles from here will be attacked by the Troops in a few days and no doubt the Kafirs and Hottentots will be effectually driven out in a short time. We, that is Sir Harry and Staff, are at present living in a house here but to-morrow we leave and shall encamp on a stream called the Blinkwater & shall remain in the Kroome until the operations are conducted moving from camp to camp of the different divisions. I sincerely hope that the War will be finished before the arrival of the other Governor, both for Sir Harry's sake and because it will be indefinitely postponed if not now brought to a conclusion.

Annot & the little girl are well at Cape Town although the heat there is very great. I must write you a short note as the Mail is going. I hope Richard is quite well and that Hyacinthe has recovered her strength

give my love
believe me
Yours affectionately
Edward Wellesley

I have sent you some papers which are amusing from the abuse they lavish upon one another in a small society, like people in a village, or the inhabitants of Hampton Court Palace

41

To his brother Richard

Camp Blinkwater
March 15. 1852.

My dear Richard

We have been encamped here since the 9th, this being a favorable position for Sir Harry to see the operations which have been going on as it faces the Kroome Range distant about two miles. These operations have under the C-in-Chief's own observation been most successful. The strongest positions of the enemy have been carried, a quantity of Cattle taken, and 150 Women amongst whom are four of the Chief Macomo's wives prisoners; and he himself reported to have lost an arm, which if the case will probably kill him as he is the greatest drunkard in the country and an old man. Nothing can exceed the endurance & fatigue which the Troops have shown in their attacks, the country being most inacessible [sic], and the positions of the strongest nature, in many instances they had to climb on their hands & knees under a heavy fire to capture a position, the women being found concealed in caves and dens where they had been secreted for safety. The practice of the Artillery has been most perfect shells having been thrown with the greatest precision, in one instance eleven bodies being found in one place killed, and more dreadful to relate children being found with their limbs torn off by the bursting of the shells and every imaginable destruction effected. The loss on our side has been comparatively trifling, one African only being killed and we have had nearly 4000 men engaged. The capture of the women will have a great effect, and the result of these successes generally has been that after the first two days no opposition of any consequence has been met with, and the Kafirs are leaving & going towards the Amatolas in great numbers; there we shall follow in a few days and when we have effectually scoured all this range, which is about 20 miles in circumference and filled with ravines and precipices, steep heights, rocks and stones of nature's most formidable forming, and in which she exceeds all the Vaubans who ever made fortifications.

Our camp is in a beautiful valley with a stream running through, this part of the country being the most fertile in the Colony. Sir Harry & Staff consists of six and we all live with him. We have our Tents with us and have consequently not the inconveniences of the ordinary Patrol.

No news of the Governor as yet, I sincerely trust he will arrive when the war has been brought to a satisfactory conclusion. There has been a fearful shipwreck of Troops on the coast here which you will see in the papers I sent you, it is a wild coast unless you know it.[58] Give my love to Mary

yours affectionately
Edward Wellesley

We shall go to the Amatolas in a few days, three marches from here and then I fancy to King Williams Town where the new Governor will probably be at the end of the month & where Sir Harry will meet him.

42

To his brother Richard

King Williams Town
April 15. 1852.

My dear Richard
General Cathcart arrived here on the 9th and Sir Harry left on the 11th, the former has concurred in the policy adopted by the latter

and issued a manifesto to the Kafirs to that effect which will at once shew them that they can expect no better terms than what had been offered them by Sir Harry and probably induce them at once to submit and cross the Kei; the friendly Chiefs and their tribes are allowed to remain on their locations –

We leave here in a few days and after visiting the different Camps in the Amatolas, eventually go to Fort Beaufort where the General will establish his Head Quarters at present. At the Waterkloof the Rifle Brigade will be established with other Troops under Somerset, and we have also Troops on the line of the Fish River. It is only at this moment that it can be said that we have Troops enough to guard effectually the Frontier inhabitants, and carry on offensive operations in the Amatolas. The Troops will all remain stationary in the Amatolas until the Kafirs completely evacuate them, all Cattle are in future to be destroyed and the men to be harassed by driving them after capture, and the General is going to erect towers in the Amatolas for defence and around which the huts are to be created. The state of occupation of the country will possibly continue for some months before a final & complete peace will be established.

General Cathcart has for his Military Secretary Seymour[59] who told me he saw you just before leaving England. Greville and Curzon[60] whom you also know are his Aides de Camp; we should have left this sooner but Cathcart was pitched off his horse the day after his arrival at his own gate and cut his head most frightfully; he seems of a good constitution for although his skin was completely exposed and a worse wound seldom seen, he was up the next day much to the surprise of the Doctors & transacting business, & wrote a dispatch to Lord Grey in which I understand he told him he concurred in all his predecessor's policy, which will place Lord Grey in an unpleasant position. Adieu, remember me to Mary from whom I have received numerous papers & believe me

yours affectionately
Edward Wellesley

43

To his brother Richard

King Williams Town
May 1. 1852.

My dear Richard

I received your letter of the 13th March enclosing the power of Attorney which I now return signed and send it to Cape Town now although there is no Mail until the end of the next month as we leave here on the 4th Proximo and may be in the field when the usual time for writing arrives. Since I last wrote affairs have remained in the same state; the Troops still occupy the Amatola Mountains, and the country adjacent to the Waterkloof, while a Force is stationed on the Fish River Line to protect the Colony from any inroads of the Enemy. There has been little or no fighting, but the Chiefs have not surrendered and although a large number of Kafirs have crossed the Kei as was hoped still the evacuation of the country has not been by any means universal. This slow termination of hostilities is the characteristic of Kafir Wars and indeed experienced Kaffrarians say that the people will still linger until September when the sowing season commences, and they will find that they are unable to cultivate, when they will en masse leave their country and cross the river to which they are now compelled to submit.

In the meantime General Cathcart has commenced building in the heart of the Amatola Mountains which will show the Kafirs that we fully intend to keep the country, and if as he hopes a population can be thrown into the mountains the Kafirs will be unable to return when once they have left. His two pet measures are at present the introduction of a Chiefs population who may be supposed to have a partiality for being amongst mountains although the climate is totally different, and the erection of square Norman towers in various parts of the same mountains to serve as a nucleus around which the huts of the settlers can cluster and from which they can command the approach of the locations against any attempt of the enemy; you thus see repeated the old system of the feudal ages, only instead of a truculent and heavy

Norman Baron sallying from these towers, you will have the English soldier who in place of a cuirass has a torn and tattered coat which once represented the national colour long since faded who in place of a <u>barred</u> helmet has a hat y clept wide awake which attempts to <u>debar</u> the sun from his face, but fails as witness his seared and battered countenance, the cuirass for his thighs are represented by a pair of patched pantaloons which time and the Mimosa bush have left barely decent; and the mailed shoe is replaced by the humble Blucher through openings in which appears glimpses of the "human foot divine" which can no longer through old age be concealed.

We leave this on the 4th and after visiting all the Camps shall go to Fort Beaufort where Cathcart will establish his Head Quarters probably for some time, he has quite recovered from his fall and seems to be hardy enough. The new Ministry[61] is the most curious piece of patchwork that was ever made I should think they would last for a month and then vanish from the political world. I should have thought we would have been able to induce one of the men like Aberdeen or Sir J. Graham to enter the Omnibus of his Ministry for it is nothing else, everyone being a stranger to every one else and to the people also.

Annot and the children are well at Cape Town, but while we are moving about so much I see little chance of our meeting for some time. Give my love to Mary

yours affectionately
Edward Wellesley

44

To his brother Richard

Fort Beaufort
May 17. 1852.

My dear Richard
We left King Williams Town on the 4th and after halting a night at Fort White proceeded to Colonel Michel's[62] Camp in the Lenya Valley in the Amatola Mountains where his Brigade are encamped;

the spot was a favourite location of the Chief Sandili and is very pretty the stream Lenya here entering the river Keiskamma. On a part of the mountain range which overlooks the valley the guns of the force have been placed, the road having been previously made with great labour by the Troops up a most precipitous path, and rocks split by lighting large fires and then pouring cold water upon them. We assembled here and rode along the ridge which divides the Amatola Basin from the Wolf Valley, we saw a few Kafirs but were not in any way molested. From this we had magnificent views of these mountains and their valleys; the country seemed deserted. On the second day we visited Eyre's Camp distant about eight miles from the other and placed in a large open valley called the Raskamina [?] Hoek; here one of the Governor's Norman towers is in course of creation and the Brigade under Eyre are also hutting themselves for the winter. The road or rather path which leads from the Lenya to the Hoek passes through the Booma pass where in the commencement of this War a Column of 600 men were attacked and suffered severely, the men were unhappily unloaded, which was a most unmilitary thing for Mackinnon to have allowed, they were taken by surprise, thrown into confusion, and the Kafirs had it their own way, we saw some of the bones of those poor fellows still on the path. The pass is surrounded by thick bush, having on one side the Keiskamma and precipitous rocks on the other, a horse can travel easily and with due measures this place is not so formidable as we were led to expect. From the Lenya to which we returned we went to Fort Cox, Fort Hare and thence on here. I saw Woodford[63] yesterday who brought me the books and told me he had seen you shortly before he left England, he was en route to Graham's Town on Court Martial duty a Paymaster addicted to peculation and other malpractices having to be tried. The Rifle Brigade are encamped near the Waterkloof where Macomo still is and which is being shortly blockaded, the Governor here as everywhere else prohibiting attacking these places and having adopted a system for occupation and blockade merely, hoping thereby to tire or starve the Kafirs into submission or evacuation of their territory, that they are unwilling to do this is natural enough and we have lately passed through country so beautiful that they are right to fight for it to the last. We shall I think remain here for some time paying visits to the camps surrounding the Waterkloof fastnesses, but eventually if the Kafirs do not go we shall have to go at them again more actively. From all this you will perceive that this War is in a quiescent state and in fact nothing has been done of an active nature since Sir Harry left. I wish you would send me Cathcart's book on the Campaigns of 13 and 14[64] in January if an opportunity offers, he is much liked by deputations and people who see him from his gentlemanly kind manner in such direct contrast to the cut and thrust style of the former representative of Majesty in this Colony. I should not be at all surprised if the Government gave some promotions for this War upon the arrival of Sir Harry at home as some compensation for Lord Grey's haste in withdrawing him and in compliment to him to whom personally they can give no new honours. This is a hot and dusty place and today the whole air is one piece of red dust a regular storm of dust and the wind as hot as if Boreas had an inflammation in his throat. Adieu give my love to Mary and

yours affectionately
Edward Wellesley

45

To his brother Richard

Fort Beaufort
June 21. 1852.

My dear Richard
In consequence of an alarm in Lower Albany the Governor went to Graham's Town for a few hours we formed a Camp six miles from the Town and rode in, the joy of the inhabitants of this would be capital of South Africa was very great at this first visit, two addresses were presented and a number of guns fired off. We also have just returned from Fort White where we formed a Camp to be near the country where operations were being carried on against Segolo and Staeth [?], they were without any success, in

83

fact the country was entirely deserted and the result of Sir Harry's last operations when the crops were destroyed was not complete and the Kafirs seem to have abandoned the locality entirely. The Waterkloof has been blockaded and a number of women taking supplies in made prisoners, there is a rumour that Macomo and his people intend to leave this moon and today we have a confirmation of it in the passing of Cattle & men from there towards the Amatolas. No attack has been allowed. A daring attack was made a few days ago upon a small escort of Sappers & Miners who were in charge of a few Wagons, the object was to capture some of the new Minié Muskets, the Hottentots 300 [?] in number fired upon the mules of the leading Wagons disabling two, at the same moment an unarmed party sprang out & jumping into the Wagon broke open the cases and barrels of ammunition which contained the arms and decamped, all this time a hot fire was kept up and the half of the party killed or wounded and obliged the remainder to retire and leave the wagons & fall back upon an old post [fort?] where they barricaded themselves, a poor soldiers wife was shot in the melée and afterwards assegaid; fortunately the arms had all been rendered useless by removing the nipples which were sent by another conveyance. These people must have received information from Graham's Town of the convoy being about to leave. With this exception the War has been perfectly passive.

Good bye I write in great haste as I have been much employed and only in a few minutes to the post. Love to Mary

yours affectionately
Edward Wellesley

46

To his brother Richard

Fort Beaufort
July 20. 1852.

My dear Richard
Since I last wrote I received your letter and with respect to the Power of Attorney I returned it signed from King Williams

Town in April. A large assemblage of Kafirs having been reported at Auckland the site of one of the destroyed military villages, the Governor sent a force and went himself; we found a number of huts which were destroyed but the Kafirs and any Cattle they may have had escaped, we returned the same day riding about 40 miles, this took place at the end of last month and there had been previously an attack upon the Rebel Hottentots who were surprised in the Buffalo Mountains and all their women and children captured with a large quantity of property. On the 7th of this month a movement was made against the Kafirs under Macomo in the Waterkloof, we left this and formed a Camp on the Kroome river under the Kroome range from whence we ascended the Kroome and united with the Rifle Brigade at the top and bivouacked on the heights. On the following day, we passed through a forest which divides the Waterkloof from Fuller's Hoek and reached an open space familiarly called the Horseshoe, this is an open plateau something the shape of what it is termed and the best fighting ground I have seen for Kafirs, the bush runs up on two sides from the Waterkloof and Fuller's Hoek on the third the forest first named abuts on the plain and on the fourth a few detached rocks and they all afford cover, it is a melancholy spot, the graves of many poor soldiers are dotted about, and you are pointed out the spot where many officers fell amongst them being Fordyce who commanded the 74th Highlanders and was a brave and distinguished officer. We however met with no opposition either passing through the Forest or on emerging on the plain and having joined another Column which had been operating on this side, in concert destroyed a large number of huts on the edge of the Waterkloof and in a skirmish one man of the Rifle Brigade was killed, the Governor subsequently returned through the Forest and we afterwards descended the range and reached our Camp on the Kroome river, the next day we returned to Fort Beaufort. The Waterkloof of which you in England have heard perhaps a great account in the papers is a valley about 8 miles in length thickly fringed with wood, from the main valley branch off numerous ravines on the left and on the right also much wooded which renders the passage of the main valley difficult as the Kafirs have thus retreats on both flanks and easy modes of access to attack men passing through, with good cover for themselves; at the head of the valley an ascent of forest paths brings you to the narrow forest which divides the Waterkloof from Fuller's Hoek through which we passed, the latter being a rocky precipitous ravine thickly wooded overlooking the Blinkwater a stream which runs into the Kat river about a mile from the hills, all along the side of the heights are a succession of ravines running from the hills to the bottom and perhaps the best description given of them was by Somerset who compared them to an immense plum pudding with thick slices cut out. The whole range is about 20 miles in circumference. On this occasion more of the Troops descended into the plains and a permanent post is to be established near the spot where Fordyce fell which is to be occupied by a large force with guns and the Governor expects that from constant annoyance the Kafirs will be inclined to leave. I told you some time ago of wild characters who appear in this War and there has just arrived here a Mr Lakeman who has enrolled a Company partly at his own expense and clothed them according to his own fancy, the Colonial Newspapers call him "the patriot Lakeman" he is a plain featured little man who apportions his H's with reckless indifference, this having served with the French in Algeria he has pleasant anecdotes to relate about the Arabs and the wild women of the Desert, his men he has clothed entirely in leather coat, trousers and a leather helmet with a crest and plume of horsehair, in this costume which is the colour of clay they resemble most the warriors in a mediaeval melodrama at one of the minor theatres, and as they are enrolled from among the lowest description of Englishman and much addicted to the strong grape of the Colony when once they get into a town it is impossible to get them out of it and these leather men are seen rolling about with their helmets the wrong side to the front and presenting a ludicrous appearance. With all this however Lakeman and his men are brave enough and when in the field where Bacchus is not, do very good service.

We are now preparing for another expedition to the opposite banks of the Kei to punish the paramount Chief Kreili who has neglected to pay a fine of cattle imposed on him by Sir Harry Smith accompanying his refusal by some remarks not palatable at Head Quarters; all the Burghers have been again called out by proclamation and they are to have all the Cattle they take, with all this temptation I am afraid very few will appear at the rendezvous on the 6th August and for which we shall leave here about the end of the month. The march to the Kei will take seven or eight days and the Governor means to pitch his Camp at this place from whence he no doubt will write a despatch the place from where dated being supposed to look well in the eyes of the Colonial Minister, whether it will have an equally good effect here is very doubtful; in the meantime the season for the Kafirs sowing is approaching and the Amatolas which have been left unoccupied by us for some time will have to be entered again to prevent this, altogether affairs do not look very happy, the active operations by Sir Harry at the end of his command having been too suddenly given up and the system of fighting from heights, and occupation merely of the country, having produced nothing.

We have cold weather here now and the Camp at the top of the Hill making the post is at present enveloped in thick fog, the other night when we were on the heights snow fell and the Winterberg range, which is the highest in this part of the country, was covered with snow, I think His Excellency was nearly frozen as from the hot days people coming here think cold is impossible and blankets superfluous.

I heard from Annot to-day who is well at Cape Town

Give my love to Mary
yours affectionately
Edward Wellesley

I send you a stanza [missing] suggested by a late visit[or?], bad enough no doubt

47

To his brother Richard

Banks of the White Kei
August 13. 1852.

My dear Richard

We left Fort Beaufort on the 29th and proceeded to the Blinkwater where a Force had been formed to accompany the Governor in the expedition against Kreili; we then passed over the Eland's Berg which we were two days in getting over and where thirty of the bullocks on the supply waggons died, and after crossing the White Kei where we were joined by a force of 400 friendly Kafirs and Fingoes under Captain Tylden,[65] proceeded to a stream called the Balatea where being joined by the Troops sent from King Williams Town on the day appointed, encamped there, and halted for three days. Some Burghers also arrived but no general assembly of these people had taken place as was expected and called for by the Governor in his proclamation. We left the Balatea and crossed the White Kei on the 10th, the Governor at the head of the few Burghers and met with no opposition, in fact saw no Kafirs. On the night previously two Messengers had arrived from Kreili offering to pay the fine imposed by the late Governor and asking what the General wanted, they were told that it was now too late and sent back. We encamped that night on the left bank of the river and on the next day all the Troops marched to an old trading station about eight miles from Kreili's great Place as it is termed, to which we marched the following morning at daylight, and the whole of the huts were then set on fire and destroyed by the Fingoes by order of the Governor.

This location of the paramount Chief of Kafirland is situated in a pretty valley near to the junction of the Black and White Kei which then receives the general name of Great Kei, the huts were very numerous which were occupied formerly by all his wives I fancy he being in possession of ten. We returned to the Camp here the same day leaving two Columns of Troops and all the Burghers to go after Cattle in which they are to be occupied a week. Two mounted Kafirs were the only beings we saw this day and the country was on fire in all directions, the Kafirs always burning the grass at this season and also no doubt doing this more at present as our Horses and Cattle are thereby deprived of all pasturage. Nothing could be more desolate than this blackness of the land, the kraals all deserted and no buck hardly to be seen. Nothing has as yet been heard from the Column engaged in Cattle hunting. We are to remain here until the 17th when we ride back to Fort Beaufort by way of King Williams Town, the Troops being left here. Our English letters leave here on the 15th until which I shall keep this open. There is a great quantity of game in this part of the country deer, partridges, and the bustard, called here the [illegible] this latter was formerly to be found in England and is a fine bird, in taste something like a turkey.

August 14. I see by the newspapers that Sir Harry Smith instead of achieving an elevated position after leaving here so grossly insulted by Lord Grey has [humbled?] to himself a dinner from a Lord seems to him sufficient atonement for being kicked out of a Government and told that he is incapable of Civil or Military Administration. Forgiveness is a Christian virtue but this appears to have been carried in his case to such a low degree as to merit the deserved contempt of every one.[66]

August 15. Our Fingoes have taken 40 Cows which is all the result of this movement at present

Give my love to Mary.

yours affectionately
Edward Wellesley

48

To his brother Richard

Fort Beaufort
September 20. 1852.

My dear Richard

My last letter to you was from the Kei; 1000 head of Cattle were taken on this and we returned rapidly from there by King

Williams Town to this place; on the 15th the Waterkloof was assailed for the third time and the operations have been so far quite successful, about 100 Kafirs are reported to have been killed, 200 Women & Children (miserable starved objects) taken prisoners. The enemy would not fight and it is also reported are all leaving the place. The Fingoes who have come up with them at their fires at night have massacred a number of them and not being particular or infected with humanity slay women, children, and all they can catch. Eyre and my Regiment as usual did all the work. The Governor & Staff were on the hills looking over where we remained for 3 days. A halt now has taken place and then the place is again to be attacked and Posts established at several points to keep the Kafirs out. I think the War is now really approaching to some termination. The Hottentots will give trouble, but as £500 have been offered for their leader dead or alive, and as they are not a race of the least principle I should not be surprised to see his best friend walk in with the leader's head in a basket, a free pardon being also granted. I believe we shall go to Graham's Town where Head Quarters are to be established about the beginning of October and I shall then be enabled to send for Annot who is well at Cape Town as long as we travel about so much.

The book that Mary sent arrived, give my best love and believe me

yours affectionately
Edward Wellesley

There is no time for more, a co-partner of Staff having shot himself by accident with one of Colt's revolvers. I have much to do and the Mail goes to-day

49

To his brother Richard

Graham's Town
October 11. 1852.

My dear Richard
The operations in the Waterkloof were successfully concluded on the 24th of last month and numerous posts having been established

to occupy the place so as to prevent the Kafirs from returning the Governor left Beaufort on the 30th and proceeded to Fort Hare, and from there we went to the foot of the Amatola Mountains where a Camp & Post was formed from which Eyre with the 73rd and some other troops had been ordered to attack Uithaalder and the Hottentots, and generally to clear the mountains of any Kafirs who might remain in them. He entered the mountains on the 4th and on the same morning destroyed in the heart of the hills the village of the Hottentots, a large portion of these had abandoned the country a day or two before, possibly when they ascertained the destination of the Troops, those who remained fled on the approach of the soldiers offering no resistance, these movements are still going on and scarcely any opposition has been met, and in a short time there is no doubt Eyre will have effectually swept the Amatolas from end to end, constructing such roads as may be necessary thus making communication easy and rendering familiar all those fastnesses. We left Fort Hare on the 4th and arrived at King Williams Town on the 5th remained a day and reached this town in two days from the former, the last day we made 45 miles & arrived late at night, much to the disgust of the inhabitants who had prepared illuminations and deputations & were astonished when they found His E. had arrived in the night. On the 8th the Chief Segolo who has caused us infinite trouble and is one of the bravest of the whole surrendered himself at Fort Murray, and is expected here to-day, he was accompanied by his Councillors and several followers who delivered up their Arms. The news of his surrender was brought to the Governor by an officer of Lancers (educated at Eton) who rode the 77 miles in 1½ hours [days?] which for this country and as the road is hilly and hard was good riding. Colonel Cloete is on leave so I am at present Chief of the Staff at Head Quarters. I think our affairs are looking very well as the surrender of one Chief will I think lead to that of others, and the Hottentots will then only remain, and with the Police now established they will some day be caught, and a good massacre of the whole . . . [words missing]

Since commencing my letter Segolo has arrived and is safely housed in a strong room, he is a fine looking Kafir about 6 feet [4?] & has a more prepossessing countenance than most of the lot. I can hardly express to you my disgust at seeing these brutes who have waged a long war against the English, it proves how much complete knowledge of the country and habits of abstinence, and endurance, can effect against our best discipline and pluck.

I am very glad that Montagu[67] has secured his election although I should have preferred his principles more if they were less democratic, I was amused at one charge which they brought against as pure a man of the people namely that he had been a pensioner on the Government for some years as an Half-Pay officer for some years, this fact although true it is denied by a local paper is true, as he is at present on Half pay as an Ensign or Lieutenant – & has been I think from the year 15 or before. An Army List is a sad tell tale. Talking of Army Lists it is rather curious and exemplifies how completely the Army is a lottery that had I remained in the 25th I should at present be only a Lieutenant with 7 above me for purchase, whereas from Lord Fitzroy's kind consideration in transferring me I have now in my present Regiment only 3 Captains above me for Majority, besides holding a Staff appointment which may lead to something else, if it does so it will not be for lack of zeal and hard work as I think we have a peculiar <u>implantation</u> in our nature which inclines us to perform those duties with which we may happen to be interested, with more alacrity than any other people, <u>because they are duties</u>. Although I am perhaps rather young in judging I perceive a much more lax principle in carrying on what are the duties of different classes of persons than at all arrives at my idea of perfection; whether this is a natural tendency which will at last complete the demoralization of our country and reduce us eventually to a second place I cannot say, you as one of experience may decide. I must bitterly complain of your want of writing, as I have not received a line for the last two mails whereas I have by tent or Camp on field of War been a most regular correspondent, you must tell Mary to write me an occasional note if you are too Foreign Office. Our mails now leave here on the 18th which obliges us to write from the Frontier on the 11th or 12th, the Steam Communication with England is now very rapid, and the constant arrival and departure will increase the trade of the Colony; the people here are all anxiously expecting their

Constitution; I hope myself Lord Derby will not give it them, as they are not yet fit to legislate for one butler and a housemaid much less for a country, Montagu would not believe this. The people are very clever in theory but [illegible] than practice.

yours affectionately
Edward Wellesley

My best love to Mary. I hope to have Annot here in a short time, I shall hardly know my own children by sight. War is an [illegible] thing

50

To his brother Richard

Graham's Town
November 4. 1852.

My dear Richard

The people of Graham's Town and generally of this division of the Colony were sent out as settlers by the English Government in 1820, at that time Lord Charles Somerset[68] was the Governor an appointment which he held for a number of years during which period he did nothing for the country except improve the breed of race horses, and introduce, they say, his own to a large extent; he in those good old Tory days looked upon the Cape as his patrimony where he would possibly have remained to this day if some disagreement with the home authorities had not sent him to England. Upon the arrival of these settlers in 1820 they were sent to this part of the Colony then a most arid waste and told off to their several lots by a Military Officer sent by Lord Charles for that purpose; all this was done in the most absolute tyrranical [sic] manner, the country to be occupied was divided by the number of people, who were then forced to locate upon the spot apportioned to him or them, & the consequence of this was that one poor devil had no water on his lot, another had no wood, a third had neither wood or water, a fourth found himself pleasantly situated in a swamp, and so on, – while some other lucky individuals were fixed upon spots where all the necessaries were abundant.

Notwithstanding all these drawbacks however these Englishmen have in 30 years made themselves the richest and most influential portion of the Colony, the town and some others have been made by them, and their flocks and herds are abundant – The most respectable of the people here have raised themselves from the lowest grades, one man now a Member of the Colonial Council and Editor of the best Newspaper was formerly a Butcher's boy, another Member of Council began life as a common soldier, one of the richest Merchants here was once a Waiter, and it is said that at his own parties he is occasionally reminded of his former days, to be seen giving a plate he may be handing a Lady at supper a preliminary dust with his pocket handkerchief. The distribution of the aspirate <u>H</u> is uncertain and guided by no fixed rules, but the little boys play at Cricket in the streets and the place is quite English.

We leave here on the 15th on an expedition which will probably occupy two months; Sir Harry Smith during his government extended our territories here in the most reckless manner not having the means of properly governing them, one of these distant provinces beyond the Orange River is now in a state of ferment and a force of 2000 men is being assembled and the Governor is going there himself, I don't think we shall have any fighting but one of the most powerful Chiefs there governed by his French Missionaries,[69] is inclined to give some trouble which the mere appearance of a large Army will quell. In the meantime Eyre has most completely cleared out the Amatola Mountains, during which Sandili had one or two narrow escapes of his life and generally the whole of Kafirland is quite deserted, and the Waterkloof being also totally evacuated, and occupied by our Troops, this part of the drama may be said to be concluded. With respect to the Hottentots a proclamation has now been issued offering to spare their huts if they surrender with the exception of the leader Uithaalder and some other dozen of the heads of the misguided people; the effect of this will doubtless be to bring some of them in as they are starving and hunted wherever seen like wild beasts. The establishment of the Frontier Police one of the Governor's first acts has been most beneficial and in every case lately attempts to steal Cattle have been completely defeated. I have taken a great interest in their formation being convinced of the great necessity for such a force and the use to which they could be put, and the Governor has ordered all the reports and everything connected with them to be sent through me; the Force is more Military than Civil, the men are all mounted and well armed and amounts to near 900 distributed along the Colonial Border, their pay is very good, and they are very active so much so that on the last occasion when an attempt at Cattle lifting was made by some Kafirs and Hottentots, although the latter had a day's start before we got the news here, by sending an express sixty miles on horseback the extreme border police were alarmed and caught & retook all the booty just as the thieves were entering Kafirland.

I received your letter of the 14th September, your confirmation about the Swiss was very interesting, I trust the Colonial Office will conform to the General's ideas on this point, at present we have conquered the Kafirs and hold their greatest stronghold by Military occupation, this to be continued will require an immense force and entail a large outlay of money, it is absolutely necessary to the country that these Mountains out of which the Kafirs used to sally for attack, or into which they would drive and secrete Cattle stolen from the Colony, should be occupied entirely by us & to effect this the plan of establishing a Colony of people peculiarly loyal not to a King, but to themselves, of sober contented habits, brave and accustomed to a mountain territory, and of agricultural tendencies also, seems to be a most admirable idea. That these people would in a few years render a territory like this (well watered, with the most beautiful climate, far surpassing any other part of the Colony, a fine soil where you might have a constant succession of crops) a most delightful exchange for their present restricted land, there can be no doubt. An Englishman always looks forward to returning home, and that his residence in a Colony is only temporary but if you could transplant a community of Swiss who would make the Amatola Mountains their home, you not only effectually render them inaccessible to the Kafirs, but secure to yourself an industrious sober population a most certain safeguard on your most exposed border.

I received a number of newspapers also Cathcart's book by the last Mail. A report which I do not believe also arrived that the Duke had died, sent by telegraph as the Steamer was leaving England, as there have been reports of this sort before I trust this one is not true, although as he has now reached Lord Wellesley's age and has gone through more hardships in his early life we cannot hope that he can live much longer.[70]

I am afraid that I shall not be able to get Annot here before we leave. our life is so nomadic that I often regret that I had not left her in England as I had at first thought best, as she would have been happier there than in this country although separated from me, however l'homme propose, et Dieu dispose, so I suppose it is all for the best.

I meet several of the soldiers of my old Regiment the 25th who are now holding situations of a civil nature, and in some instances have become Officers of the Colonial Levies now employed and as such have come under my notice as most official men, they one and all recur to the name of their poor Colonel[71] with an affection and reverence which is most delightful though painful for me to hear; and the more I see of Commanding Officers in general, who are naturally entrusted with the entire happiness or misery of some thousand of their dependent creatures, the more I am convinced that no one had so conscientious an idea of his duties, or could have performed them in a more perfect and admirable manner. With my love to Mary

ever yours affectionately
Edward Wellesley

51

To his brother Richard

Camp Burghersdorp
November 29. 1852.

My dear Richard

We left Graham's Town on the 16th and after twelve days march reached this place the capital town of the division of Albert as you will see by the map if you have one, and about 20 miles from the

Orange River. Here we found encamped 2000 Regular Troops being the largest number ever assembled in the country, and the Troops commenced moving across the river yesterday. We leave to-morrow morning at 8 [3?] and shall cross the river and a permanent Camp for the whole Army will be probably formed about 20 miles on the other bank from whence any other operations which may be necessary will be carried on. A Kafir Chief named Moshesh is inclined to be refractory but will not I think fight when he sees the number of Troops, and independently of this there are numerous affairs to be settled by the Governor naturally in a perplexed confusion incident on the addition of territory made to the Colony by Sir Harry Smith and peopled by totally distinct people such as English, Dutch, Kafir, Bastards[72] of all sorts & so forth. The country is more ugly than anything you can imagine, no grass, no trees, rocks springing from the earth & lack of any water, swarms of Locusts literally darken the air at times and the destruction of crops and all green appearance is very great, in Camp cow dung is used for fuel no wood begin obtainable. This town is inhabited principally by Dutch and by a peculiar class who from their religion & dress are familiarly called Doppers[73] their reception of His Excellency was very enthusiastic and manifested in the curious manner of firing off their guns in the face or under the nostrils of his horse, this was occasionally diversified by frequent spills from their horses not yet accustomed to fire, cheering was immense & the broadest trimmed hats contemplated by any despairing matron were waved in triumph at our entrance.

The heat is now intense and writing in a bell tent with the thermometer at 100 is no joke, everything curls up except one's hair, hot puffs of wind scatter your papers about, put out a melting candle when you attempt to read your letters, locusts hit you in the eye as you march, and other little annoyances of this nature.

I am sorry to see that Lord Hardinge[74] is made Commander in Chief in place of the poor Duke, I should have wished to see Lord Fitzroy who has indisputably more claims & has always been so kind to me, perhaps the personal feeling is the strongest. I cannot say how long we shall be in this part of the world, but if all goes on well we shall probably return in a fortnight leaving the Troops for some time longer. Eyre commands the whole & my Regiment are as usual pre eminent in appearance & all other qualities of Soldiers..

Adieu as the post is going
My love to Mary &
yours ever affectionately
Edward Wellesley

52

To his brother Richard

Camp Caledon River
December 3. 1852.
(27 miles from the Orange River)

My dear Richard

As there is a chance of this letter reaching the Colony in time for the Mail I follow up my last which I wrote to you from Burghersdorp and which place we left on the 30th. We reached and crossed the Orange River 27 miles the same day the river being very low, its width is about 170 yards and the banks are well wooded with willow trees and exceedingly pretty, the river itself being the only one in this part of the world deserving the name. We encamped on the right bank where the Governor was received by a deputation of Boors [sic] belonging to the Orange River Territory who demonstrated their joy by firing off their guns as usual, but their horses not being so well accustomed to the noise as they might be immediately bolted in all directions, occasionally pitching off their riders who were then seen pursuing their steeds in the most undignified manner. On the following day we marched here & crossed the river not of any magnitude and are encamped on the right bank where all the Troops except one Brigade of Infantry are also arrived; we are about 100 miles from the residence of the Basuto Chief Moshesh who is accused of Cattle lifting & other misdemeanours, and we shall remain here for some days until the terms which the Governor may offer him are accepted or refused, if the former we shall return to the Colony leaving the Army here for some time, if the latter we shall immediately advance on his location and a war will commence the result of which there is no doubt, but the termination of which maybe as tedious & uncertain as the one we have been engaged in at the other end of the Colony. This Chief is said to be enormously rich in Cattle, and his people are well armed, on our road the reports stated him to be decided on fighting but since our arrival it is said he will submit to any terms rather than engage in hostilities with us. It is confidently reported that the Home authorities are inclined to give up this country confining our frontier to the Orange River, it was added to the Colony by Sir Harry Smith after a rapid visit upon his arrival in the country and has been since a constant source of annoyance and trouble, the population are partly Dutch who would be glad that the English should give up the territory in order that they might join their country men whom we have lately allowed to found a Republic[75] some distance more in the interior; – a parcel of low Colonial English who have got up the present war cry in order that they might reap the benefits of a large Army subsisting in their country for some time, with the chance of some portion being left behind permanently; – and several Kafir Chiefs with whom we have entered into friendly alliance, – and a Tribe of people descendants of Boers and Hottentots, with whom Sir Harry Smith also made treaties upon his first arrival.

The Kafir of which race the Basutos under Moshesh are a tribe, always robs, restitution is demanded, he evades, & 200 English Troops are now required to enforce obedience, who proceed under humane & systematic Military Laws to make war if necessary. The Boor [sic] a Dutchman of total indifference and hatred to all Blacks would practice on these occasions a totally different measure, he would invade the country from which the robbers had come and butcher every man woman and child he could meet and create such terror that no second attempt would be made for some time, none being left to make it. We treat the Kafirs as a power like ourselves to be treated with and to make war against as highly civilized and humane people, we are taught this by Exeter House[76] and the Aborigines Protection Society, divine laws do not go to this length, and in return for our humanity the Enemy murder us in their old accustomed barbarous manner, and we spend several millions yearly. We have had very hot weather but to-day we have had rain and thunder which have made the tents much cooler. Our Camp presents a fine array of canvas, the Men and Horses being alike in good health and condition, and our whole Force complete in all respects.

The farms are all occupied in this part and the country is admirably adapted for pasturage. The farmers all seem rich driving their six and eight horses in well built wagons and their houses of a good description. We have seen little game, but the Orange and Caledon possess fish, the flavour is to be compared to eating several wet towels, and they are also painfully full of bones, but still they <u>are</u> fish, and imagination does or should make up for the deficiency of our ideas of what a fish should taste like. The English Mail arrived here this morning, bringing me however no letters. I am sorry that Lord Hardinge is appointed Commander in Chief above Lord Fitzroy, the Queen's Order respecting the poor Duke's death is very good.

yours affectionately
Edward Wellesley

The Colony has been very quiet since we left, and there is a report that the Rebel Hottentot Leader Uithaalder has been killed in the Fish River Bush.

Please buy me a Hart's Annual Army List for 1853 & send it out.

53

To his brother Richard

Camp Orange River
December 30. 1852.

My dear Richard

By the enclosed Gazette you will see that I was wrong in thinking that Moshesh would not fight as we have had a hard combat with him and I was wounded and had my horse killed at the end of the day, the paper gives as complete an account of

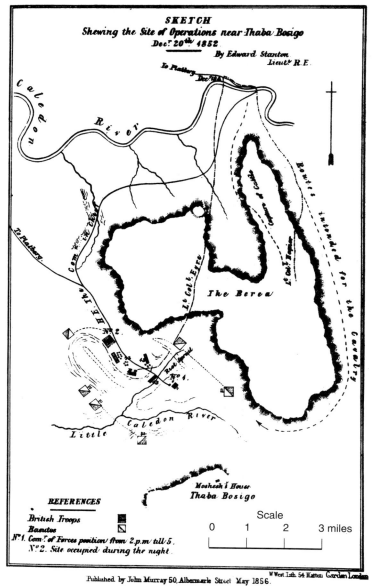

SKETCH
Shewing the Site of Operations near Thaba Bosigo
Dec.r 20th 1852

By Edward Stanton
Lieut.r R.E.

The action at Berea, December 1852

everything that occurred after our arrival at the Platberg that by reading it you will become as well acquainted with the subject as I am myself, nothing has been suppressed. You will perceive that Moshesh in his remarks at the conference displays great shrewdness, in fact he is a superior man and throughout behaved with much discrimination and a courtesy beyond most savages. I imagine that he was to the last moment disinclined to fight but his people were determined to try their strength with the English. The report of Colonel Cloete[77] gives the account of the proceedings of the Troops who went with the Governor and we were joined by Eyre's force at 5 in the afternoon. The plains were then covered with masses of Horsemen in our front and on all sides of us the appearance of whom was picturesque in the extreme and of a totally different character to any other Kafir contest. When we had fixed upon a spot for our bivouac for the night which was done for our own protection & in order to prevent the Cattle Eyre had taken from being re-stolen amongst some enclosures and stone Kraals on a Knoll having on one flank a perpendicular precipice which was thus guarded; - the Troops were all called in to occupy the enclosures this was about ¼ past 7 and the Governor rode forward to where the 43rd Regiment were holding some other stone Kraals about ¾ of a mile in advance of the place fixed for our bivouac, when he got to them he ordered them to retire, the firing was very sharp all about us as the Basutos were on both flanks as well as in front and I expected the Governor would have been hit every moment, after giving the order he turned his horse and I did the same being close to him, at that moment I was cut over as we used to say at Eton the ball entering my right leg at the calf and coming out at the other side and entering my horse's stomach, I was not aware the horse was wounded he however made one or two paces forward staggered and fell upon his head. I had just time to pull my wounded leg out of the stirrup and was thrown on my shoulder. I then got up and was put on a Lancer's horse and went to the Camp with the Doctor who dressed my wound the shots flying over our heads all the time; you may fancy the firing was hot enough where I was wounded as a Sergeant of the

43rd who wanted to get my saddle off my horse was obliged to discontinue trying, one or two balls entering it as the saddle was lying on the ground. We all slept that night with our heads against a low wall of one of the enclosures of the Kafir huts, the men with their Arms at their sides expecting an attack but no firing took place after 8. The Infantry consisting of the 43rd & 73rd & Rifle Brigade/Company behaved in the steadiest manner throughout a most arduous day, the 73rd & 1 Company of the Rifle Brigade had not anything to eat from daylight and there was no water where we bivouacked at night. I suffered much pain that night but since then have been progressing in the most satisfactory manner, there has been scarcely any inflammation and the wound is now looking very well indeed, most fortunately no bone was touched. I have a very attentive little Scots Doctor on the Staff attending me. We returned to Platberg the day after the fighting [which was on 20 December] and then left on the 24th - on our return we travelled very slowly I in a Mule Wagon with a stretcher slung on it, we reached here yesterday & as the river is very full the Wagons & everything else have to be punted over. I expect we shall reach Graham's Town about the 10th by which time I hope to be able to make use of my leg again at present I am obliged to be carried from my Wagon to my Tent. I am very sorry for the loss of my Horse he was a nice creature & I had been on his back since ½ past 2 in the morning he formerly belonged to Sir Harry Smith. Eyre had a narrow escape in the morning, he as well as poor Faunce[78] got amongst the Kafirs and they tried to get him off his horse, he fired off 10 barrels of a revolver and by hard riding escaped, poor Faunce not being a good rider fell into their hands and they killed him. He was found and the sons of Moshesh made a grave for him.

Give my love to Mary and believe me
yours affectionately
Edward Wellesley

54

To his brother Richard

Graham's Town
February 12. 1853.

My dear Richard

We returned here from the Orange River Expedition on the 10th of last month, having left the Troops and travelled back as fast as we could. I am happy to say my wound is now nearly well, my leg which at first had assumed a size which would have been the envy of the most gigantic of London footmen has now resumed its natural dimensions, I had successively discarded crutches, and then sticks with which I used to crawl about like the Diable Boiteux and can now walk tolerably well with only one, and in another month I hope to be able to ride & walk as usual. Whilst we were away everything was quiet in the Colony with the exception of an attempt of some Hottentots to enter and steal, but they were pursued and lost half of their number. It may now be said that we are actually at peace, no Kafirs are to be met in the Amatola Mountains, the principal Chiefs including Sandili and Macomo have crossed the river Kei, the alternative offered them, and the Hottentots seem to have ceased their depredations, and the few that have [not?] surrendered themselves are probably in a starving condition and without ammunition. Still no direct offers of peace have been made by the principal Kafir Chiefs, and no acknowledgement that they have been beaten or that they repent having rebelled against us; consequently although no hostilities are being carried on, there is a state of great uncertainty prevalent, and to bring things to some satisfactory conclusion the Governor left this place for King Williams Town from where I have no doubt some arrangements will be made with Kreili the paramount Chief so as to enable the Governor to proclaim peace. To expect a positive and definite peace as if one was dealing with a potentate of an European power, is of course absurd, but a tolerably sincere desire on the part of the principal Chiefs for peace, and a desire on their part to restrain their followers from committing depredations may be arrived at, and must then be maintained by the constant presence of a large armed force in the country ready to break up at once any combination for hostile purposes against the Colony, or to severely punish any attempt at marauding. As respects the Hottentots I think they will gradually disperse and as there are no means in any of these frontier towns or villages of preventing people from coming or going as they may think proper, the rebels will amalgamate with the other Hottentots who are scattered about everywhere in the Colony. It would be of great importance if we could however catch Uithaalder their leader as he must be far superior to any of the others, and we know from many who have surrendered that he prevents many of his followers from giving themselves up who would otherwise be too happy to make their peace with the Government. If he was hung it would also inspire such terror amongst the Hottentots, who are naturally of much less boldness and courage than the Kafirs, that they would not be inclined to rebel again. The whole of the Colonists as you will see by the Cape newspapers I send if you take the trouble to read them, pretend to be afraid that peace will be made and are all alarmists, but unfortunately every man in the Colony is more or less interested in the continuance of the war, immense sums of money being expended for the Troops and Levies all of which find their way into the trouser pockets of the merchants and others, the sum for waggon hire alone for merely one Division of the Army was £100 a day, and when money is thus spent in large amounts and benefits every class, their interest is apt to appear as good sense and patriotism and they try and impose it as such upon their neighbours. The only people who really suffer by the Kafir wars are the Soldiers who have immense toil and wearisome marches to undergo, and scarcely any glory or exciting battles in their favor. Eyre has gone home on leave, and it is to be hoped there will be no more occasion for such services as he has rendered, for between you and I and the crutches there are a great many Lieutenant Colonels in this country but there was only one Soldier.

I received all your letters and newspapers which are very interesting as memorials of the poor Duke's funeral. My love to Mary and believe me

yours affectionately
Edward Wellesley

55

Richard Wellesley to their mother, Mrs Richard (Jane) Wellesley, received by her on Tuesday 1st March 1853

F.O.
Monday

My dear Mama,

You will see by Eddy's letter that they have had a severe fight with the Kaffir's which I think will be a finisher for them. I am happy to see that Eddy came out with such honour & glory. He must be quite happy at having had an opportunity of distinguishing himself, and it is most satisfactory to see the way in which he is mentioned in the Despatches. You will see he did not escape without a slight wound thro' his leg which luckily has not touched any Bone & he talks of being able to walk again very soon it is evidently going on quite satisfactorily – We must be very thankful for this opportunity he has had of distinction without any more serious mishap & I am in hopes the lesson they have given the Kaffirs will put a stop to the War – & enable him to join Annot at Cape Town – Love to H

yours affecly
RW

56

Edward Wellesley to his brother Richard

Graham's Town
April 19. 1853.

My dear Richard

Since I last wrote to you everything has been going on here quietly & this Frontier gradually assuming a tranquil & peaceful aspect, the Farmers are returning to the Border farms and security is commencing to be felt, we have reduced all the Irregular Forces employed during the War, and with the exception of 200 Fingoes enrolled for service on the Border, have no Troops now except H.M. Army. The Kafirs are perfectly tranquil & have made no attempts to enter their old Territory now to be called as you will see by the papers I have sent the "Royal Reserve" & there have been no depredations by Hottentots who seem to have dispersed, of the latter we have tried many by Courts Martial & several have been tried by the Civil Courts, those who have surrendered themselves are awarded 2 years Imprisonment – sufficiently mild punishment – fixed by General Cathcart – for their treason & rebellion. Our old friend Moshesh of <u>Berea</u> celebrity is more civil & contented than he has been for years & altogether the Governor can congratulate himself upon having in a comparatively short space of time pacified an immense tract of country which was at his arrival in utter confusion & war, his own indefatigable mind & thoroughly independent character have aided him in doing this, for he has had to contend against not only open enemies but a whole mass of Colonists every one of whom is more or less interested in keeping alive alarm & agitation that they may benefit by the enormous sums expended in the country during hostilities. The Constitution for the Colony being expected by the next Mail I fancy we shall go to Cape Town to receive it as the Governor's presence there will no doubt be necessary, but I do not think he will remain there for any length of time as he has a marked aversion to Colonial Towns, and their consequences such as influential men with hints as to the best mode of governing the Cape, & avoiding future Kafir Wars and petitioners for employment in any branch of service, for all of which they may be totally unfit. We have just received the news from England to the 2nd of March by which we see the account of the Orange River Expedition has been received & favourably viewed, I only hope that now all the business is settled they will give the Army some token of approbation, personally of course I am most anxious as I have only looked for promotion in my own profession all my life, and also for the Officers & Men whose exertions have been very meritorious although exhibited in an inglorious contest, of which I can possibly speak more than any one having had more opportunities from my position of knowing what has actually been accomplished. This is the commencement of the winter here & you have no idea what a beautiful climate this place enjoys. I should think as fine as any in the world; if that were the only thing needful one might live here for ever. There is a report that Gold has been discovered at the mouth of a river some 20 miles from here, if true it will be disastrous to the country which already suffers from a complete scarcity of farm labourers artisans &c & would then become quite bereft of those useful & necessary portions of population who would naturally all flock to the diggings leaving agriculture & carpentry, building &c to take care of themselves. Give my best love to Mary. Annot is at Cape Town where latterly she has not been well, I imagine we shall be there at the end of the month.

Yours always
Affectionately
Edward Wellesley

57

Note from Richard Wellesley to his sister Hyacinthe Wellesley

F.O.
Thursday

My dear Hyacinthe
I send you a letter from Edward giving a very interesting account of the campaign in Kaffirland & you will see by the enclosed Newspapers that his name is honourably mentioned – Ask Mama to return them when done with

yrs RW

58

Edward Wellesley to his mother

Graham's Town
May 6. 1853.

My dear Mama
I received your letter of 12th March and I send you another of the accounts of the Berea fight as you wished to have one. My leg is now perfectly well and I have lately been playing at Cricket with

no inconvenience, I was fortunate in having the services of two most kind and attentive Surgeons to whom I feel very much indebted. We have received news that the home authorities have acknowledged the services of the Army and the Queen has expressed her approbation of their services, but as yet have not heard of any more tangible mark of the Royal pleasure being about to be given, I hope however that this will be done as the Troops have really throughout the whole War undergone hardships and privations which in a more unfavourable climate would have been most harmful to them, and although the effects have not been so evident, and the results not so apparent yet this must always be the case in a war against savages from whom there are no towns to gain, & who will never meet you in open battle.

At present all is peaceful and the arrangements made by the Governor will it is hoped tend to make this perpetual I think however that all will depend on a strong force of regular . . .

[page missing]

much I sympathize with you in the affliction.

I suppose you will be very sorry to leave Moulsey where all the people seem to have been very thoughtful and better than most country neighbours. I fancy it must have been however too damp for Hyacinthe and for yourself ever to have lived there in the winter. Augustus must have enjoyed himself very much in Italy & Sicily where Music is so much loved; this land is very barren in that respect, your Colonist being more intent on making money than in anything of the softer acts of civilization, or to appreciate anything of this sort in the female members of his family. Since a good Regimental Band is not to be heard and all the best players in my own Regiment were unfortunately killed during the War.

Richard is a very good correspondent as I generally hear from him every month and write in return. At present we have not so much to do as during hostilities, for then the country was directed from the Head Quarters of the Army, but now all is returning to peace and the Civil functionaries to resume their own duties. I have been expecting to go to Cape Town for some time, and now that the Constitution for the Colony has arrived I fancy the Governor will go there immediately. Annot & the children are there where they are better than anywhere else as I have been so constantly in movement since I came out.

With my love to Hyacinthe
yours affectionately
Edward Wellesley

59

To his brother Richard

Graham's Town
May 7. 1853.

My dear Richard

I received yours of March 14 when you had received the news of the Berea fight, the Secretary of State for the Colonies also by the same post acknowledged the receipt of the intelligence and conveyed in the usual old stale official terms Her Majesty's "marked approbation" with the conduct of the Officers and Troops, this staid official style which seems a condensation of all the inkstands, rulers and penknives of an office with about as much feeling or sympathy, is cold enough, but I trust that something more tangible will be awarded the Army, and that the gracious act is merely delayed, for the Troops really and well deserve any special mark of distinction, and I see moreover that naval promotions have been given for the Burmese Campaign[79] which has occupied but little time, and during which no one has had to undergo half the toil & fatigue or hardships that the Army of South Africa has endured. Everything on the Border is going very well, all the Farmers are returning and large sums are being given for farms, the Kafirs are quiet and Sandili has established himself on the bank of the Kei, a very good position, as if his people prove unruly hereafter or attempt to steal Cattle, they must cross a large tract of open country before they can enter the Colony which can be easily guarded & prevented by Cavalry, or he could at once be driven across the river. A Commission is expected out to assist in finally settling the border and territories, it is expected that the Sovereignty as it is called will be given up, in fact the territory so recklessly added to the Colony by Sir Harry Smith has only proved a source of continual annoyance trouble and expense & to be properly governed would require a separate Government, it being such an immense distance from the seat of the Colonial Government. I hope that there will however be no attempt to give up Kaffraria as was done before for that would inevitably bring on another war in perhaps a few months, by holding the Amatola Mountains and the Waterkloof you deprive the Kafirs from having any secure strongholds into which to drive and secrete their booty when taken, and thus is much safer & in fact the only practicable means of policy, the attempt to keep any frontier from being passed by savages except by an overwhelming force, being impracticable.

The Constitution for the Colony has arrived and is to be soon given to the people, like Holloway's Ointment or Paris [Pan's?] Life Pills it is expected to heal and keep in vigour all the ills of this crazy carcase of a Colony & I believe people are so sanguine that bald headed Independents even think it would make their hair grow again like Macassar oil and smoky Radicals that it will give their teeth "that pearly appearance so much desired" like the Odonto its first effects will however be division and dissension.

We have had some Cricket here lately, we played the Inhabitants in this Town who licked us in one innings in the most disgraceful manner (vide Newspaper which I send) we had not played much together and when we came to play found out that the greater part of our Eleven were impostors of the deepest dye, and quite hopeless at the manly game. Will you be so good to get this Cheque cashed and adding the difference from monies which I think you have some of mine in your hands pay the enclosed bill of my saddler, & send me the receipt & also the other enclosure to Mama

We expect to go to Cape Town shortly as His Excellency's presence will be required there to arrange the Constitution question & future Parliament of the Colony.

My love to Mary
yours always affectionately
Edward Wellesley

P.S. Officers can be elected Members of a Colonial as of an Imperial Parliament; do you think it is worth while working up for a Constituency here, what do you say to D.A.A.G. and M.C.P.?

60

To his brother Richard

Graham's Town
June 13. 1853.

My dear Richard
I have not much news from here this month everything has been going on quietly and satisfactorily and there have been no attempts of Kafirs to disturb the peace, & only in one instance of Hottentots which latter must of course be expected where there are so many facilities for marauding which exist in the dense bush which covers so much of the country. We have been stationary here with the exception of a short excursion to the coast which His Excellency took but merely accompanied by his personal Staff. A Sir George Clerk has arrived here ostensibly as a Commissioner for the final adjustment of our old friend the Orange River Territory question and to decide whether it is to be abandoned or not, but it is imagined he will eventually succeed the General who is I fancy anxious to return home now that the War is over. Clerk was formerly & in part is now, in the Company service and was formerly Governor of Bombay, how good a proof it is of the inferiority of this service over others when you see the Government at home so frequently select them for different missions to countries with which they are entirely ignorant, in this Colony they have twice selected within the last four years two men of this service to send here in times of peculiar emergency; I always regret when I think of this that Augustus could neglect an opportunity of entering a service the duties of which are not confined to one hemisphere, but from which talents you may possess may send you to any post of honor & greatness.

I received yours of the 14th April & hope the contemplated ball at the F.O. has not brought down the oldest inhabitants of

Downing Street. I saw Charlie Woodford the other day who is on Detachment near Fort Beaufort, he told me that Johnny was very ill which I was sorry to hear, the Rifle Brigade expect to be sent home immediately, the Government will however I trust not commit the same faults they did at the end of the last war and reduce the Force here too speedily. What a fight they have had in Ava,[79] I fancy Mea Toon is the Sandili of that part of the world we never can get rid of our "little wars" but have been continuously fighting since the European peace somewhere or other.

We had a grand dinner at the Governor's on the Queen's Birthday and were the only people who illuminated in the town, I felt much inclined to smash some windows but prudence prevailed over excess of loyalty. They have found some coal in the Orange River Territory a specimen of which I was sent, it burns very well & may be found eventually of immense benefit to the country. Many thanks about the money & my Majority, but I can say nothing positive on the subject at present as I shall wait the course of events which may arise after the war, and perhaps I shall not require to purchase that step at all, therefore do not think of me. Please pay the enclosed by a Post Office Order on Dublin & for which I think you have enough money of mine & get a receipt from the man. My love to Mary

yours affectionately
Edward Wellesley

I have written to Hyacinthe, they seem sorry to leave Moulsey, leaving any place or the last of anything is always painful

61

To his brother Richard

Graham's Town
July 13. 1853.

My dear Richard
We have been going on very quietly here since I last wrote, the only event to disturb our monotony has been the arrival of the

special Commissioner Sir George Clerk who has also become invested with more interest as rumour points to him as the successor of General Cathcart, whenever the latter does go I personally shall much regret him as he has been very kind to me and I admire him for his high tone of independence, honor, and his truly gentlemanly demeanour. Sir George Clerk has come here specially to arrange the affairs of the Orange River Territory and I have no doubts that country will finally be abandoned. The whole country is now in ferment from the near approach of the Elections, this Eastern portion of it is more peculiarly interested than any other as being anxious for a strong local government on the spot and no provision for this having been made in the Royal Ordinance forming a Constitution, the only hope the people here have is to make as strong parties as possible in both houses of legislature in order to propose and carry out this measure on which they are so bent – I have no doubt myself that if there had been a good Government here instead of all being referred to Cape Town 600 miles off there would have been no Kafir Wars. In one of the newspapers I have sent Mary you will find a minute of His Excellency's on his policy since his arrival if you read it you will agree with me that it is a most able paper and most clearly sets forth all that he has done (& that not a little) since his arrival, its production has very much raised him in public estimation all the different shades of people as represented in the local papers having more or less praised it – in one point – all must be unanimous namely to prevent further wars you must keep the Amatolas – if there were no receivers of stolen goods there would be no thieves, if the Kafirs have no more strongholds to drive stolen cattle into, they will rob no more.

The next mail is expected to be very interesting as Peel[80] said in the house the future policy should be announced before it could leave, until one knows what is eventually to be done with the Head Quarters & Staff & where we are finally to be stationed one is in an unsettled state & I have consequently left Annot at Cape Town until our fates represented by Lord Hardinge & the Duke of Newcastle[81] shadow forth our destiny. I have written to Mama. My love to Mary.

Always yours affectionately
Edward Wellesley

62

To his brother Richard

Graham's Town
August 14. 1853.

My dear Richard

I was very much surprised to hear from a letter from Mary the only one I received by the last mail that you had not heard from me since February whereas I have religiously written every post and can't imagine what can have become of my letters. We received four days ago the Brevet for the War by the Mail, they have been very generous in some points and have left others out, and I regret one most particularly Seymour the Military Secretary who is one of the best fellows I ever met and more deserving of some mark of favour than many others promoted. Herbert was a Major one day and then made Lieutenant Colonel, I imagine the only case on record. My promotion will necessitate my resigning my present appointment which can only be held by a Captain & although I might perhaps continue to hold it do not wish to establish a precedent in my own person which might hereafter be injurious to others. I have not said anything about this yet as the General has been too much occupied in writing for the English Mail which leaves to-day but to-morrow shall mention the subject & let you know the result by the next post which may possibly be in time also for the steamer and despatch this in order that you may not feel surprised if I come home on leave if I vacate my Staff appointment which I should apply for immediately.

We paid a visit the other day to the celebrated Waterkloof now perfectly peaceful, we remained out one week and then returned here. All the . . .

[rest missing]

63

To his brother Richard

Graham's Town
September 10. 1853

My dear Richard

I did not hear from you by the last Mail but heard from Mama that you had gone abroad and hope Mary and yourself enjoyed the excursion. We had expected to have heard by the last post what arrangements had been made for the permanent Staff here, but the intelligence did not arrive consequently must wait for the next, I told you in my last letter that I could not keep my present appointment with my present rank, but shall continue on until we hear what is finally decided upon at home. We have just returned from King Williams Town where we remained a week and during which the Governor had a meeting with the Gaika Chiefs including Sandili and Macomo, this was the first time I had seen these men, Sandili is tall but has a shrivelled leg which he conceals in a pair of trousers, he spoke much the burden of his speech being repeated requests for his old country the Amatolas. Macomo also spoke and very well, he has the talent of the nation & when he spoke all the Gaikas appeared to listen most attentively, he is an old man but with a very acute and clever countenance, he said very coolly that he had gone into the Waterkloof to avoid the war, he also prayed that the Amatolas might be given back, that Sandili had been punished, was a child who had lost his father, had erred, should now be forgiven and so forth. The Governor who was lying down in a circle formed by ourselves and the Gaikas held out no hopes of restoration of the forfeited lands and the meeting broke up I think with much dissatisfaction upon the part of the Chiefs. Amongst the Kafirs were some fine specimens Klu Klu a brother of Sandili was a very handsome native, and a son of Macomo who stood behind his father with his blanket disposed in a most graceful toga–like fashion was one of the handsomest of any native I had seen. After all however the scene was curious that the half naked savages should have held out against us so long only shows the absurd plan upon which we have treated them for if we had not taught them how to fight and had not permitted the transport and traffic of gunpowder, and arms into their country they would always have remained as innocuous as when first we came into contact with them. The Colony is in a state of wrath and excitement because of the abandonment of the Sovereignty which has been proclaimed, loud cries of British faith and honour having been broken and lying prostrate in the mud, scurrility reigns in the Colonial press, one paper tells the Governor that he was licked at Berea and that he then told the Colonial Secretary that the country could not be held except by 2000 men, although he (the Editor) would undertake to keep it with half the numbers. Traitor recreant and so on are plentiful in the papers, in the meantime the troops stationed there are to be withdrawn and the absurdity of a frontier 400 miles distant from this place be done away with. I trust my missing letters have re-appeared as I have scrupulously written each month. Annot remains at Cape Town until it is decided what I am to do. Love to Mary.

yours affectionately
Edward Wellesley

Send enclosed to Mama

64

To his brother Richard

Cape Town
December 31. 1853.

My dear Richard

I write you a line to say that we have taken a passage in the "Coromandel" a sailing vessel from China and bound to London as I was tired of waiting for the next Steamer which may however arrive in England before us so I shall send this by her as you would be surprised perhaps at our not arriving. We have very good cabins on board and are the only passengers with the exception of one person. We go on board this morning & shall sail in the evening if the wind is favorable.

Adieu therefore and with love to Mary whose letter I received after Annot had written.

yours affectionately
Edward Wellesley

Annot desires her love and the children are delighted at going on board which will no doubt do them much good.

If the winds & waves are propitious we should arrive in England about the 20th of February.

65

To his brother Richard

"Coromandel"
March 7. 1854.
off Falmouth. 12 noon.

My dear Richard

We have arrived in the Channel after rather a long but a fine weather passage. I am sorry to say that Annot has been ill the whole time more or less and on Sunday last was attacked with very severe hemorrhage (technically I believe called <u>flooding</u>) which we had great difficulty in stopping, fortunately the Captain's wife is on board & a most capital doctor & nothing can exceed their kindness & attention, & Annot is better but of course very weak so much so that she will only be able to travel from the Docks to your house & in a carriage but not by the Mail that is to say when we arrive in London. I received Mary's letter asking us to come to you after I had written from the Cape before we left. I am not certain whether Annot's illness is attributable to a miscarriage or not and we cannot tell until a Doctor has seen her. The children are quite well and improved by the sea voyage; Courtenay is a man of tar and quite a sailor assisting in pulling the ropes &c. I write this as we may at any moment have a chance of sending a letter on shore & shall put in where we are at the moment of dispatching it when an opportunity occurs, & when you receive it send on & let Mama know we are arrived. We shall be two days or a day and a half going up the river from the mouth. We have had a fine breeze from the South West in entering the Channel & hazy weather & have not as yet seen any land but several vessels. Adieu my best love to Mary.

yours affectionately
Edward Wellesley

8th. Passed the Isle of Wight at 12 & going 10 Knots with a splendid breeze & shall be in the Downs to-night & enter the river to morrow morning, if the wind holds.

1.P.M. Very hazy weather & have lain to all night.

Off the Foreland. March 9.

I shall write when we get to the Docks as I shall most likely have to ask you to have a carriage sent for Annot who although better will require great care in being moved. E.W.

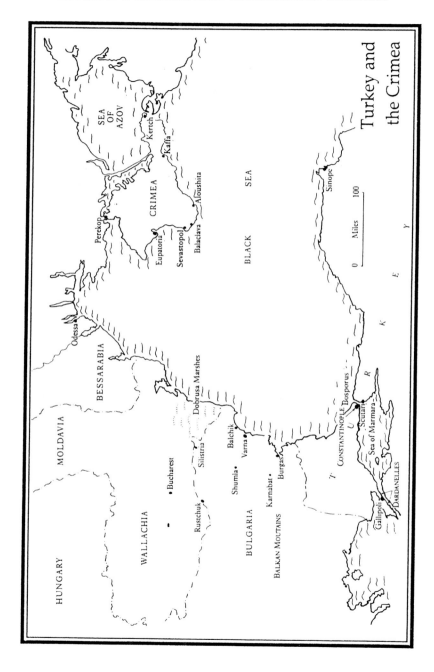

Turkey and
the Crimea

II
To the Crimea 1854

The weakness of the Ottoman régime in Turkey in the 1830s, threatened not only by independence movements in Greece and the Balkans, but also by Mahomed Ali in Egypt, was exploited by Tsar Nicholas I of Russia, to whom the Sultan Mahmud II appealed for help. The threat this posed to their interests brought Britain and France, rivals in the Near East, together. These three nations, together with Austria and Prussia, agreed in 1839 to 'settle the eastern question', while the Sultan was on his deathbed. Mahomed Ali was forced to return Syria, Crete and Arabia to Turkey, but was confirmed as hereditary ruler of Egypt in return for an annual tribute to the Sultan. Two years later the Powers signed the Straits Convention which respected 'the ancient rule' that, while Turkey was at peace, the Bosphorus and the Dardanelles were closed to the warships of all nations. This would allow Turkey to open them to friendly powers when she was at war; whereas Nicholas had pressed for their closure to all warships in those circumstances. His support of Turkey having brought no dividends, he began to contemplate its partition and to build a major naval base at Sebastopol.

The apple cart was upset by the ambitions of Louis Napoleon, nephew of the great Emperor, who, elected President of the French Republic after the revolution of 1848, had become Emperor as a result of the coup of 1851. Intent on emphasizing the status of France, and therefore of himself, he laid claim in 1852 to a special position as defender of Roman Catholic interests in the Holy Places of Jerusalem. Tsar Nicholas retaliated with a similar claim for the protection of Orthodox interests. When this was not recognized by Turkey, the Russians decided to invade the Danube Principalities of Moldavia and Wallachia, modern Romania, then formally part of the Ottoman Empire.

Tension mounted, and the British government, headed by Lord Aberdeen, with Lord John Russell as Foreign Secretary, vacillated, as did Napoleon III, although he tended to take a firmer line. Lord Palmerston, then Home Secretary, demanded action. In June 1853 a British fleet was despatched to Besika Bay, at the mouth of the Dardanelles, which did not deter the Russians from crossing the River Pruth and advancing into Moldavia. A conference of the great Powers was held at Vienna in July, which drew up 'The Vienna Note'. This stipulated that the Sultan would 'remain faithful to the letter and to the spirit of the treaties of Kainardji and Adrianople relative to the protection of the Christian religion' and that no modification to the existing rules would be allowed without the consent of France and Russia. The Russians accepted this, interpreting it as giving them the right to interfere in the interests of the 12 million Christian subjects of Turkey, most of whom were Orthodox. The British government told its ambassador to the Sublime Porte, Lord Stratford de Redcliffe,[82] to advise the Sultan to accept the note, although he himself was opposed to it. But, as it appeared to give France and Russia the right to interfere in the internal affairs of the Ottoman Empire, the Sultan insisted on an amendment which promised that he would be faithful to the treaties 'relative to the protection *by the Sublime Porte* of the Christian religion.' Britain and France refused to accept the Russian interpretation and took the view that Russia was exerting undue pressure on Turkey in pursuit of her own ambitions. In September Tsar Nicholas met Francis Joseph, the Austrian Emperor, whose Foreign Minister, Buol, proposed a compromise: that the Turkish amendment should be agreed, but that it should be accepted that Russia had the right to ensure that the engagements of the Treaty of Kuchuk Kainardji[83] were carried out. The British cabinet rejected the compromise, believing it to be a trick, devised by Russia and Austria to gain acceptance of the Russian interpretation of the original note. When the Crimean War was over, Lord Aberdeen said that he wished he had accepted it.

Confident of the support of Britain and France, although Lord Stratford, against instructions, made several efforts to stop British and French naval movements encouraging it, Turkey declared war on Russia on 4 October 1853, and, on 23 October, their Commander-in-Chief, Omar Pasha,[84] attacked the Russians in Moldavia and, against Lord Stratford's advice, the Turks sent a light flotilla into the Black Sea, an act which the Russians interpreted as designed to stir up rebellion in the Caucasus. They retaliated by destroying the Turkish ships and, it was reported, continuing to fire on their helpless crews. This inflamed British public opinion, which accused the government of cowardice. Palmerston resigned, in fact on another issue: he returned to office a fortnight later. The cabinet feared that, if Britain did not openly come to the support of Turkey, France would act alone, to the prejudice of general British interests in the Near East. On 22 December agreement was reached with France to combine with them in keeping the Russian fleet bottled up in Sebastopol, provided that the French would cooperate in making more peace proposals; meanwhile their two navies would protect Turkey from Russian attack. The French agreed, and the fleets were ordered into the Black Sea in January 1854. Reacting against their intention to confine the Russian fleet to Sebastopol, the Tsar withdrew his ambassadors from London and Paris in February, and, while Austria was again trying to devise a compromise, Britain and France sent an ultimatum to Russia to withdraw from the Principalities. No reply was received. On 12 March, two days after Edward Wellesley arrived home from South Africa, Britain and France allied themselves with Turkey, and a fortnight later were at war with Russia.

A month before, Lord Raglan had been appointed 'General Officer Commanding the Forces eastward of Malta', and orders given for 10,000 troops to be sent to the island. On 10 April Raglan set off, accompanied by Wellesley, to confer first with the French in Paris [71]. His secret instructions from the Duke of Newcastle, Secretary for War, stated that his first duty was to prevent a Russian advance on Constantinople, but that it might become 'essential for the attainment of the objects of the war to undertake operations of an offensive character and that the heaviest blow which could be struck to the southern extremities of the Russian empire would be the taking and destruction of Sebastopol.'[85]

When he and his French colleague, Marshal St Arnaud,[86] arrived at Constantinople at the end of the month, both were thinking in terms of the defence of the Bosphorus and the Dardanelles, almost all of the French troops and 5,000 of the British having already been deployed at the latter, which they were busy fortifying. At that time, the Russian army, under the command of the veteran Field Marshal Prince Paskevich,[87] had advanced to the Danube and was laying siege to Silistra on the southern bank. Omar Pasha tried to persuade Raglan and St Arnaud that they should deploy their troops into northeastern Bulgaria in order to free his to take the offensive against Paskevich. They agreed to do so, and began to move troops there in June. At the same time Austria moved troops into her provinces adjoining the Principalities. On 23 June Paskevich, who had never been enthusiastic about the campaign, abandoned the siege of Silistra, and began to withdraw from Moldavia altogether.

The object for which Raglan's expeditionary force had been dispatched appeared to have been achieved, but the British public was in a bellicose, jingoistic mood and the Emperor Napoleon was not going to be deprived of his chance to earn some *Gloire*. Omar Pasha wanted his allies to join his forces in pursuing the Russians to, and perhaps beyond, the River Pruth, but neither were keen to do so. Both wished to escape from the fever-ridden lowlands of the Danube valley and were strongly backed by Newcastle in their refusal. Aberdeen and many of his colleagues would have been glad to have called it a day, but Newcastle, aided and abetted by the thundering of *The Times*, knowing that public opinion was behind him, persuaded them otherwise. On 29 June Newcastle wrote a despatch to Raglan, reminding him of the mention made in his secret order of 10 April and continuing: 'The circumstances anticipated in my despatch [of 10 April] have therefore now arrived; and I have, on the part of Her Majesty's Government, to instruct your Lordship to concert measures for the siege of Sebastopol, unless, with the information in your possession, but at present unknown in this country, you should decidedly be of the opinion that it could not be undertaken with a reasonable prospect of success . . . the difficulties would be increased rather than diminished by delay . . . as there is no prospect of a safe and honourable peace until the fortress is reduced, and the fleet taken or destroyed . . . nothing but insuperable impediments . . . should be allowed to prevent the early decision to undertake these operations.'[88]

The despatch took a fortnight to reach Raglan, and when he had read it, he handed it to General Sir George Brown, who was visiting him, and asked him his opinion. Brown replied: 'You and I are accustomed, when in any great difficulty . . . to ask ourselves how the Great Duke would have acted and decided under similar circumstances', and said that, without better information than they had about the Crimea 'that great man would not have accepted the responsibility of undertaking such an enterprise'; but that nevertheless, as it was clear that the government had made up their minds, Raglan had better agree, or they would send someone to replace him who 'will be less scrupulous and more ready to come into their plans'. So Lord Raglan replied on 14 July that 'it was more in deference to the views of the Government and the known acquiescence of the Emperor Louis Napoleon than to any information in the possession of the naval or military forces' that the decision had been taken 'to make a descent upon the Crimea' and went on to stress the lack of any intelligence about the strength of Russian forces there.[89]

The die was cast which was to send Edward Wellesley and many others to their death, although cholera might have struck him and others down in any case.

66

Edward Wellesley to his mother at Bushy Cottage, Hampton Court

5 Spanish Place
Thursday [March 17.1854]

My dear Mama

I am sorry I shall not be able to come to-morrow as I have got a swelling in my face and do not want to expose myself more than I can help. I saw General Wetherall[90] at the Horse Guards to-day he is the acting Adjutant General, he was very civil and kind and had a letter about me from Sir George Cathcart which he said he would take to the Military Secretary to Lord Hardinge which I trust will be of some avail in providing me with an appointment on the Staff to the Army destined for Turkey & Colonel Eyre also forwarded for me an official application to the same effect. The kindness of Sir George in thus writing home so much about me I can not sufficiently appreciate. Annot is going on well and the children are quite well. Augustus has gone to the Ordnance and I have not seen him yet to know the result.

yours affectionately
Edward Wellesley

Arthur[91] is laid up from Sciatica I saw him to-day and he is quite immoveable

Excuse the writing as I am sitting in Annot's room writing on my lap

67

To his mother

Friday night [March 18.1854]

My dear Mama

I shall not be able to go to you to-morrow as my face is not quite well but much better. Annot is getting on very well and the children are quite well. I have heard nothing about going out yet.

yours affectionately
Edward Wellesley

68

To his mother

5 Spanish Place
Monday night [March 21.1854]

My dear Mama

I saw Lord Hardinge at the Horse Guards this morning and he has appointed me Assistant Quarter Master General to the Head Quarters of the Army proceeding to Turkey, he was very kind, told me that he had heard very highly about me from Sir George Cathcart and altogether treated me with the greatest consideration although I had never seen him before, Colonel Airey[92] the Military Secretary had told me to call when I met him yesterday at Lord Raglan's. Of course poor Annot is very sad but the appointment is very good indeed in point of emoluments and it is so flattering that I who only arrived the other day should have been selected at once from amongst the many applicants assisted by the most powerful interest. Lord de Ros[93] is my immediate Chief I met him to-day and shall call upon him to-morrow morning by his own request & make myself as useful as I can before we go which will be soon and I shall consequently have plenty to do before we leave. I saw Lady Charles[94] yesterday looking much better than ever.

In haste
yours affectionately
Edward Wellesley

69

To his mother

United Service Club
Tuesday afternoon [?5 April.1854]

My dear Mama

I received your note & had previously been to Abbot & Jenkins who told me the case was postponed until to-morrow when I shall go. I hope to be able to go to you some day at the end of the month but have been very busy since I saw you. I met the Duke of

Cambridge[95] at the Ordnance just now who recognized me & shook hands. I am glad to say Annot is much better & was out with me for some time to day the children are also well.

Is Hyacinthe coming to London any day this week. Excuse the scrawl to raise the post.

yours affectionately
Edward Wellesley

Richard is looking very well

70

To his mother

Friday night.8 April.1854.

My dear Mama

I could not go to the Rolls as I was obliged to go to a meeting at the hour named but a note came from Abbot & Jenkins that we were not required and we have not heard what was the result. I was very busy all day & write to-morrow.

We purpose to pay you a visit on Sunday & shall come early. I am to go with Lord Raglan by Paris & I fancy we shall soon leave. I was in the House of Lords to-night where there was a debate about the Army, Lord Grey proposing that the Administration should be vested in a similar way to the Navy.[96] Annot is going on well as well as the Children. I hope Hyacinthe got home safe the other night.

yours affectionately
Edward Wellesley

71

To his wife

Embassy. Paris.
Tuesday 4.P.M.[11 April. 1854]

My dearest Annot

Richard will have given you an account of our start from London therefore I will commence from there.

127

We arrived at Dover at 11¼ [on 10 April] and immediately went on board the "Vivid" Government steamer waiting to receive us, great enthusiasm was manifested here, and we steamed across in one hour and a half in a lovely moonlight, and the sea quite calm. When we arrived at Calais the Duke [of Cambridge] was also cheered and after a supper at the station of the Railway we left for Paris, – we halted at a place called Longueau at 6 in the morning and had a cup of coffee and arrived in Paris at 9. Lord de Ros and I occupied the same carriage and slept incessantly, the night being fine and cold, but the latter one does not feel as they provide you with feet warmers in the shape of long leaden boxes which are replenished as they require it with fresh hot water. At Paris we at once drove to the Embassy amidst the multitude who had assembled to receive the Duke, an escort of the guides received him and we went in the Emperor's own carriage which had been sent for us. Lord de Ros had a note from Lady Cowley at Calais saying that I was to have a room at the Embassy in which (a most comfortable room too) I am now writing. I was introduced to her and Lord Cowley[97] and made the acquaintance of several children cousins all most attentive to me bringing me my boots and looking after me quite like a Courtenay. At 1 the Emperor's carriage again appeared accompanied by the usual escort of the guides and we all proceeded in full dress to the Tuilleries [sic] where His R. Highness was received with all honour and we were then introduced to the Emperor who was gracious enough, speaking to those whom he knew and in English. We afterwards went up a story higher and were then all presented to the Empress, the Emperor being also present, she also spoke in English and is really a most charming person and very pretty. We then went to the apartments of the Duchess Stephanie of Baden[98] where the same ceremony of presentation took place, and afterwards to the Prince Jerome Bonaparte uncle to the Emperor to whom we were also presented, the meeting between this prince and Lord Raglan struck me as curious as probably the last time they were so near each other was at Waterloo where Jerome commenced the first attack under Napoleon upon the Chateau of Hugoumont.

I had but got as far as this when Lord Cowley rushes in and

says that he expects the Emperor will call upon the Duke and that some one ought to be in uniform to receive him and I and an aide de camp have therefore to re-harness ourselves.

After we left Jerome we returned here and the crowds of people who had assembled to see us, were most civil and respectful taking off their hats and bowing. We all dine with the Emperor to-night in plain clothes and to-morrow there is to be a Review on the Champ de Mars of about 30,000 men for which His Majesty provides us with horses. Paris looks bright and the buildings and everything look quite gay after the smoke of London. I do not know when we go on but imagine in a day or two. I hope this will find you in better spirits than when I left. You must not give way to crying and the sooner you can change the air for Brighton the more I shall like it. I hope Courty's cough is better, the change of air will also benefit him. I shall write and give you an account of the Review to-morrow and in the meantime adieu and mind no more crying but try and make yourself as rapidly quite well as you can. My love to Mama who will be happy to hear that I am so comfortably provided for at the Embassy. The post is about to close.

Yours ever affectionately
Edward Wellesley

You can write on Wednesday and tell me how you are which I shall get on Thursday but not afterwards as we may be gone and Richard will send it from the F.O. E.W.

72

To his wife

Embassy. Paris.
Wednesday 4½ P.M. [12 April]

My dearest Annot

The Duke of Cambridge and the whole of us dined with the Emperor at the Tuilleries last night at half past 7, the Empress and about 40 people were there, an Infantry Band played during dinner very well, and it was a very good repast with a profusion of wines of every description. The Dinner did not last very long and after coffee in the other saloons, we all went to the Opera Comique where the royal boxes had been set apart for us, and saw one act of L'Etoile du Nord in which Caroline Dupres a daughter of the Dupres sang, but she has not a very good voice although well taught, - the orchestra was very good and the choruses. The Duke got tired after one act and we then came back in the royal carriages which were waiting to the Embassy. This morning at 12 we went in full dress to the Tuilleries in the same carriages and after being presented to the Emperor mounted our horses to go to the review, - the Emperor had provided us all with horses and you found a groom with your name on a piece of paper and the animal you were to ride. I had a very nice little chestnut and all the Staff were well mounted, indeed the whole of the Emperor's carriage and horse departments seem in complete order and in perfect taste the liveries &c being dark green and gold, the carriages lined with the same as well as horse equipments. An immense staff had assembled to accompany the Emperor and we then proceeded to the Champ de Mars where the troops were assembled. The road through which we went was lined with people, and the Emperor was received with much enthusiasm, - he rode with the Duke on his right and nothing could have been better received than we were, the cries of "Vivent les Anglais", "Vive la Reine d'Angleterre", "A bas les Cossaques", were frequent both on going and returning. The Champ de Mars is a large plain of sandy soil and here were assembled about 30,000 men of all Arms, Cavalry, Artillery and Infantry. The Emperor first rode down the ranks being received by the troops with loud cries of Vive L'Empereur. This occupied some time and after it was finished, we took up a position in front of a pavilion where the Empress accompanied by Lady Cowley the Grand Duchess Stephanie of Baden, the Duchess of Hamilton[99] &c were retiring [sitting?]. and the whole of the troops then defiled past him, - as each Battalion came by they shouted Vive L'Empereur et L'Imperatrice, and after the whole had gone past, the Cavalry were advanced and 5,000 in number charged up to nearly the feet of the Emperor, this was a very fine sight and much applauded by the populace of whom there must have been 200,000 on the Champ de

Mars, – we then all returned to the palace, the cheering being as loud as ever, and after dismounting returned in the last carriages here, where I have just had lunch, not to be despised as the review lasted 3 hours. The day threatened rain but cleared up after a little sprinkling and they say the Emperor is as fortunate in these small things as he has been in greater, in fact when we see this man surrounded by all sorts of pomps, apparently loved by the people, and the troops, one must esteem him as an extraordinary man, more particularly when we recollect that he had nothing in his favor except that he was the Emperor's nephew, an Emperor who gained his name by Military talents while the present one must retain his by those of peace as a successful general would be a dangerous rival against him should such an one arise amongst a people so fond of glory as the French.

We all dine at the Tuilleries again to-night. I have seen very little of Paris since we came but it is greatly improved since I was here before and the Emperor is adding to its beauty every day. We have certainly nothing like the Place de la Concorde and French shops beat ours very hollow indeed, and then there is a certain brightness and vivacity in the air which one has not in London. It is not certain when we leave and I think you may venture to write as soon as you receive this which I shall receive on Friday morning. I don't think the French Troops are in any way to be compared with ours either in appearance, the horses or anything else. St Arnaud who is to command the French Troops in the East was with the Emperor to-day as also Marshal Vaillant Minister of War, the review was under Marshal Magnan who commands all the Troops in the vicinity of Paris, the Cavalry here manoeuvred in very fine order and most rapidly.

The Infantry are not habitually so steady under arms as our men are, nor do they march past in such a correct way as we do, and the fact of their being bound to cheer whilst in the ranks no doubt adds very much to unsteadiness. The Emperor rides very well, and is well mounted, his horse trappings being of red velvet of a most gorgeous description, a soldier of the line stepped out of the ranks and presented a complaint as he was passing which was the only mal a propos occurrence of the day.

I trust this will find you in better health and spirits and my only regret to-day was that you could not witness the scene of to-day which I would not have missed, and which was perhaps as curious from the association between the French and ourselves and the cries of Vive Napoleon being joined with those of Vive les Anglais by French people and in Paris, – as has ever been seen. You must read this to Richard Mary &c and tell them I have no time to write separate letters a special messenger being sent at the request of the Duke with these and the time nearly up.

Ever yours affectionately
Edward Wellesley

73

From Anne Bentinck to Mrs Richard (Mary) Wellesley

Hotel Richepause
Rue Richepause[Paris]
Wednesday 12 April 1854

My dear Mary

I cannot help writing you a line to say that we are just returned from the review in the Champs de Mars & saw Edward on his way there looking so well in his red uniform we saw him yesterday in the Royal Carriages on his way with the Duke & Lord Raglan to pay his first visit to the Emperor they were very much cheered by the people and I should think the English officers have every reason to be pleased with this reception. I feel quite proud to be able to say I have a Relation going to the War and I cannot tell you the pleasure it gave to Mamma to see Edward looking so well & so handsome & happy.

What a gay place this Paris is I hardly know if I have been standing on my head or my heels since I have been here and Mamma says that her nerves are too much excited to bear it any longer than a fortnight the weather is as fine and warm as in the middle of summer the Tuileries are filled with people sitting under the Trees & eating ices. We went to see the new opera L'Etoile du Nord the music is beautiful. We saw the Duke & Lord

Raglan in the Emperor's box but I could not make out if Edward was there.

We hope Mrs Edward & the children are going on well we were sorry to have missed seeing her when she called before we left Town – When you write to Bushy give our love & kind remembrances to all there with Mammas and my love to yourself and Richard I remain, dear Mary, yours affectionately

Anne C. Bentinck

Arthur is at Bath for his sciatica as cross as two sticks that he is not going to the East

74

Edward Wellesley to his wife

Embassy. Paris.
Thursday 13th. [April] 4 p.m.

My dearest Annot

We all dined with the Emperor last night – the dinner going off in precisely the same manner as in the former night, except that the band of the Guides played during dinner and is the best military band in Paris. We afterwards went in the Royal carriage to the French Opera and saw part of the "Vertace" and part of a balet [sic] in which Rorati danced very well. Cerito was also in the house, our party occupied the Royal boxes and that of Jerome, the Duke went away early and unfortunately just as we had gone too far to be recalled the orchestra played "God save the Queen" the people all applauded violently and demanded an encore which was complied with and they played it again amidst much applause some of the Aides de Camp and I had remained and did not exactly know what to do, so we did nothing but remained at the back of the box which was perhaps the wisest plan under the circumstances; the orchestra played it very well indeed and had evidently been practising for the anticipated occasion so the absence of the Duke was unfortunate.

I forgot to tell you yesterday that several of the Regimental Bands played God save the Queen at the Review and very well. I was introduced last night to St Arnaud the French Commander in Chief who remarked that he hoped I should find the War as interesting as that at the Cape. The rise of some of these men is amusing. Marshal Magnan who commanded yesterday at the Review was a Sergeant Major in a French Regiment at Almeida and also fought against us at Vittoria. I heard him attributing the latter defeat to the illness of the French Marshal Jourdan, anything but British pluck, however vanity is all powerful more particularly amongst the French. The Duke went early this morning to see the guides but only with an Aide de Camp and at half past one there was a conference of the Emperor, Lord Raglan, Marshals St Arnaud and Vaillant and Lord de Ros, in which I presume the future plans of the campaign were settled, and to-night there is a grand dinner here.

I passed the whole morning until now in the "Louvre" rather a long time you will think but one might pass several weeks there if one chose. The galleries are filled with sculpture, paintings, Egyptian Sarcophagi, Prints, Pompeian relics, instruments, armour and curiosities of every and various descriptions, – in looking at the furniture for the houses of the kings Louis IV & V I remarked that the Emperor has adopted the very same colour and designs. I don't give you an account of the paintings as this letter would be as long as a catalogue, but tell Richard that a fac-simile of the man in the drawing room with the infant figure is in the Louvre, without the child and by Guilio Romano probably by some friend of his or perhaps himself. I send you a Galignani[100] giving an account of our proceedings amongst all of which I regret I don't speak more or better French, however I manage to get on and occasionally one meets with people who speak English. Paris is very hot much more so than London. I believe there is no messenger to-night so must finish this as the common post leaves at half past four. I hope Courty's cold is quite well and also that Cynthy is well. Give my love to all.

yours ever affectionately
Edward

75

To his wife

Embassy. Paris.
Friday April 14.

My dearest Annot

I received your letter to-day and am sorry to hear that you have all been so ill but I am glad to hear that you think of going to Brighton to-morrow as I am certain that the change of air will make you all well and I trust put you in better spirits than when you wrote and you must try and look on the brightest side of things always recollecting that you are not the only one situated as you are.

After I wrote yesterday I met Lady Charles and Annie[101] walking in the Rue Rivoli and it seems that they had seen me at the review the day before and Annie told me that she had written to Hyacinthe about me. I was glad to meet Lady C to explain my uncivil conduct and shall call upon them as they gave me their address. We had a large dinner party here last night – all English with the exception of two officers of the Emperor's. The Duke and Duchess of Wellington[102] were here as well as the Duke[103] and Duchess of Hamilton, Lord and Lady Ely Seftons, Lord Wellesley[104] &c. After dinner the Duke of Cambridge proposed the health of the Emperor in a short speech. The band of the Guides played at dinner, the rooms of the Embassy are very nice and all went off very well. I made the acquaintance of the Duke and Duchess of Wellington tell Mama and also Lord Wellesley. We had service this morning in the Embassy Chapel where all the English in Paris attend, but you would not think from the appearance of Paris that this was Passion Week, and to-day is the great day for Longchamps where all the new fashions make their appearance.

We are to go on Monday which I am glad of as I am anxious to reach our destination, so you need not write any more until I tell you. Give my love to Mama and Hyacinthe with whom I hope this will find you. The Cowleys have two very pretty little girls and two boys, one of whom is at Eton and Lady Cowley who is a delightful person sister of Lord de Ros asked me to be kind to the other son[105] who is in the Guards and at present with Omer Pacha Commander-in-Chief of the Turkish Army.

yours ever affectionately
Edward Wellesley

I have written to Mary, telling her of a most complimentary speech made by Lord Malmesbury[106] last night about Richard Lord M not knowing I was his brother.

Kiss the children

76

To Mrs Richard (Mary) Wellesley

Embassy. Paris.
Friday April 14.

My dear Mary

I know you will be glad to hear of the following rather amusing incident which occurred last night – inasmuch as it was so complimentary to Richard & shows the estimation he is held in by successive Ministers, Lord Malmesbury who dined here was after dinner talking in the drawing room about the Foreign Office & told an amusing anecdote about Hammond[107] who insisted in having the word outrage inserted in some official despatch in place of assault which Lord M wanted as Hammond said that Lord Palmerston always used this word upon similar occasions of a British subject being maltreated abroad – Lord M. continued the conversation by some remarks about the other Chiefs old Bidwell[108] Cunningham &c which I did not take any note of but he then said "some of the younger ones are very clever. Wellesley is very good" – Lord de Ros called out do you hear that Wellesley & then said his brother is just behind you, – Lord M. then stopped but as the whole was spontaneous & he was not at all aware of who I was I think Richard may consider himself very well flattered. We had a large party of English including the Duke & Duchess of Hamilton, the Duke & Duchess of Wellington, Lord & Lady Ely, Lord & Lady Sefton the former of whom took too much wine, Lord Wellesley, Lady Granville &c, the band of the Guides attended & played some music from "L'Etoile du Nord" which is very pretty if Richard ever comes across any of it, the opera is by Meyerbeer but only recently brought out here & one hears nothing else. We are to leave here on Monday & I fancy get as far as Chalons the first night & the second at Marseilles. Fancy meeting Lady Charles & Annie the latter with the usual dog in the Rue Rivoli; they are stopping in some remote hotel in an equally remote quarter & had seen me at the review the day before. I went yesterday to the Louvre where some of the most interesting relics in the Salle des Souverains are those belonging formerly to Napoleon & it is also amusing enough that in order I suppose to keep the succession & excuse the present man from assuming the title of III instead of Napoleon II, a quantity of little things of the Duc de Reichstadt who died very young at Vienna are preserved amongst the most conspicuous of which are a little white cloth jacket with combinations of the same colour & quality. Hubert de Burgh acts here in the capacity of English Aide de Camp to the Emperor for which he receives a salary & as I believe he has run out [of] all his own fortune must find the allowance useful, – the Emperor has very good horses thanks no doubt to de Burgh's choosing & indeed all his equipages are in very good taste the colour being green which the former Emperor used. I send a Galignani & if Annot has left you can forward it on to Brighton where I am sure the change of air will be of the greatest benefit to her & the children

with love to Richard
yours affectionately
Edward Wellesley

77

To his wife

Embassy. Paris.
Sunday April 16. 1 p.m.

My dearest Annot

There is no post or messenger from Paris on Saturday so I could not write yesterday. We had a small party at the Embassy the night before and yesterday the Emperor called on the Duke here and we all afterwards drove in the Emperor's carriages from the Tuilleries to Vincennes at a short distance from which was a new Pontoon bridge for passing troops over rivers which the Emperor wished the Duke to see. All Paris turned out to see us pass but there was not much enthusiasm for the Emperor, but on our arrival on the banks of the Seine where the bridge was placed and where a large crowd was assembled he was much cheered. I will not weary you with the details of the business suffice it to say that a squadron of Cavalry, a Battery of Artillery and a Battalion of Infantry were successfully passed over in a short space of time and with no accidents. His Majesty afterwards decorated with the Legion of Honour one of the Engineer Officers and we then drove to the Chateau of Vincennes, on the right of the gate through which we entered is the castle ditch where the poor Duke D'Enghien was shot by the orders of the former Emperor and Immediately on alighting His Majesty proceeded followed by us also to the Chapel and to the tomb of the poor Duke adjoining, he went in to the crypt and when he came out his eyes were filled with tears whether from real emotion or a theatrical effect I cannot say, but perhaps he might have felt this great blot on his uncle's fame and wished the English to see his feelings on the subject.

We afterwards went all over the Armoury in the Chateau and inspected the Stables &c. Loud cries of Vive L'Empereur proceeded from the Soldiers quartered there. On returning to Paris we drove along the Boulevards crowded with people all of whom pointed out to each other the English. The dust was terrific but with that exception the drive was very delightful. We all dined with the Prince Jerome at the Palais Royal on our return, he has beautiful apartments and is a good giver of dinners, I hear. After dinner I was introduced to Brouyn de Lhuys the Foreign Minister who speaks English a little and has asked us all to dinner on Monday for it is now decided that we are not to go until Tuesday morning as there is a Grand Fete at the Elysee Bourbon on Monday night at which the Duke is expected to be present. After dinner we went to the Palais Royal Theatre to the Emperor's Box but seeing the Duchess of Wellington in a box opposite I went and sat with her, the Duke was there and brought in poor old Lord Charles who is nearly blind and is come here for Medical advice, two comic actors Ravel and Levasson were amusing and after the play was over I had an ice in the open air which is one of the features of Paris and went to bed. We had prayers in the Embassy Chapel this morning and are to go to Versailles at 2 if the weather is fine but it has been raining this morning and as we shall not be back until late I write before I go. The Grands Eaux are to play there and every time this is done the cost is £500 rather an expensive set of fountains. I heard from Mary just now and am delighted that you have left for Brighton and recommend the sea baths which I am sure will do you good and also the children.

My love to all and believe me
Ever affectionately
Edward Wellesley

78

To his wife

Embassy. Paris.
Sunday Night. [April 16]

My dearest Annot

I write you a line to-night because after we returned from Versailles I was directed to precede Lord Raglan as far as Lyons and leave to-morrow morning instead of Tuesday and you may not therefore hear from me for some days as I shall be on the road to Marseilles. We had a most pleasant excursion to Versailles and went over the palace there and the grounds the whole of which are very beautiful and with which we have nothing that I know of to compare in England. The people of whom there were vast crowds in the grounds of Versailles were very civil and a band of Cavalry which happened to be playing there played God save the Queen as the Duke passed in one of the Emperor's carriages, the fountains are magnificent and the country most beautiful. We dined to-night at the Tuilleries, the Emperor and Empress and about 50 people the same thing as usual and a great number of English. I leave to-morrow at 10 and shall remain at Lyons until Lord Raglan arrives and we shall all reach Marseilles on Thursday evening and I fancy embark on board the Caradoc the same night for Malta or on Friday. I have not had a moment to see Lady Charles unfortunately and she will think me more uncivil than ever. I hope the children are well and you.

yours affectionately
Edward Wellesley

79

To his wife

Lyons, April 18. 1854.

My dearest Annot

I arrived here 2 hours ago having left Paris at 10 on Monday morning and slept at Chalons sur Saone last night after a long railway journey of 10 hours. This morning I embarked in a steamer on the Saone and came down the river in 7 hours. Some parts of the banks of the Saone are very pretty and the hills are cultivated to the very top. We stopped to land some passengers at Macon, and passed on the river several steamers and other boats laden with coal, coke etc. I travelled in company with a certain Admiral Boxer[109] who is going on to Constantinople with us to command and have charge of all Naval Stores &c there. I have just called on Marshal Castelnau who commands here and is a very fine looking old soldier covered with orders. I remain here to-night having made enquiries how Lord Raglan who arrives to-morrow is to get on, the ordinary way is down the Rhone as far as Avignon in Steamers but the river is scarcely navigable, so that we shall have to post unless a fortunate and heavy thaw melts the snow in the mountains and brings down the river.

From Avignon there is a railway to Marseilles the whole line not being yet open. I am stopping at l'Hotel Univers recommended as the best and kept by an Englishman. I am happy to say old Boxer is going to Marseilles to-night as he is an old bore and forgets his H's. Lyons is a fine town at least what I have seen of it not much as the post leaves early. I hope this will find you all well. Pray try sea bathing. My love to all and tell Mama I should have written to her but know you will read them my letter. Adieu. We shall leave this to-morrow night or Thursday morning and I will write on arrival at Marseilles. Mind and take care of your health. They were all sorry to say good-bye to me at Paris including the children and my cousins.

Yours always affectionately

Edward Wellesley

80

To his brother Richard

April 19. 1854.

Hotel L'Univers

(very good) – Murray!

My dear Richard

I left Paris at 10 on Monday morning having when we returned from Versailles been ordered on before Lord Raglan to this place to see how he was to get on to Marseilles as the ordinary navigation down the Rhone is not yet open & if the river does not increase we shall have to post as far as Avignon where the rail takes you to Marseilles. From Paris to Chalons sur Saone where we slept last night is 8½ hours by rail through a pretty country more particularly near Dijon where we poured as much soup & asparagus well oiled into ourselves as the rail would allow us, I say us as it was my misfortune to travel with a certain Admiral Boxer who is going to Constantinople to command there & have charge of naval stores (in the Caradoc with us) & who was on this occasion confided to my charge, his Secretary, Flag Lieutenant & himself not speaking or understanding one word of French & having an Irishman named Sullivan to assist them, the Admiral's impression of Dijon was that every Frenchman who at dinner handed him the bottle of Bordeaux with much civility wanted him to drink wine with him & he kept continually replying "with much pleasure" & was much astonished when the foreigner went calmly on eating his dinner after performing this act of civility. Chalons I did not see much of as we arrived at 9 & left at 5 a.m. & had to get up in the dark, <u>Boots</u> of course calling you long after you were up & stating a direct falsehood by saying it was 4 when it was on the verge of 5 at which hour a small & narrow steamer was crammed as full as it could contain & started down the Saone. Before it started I witnessed with much satisfaction the advantage of travelling with little luggage which I recommend to attention of all families who <u>will</u> take their fifteen pieces with them aboard & expect to get on quick, – before leaving at the Paris station I remarked a young French Officer in uniform calmly walk in to the Train with his hands in his pockets & no other perceptible luggage, I viewed the delightful traveller again at Chalons on alighting, again with his hands in his pockets et point de baggage, on the quay at Chalons as the boat was about to start behold him again still with his hands in his pockets, he steps to the side of the quay & has his boots cleaned by a professional who is in waiting there for that purpose & that is all, to him his imperials, his carpet bags, his washing, his everything for days this simple act of boot cleaning. By the by a party at the Emperor's the last night I was there asked me where Lord Raglan lost his arm & I was obliged to confess it was at Waterloo. The Admiral's secretary would order breakfast on board the Steamer so of course there was enough for twenty moderate shore goers. We have had trout, cutlets, sardines & all sorts of useless food. On board there are the usual priests, nuns, officers of the French Army who always travel in uniform & go on board boats in spurs, Germans & a few English, – we reached Lyons at 12. I then called on Castelnau Marshal of France who commands here a fine old soldier & with more of the appearance of a gentleman than those we saw in Paris. Lord Raglan arrives to-morrow & we leave to-morrow or Thursday morning, thank god old Boxer is gone & I am just going to dine at the table d'hote & this has to go immediately after, to-morrow we are all to dine with Castelnau. Adieu. Love to Mary.

yours affectionately
Edward Wellesley

I congratulate you on your step & tell Mary that allthough you have too much to do, I expect to hear most constantly from her & promise to answer all her letters. E.

81

To his wife

Avignon Thursday
4 p.m. [April 20. 1854]

My dearest Annot
We have just arrived here from Lyons having parted from there I slept last night at Valence half way, we came at a hand gallop with fine horses the whole way, but arrived too late for the train we wanted to catch & have to wait here 2 hours & shall dine here, & so Lord Raglan intends to go on board the Caradoc as soon as he arrives & sail to night I shall not have time to write at Marseilles therefore send you this to say good bye from France I shall write when we arrive at Malta where we should be in about 4 days. I trust this will find you & the children all well & that Brighton agrees with you in which case pray remain there as long as you like. My love to Mama & Hyacinthe in haste
Yours always affectionately
Edward Wellesley
The Duke of Cambridge is not with us having gone by Vienna from Paris

82

To his brother Richard

Marseilles
April 21. 1854. 3 P.M.

My dear Richard
When we arrived here last night it was blowing so hard that the Admiral said we had better not embark, the wind is high to-day but moderating & we shall go on board this morning & sail for Malta. I have seen the Caradoc & there is plenty of room. If we do not go to-night we are to dine with Marshal St Arnaud who is also waiting here for embarkation. There is a report here that the Russians are at Shumla, if so we shall not be too soon. This is a fine town & plenty of shipping in the harbour. Napier formerly at

the Cape & now on the Staff in Canada takes this & you can send on & let Annot know we have not yet sailed as I have no time to write more the Diligence being on the point of going I wrote to you from Avignon.

yours affectionately
Edward Wellesley

83

To his wife

Malta
April 25. 1854. 10 a.m.

My dearest Annot
We have just arrived from Marseilles having made a very good passage in the Caradoc & are going on this evening at 6 to Constantinople & I am writing this in the Governor's Palace formerly belonging to the Knights of Malta & we dine here in the afternoon before going on board. I flattered myself that I should not be ill in the Caradoc but she went so fast & rolled about so much that I was so but not so bad as all the others who were all very ill the first day. We passed the Straits of Bonifacio between Corsica & Sardinia both of which islands looked barren enough, we this morning landed at 8 having passed close to Sicily yesterday which looked more inviting – all the troops have left here except the regular Garrison & we are to be I hear at Scutari & not at Gallipoli the former far preferable to the latter which is an unpleasant place.

Malta is most strongly fortified & the ramparts as we steamed in were crowded with soldiers who cheered lustily responded to by our sailors who manned the yards for this purpose there is not too much room on board the Caradoc & the washing consequently very indifferent the Captain however is very civil & the feeding sufficiently good.

This palace is very fine with large rooms of lofty galleries & the walls so thick that the Sun cannot penetrate a great point here when it is so hot in the Summer. A French steamer is coming in from Alexandria which will take this to Marseilles this evening I fancy we shall touch at Gallipoli for a few hours & then go on to Constantinople. The "Euxine" has not yet arrived but could hardly have been . . .

[rest of letter missing]

84

To his brother Richard

Malta
April 25. 1854. 11 a.m.

My dear Richard

We did not leave Marseilles until Saturday at 2 & reached here this morning at 8 having passed through the Straits of Bonifacio between Sardinia & Corsica & sighted Sicily yesterday. We had a good passage but the Caradoc as is the case with all quick steamers rolled so much that we were all ill including myself, Lord de Ros being the only one who escaped. We go on to-night at 6 either in the Caradoc or the "Queen" as the former is slightly damaged as is invariably the case with Government Steamers. All the Troops I am happy to say have left this & are cantoned about Gallipoli & also at Scutari on the Asiatic side of the Bosphorus a preferable position to the former which report says is unpleasant.

We are in the Governor's palace here until we leave, formerly belonging to the Knights of Malta who had to ride their horses it is said up & down the stone staircases a sufficiently easy feat as they are not steep. A messenger is to leave the F.O. every five days for the Army & I suppose you will be able to send my letters by him & a bag will be made up at the Horse Guards and my letters if sent to the Quarter Master General's Department these will also go if you cannot send them, they should be addressed to me, Head Quarters Army in Turkey.

Adieu I am now going to indulge in the hot bath of Malta as I regret to confess that we had only one basin amongst about fourteen of us in Caradoc & I don't expect to get another <u>cleaning</u> until . . .

[rest of letter missing]

85

To his wife

On board Steamer "Queen"
Constantinople April 30.

My dearest Annot

We left Malta on Tuesday night having there changed our ship the Caradoc requiring repairs and embarked in this a fine screw Steamer and arrived here yesterday morning after a capital run the Steamer going all the time upwards of 11 knots.

We stopped at Gallipoli for a few hours, a division of the Army and also 20,000 French being encamped there and dined with Sir G. Brown who commands there and Lord Raglan visited the French General and the Admiral there being four line of battle ships of the French at Gallipoli. Gallipoli is a miserable little town, our troops being encamped in two bodies there and seven miles from it, and a line of entrenchments is being made from shore to shore to protect the narrow slip of land of which Gallipoli forms a part. The approach to the Dardanelles as far as Gallipoli and in fact all the scenery from Cape Matapan at the point of the Morea, is more or less striking and beautiful. The Asiatic side however is more fertile than the European and more wooded.

We left Gallipoli at 10 at night and anchored here at 8 in the morning and found the Regiments of Guards on the point of disembarking from their Steamers; the troops are all at a village called Scutari on the Asiatic side and opposite to Constantinople – some of them are in barracks and some in tents, at present. I and some others still remain in this vessel which is taken up by the Government as the "Euxine" with my things has not yet arrived. The Barracks are sufficiently dirty having been occupied by Turkish troops and contain more inhabitants than the soldiers as is the case with most Turkish houses I hear. At present all is in confusion as Lord Raglan has not yet put the Army into Divisions and Brigades and no one knows what he has to do. In a few days there will be I hope more regularity.

We have all heard of the extreme beauty of Constantinople but I confess the first view of it disappointed me, it was however a dull day and this which is very sunshiny and bright makes the scenery come out in finer relief. The peculiarity of this place is that the sea actually washes the houses and is deep quite up to the shore. The houses are all built of wood, the mosques being exceptions which with their tall minarets look very graceful and light. We are anchored near the Seraglio point and the gardens of the Harem with the cypresses mixed with the piles of irregular buildings look very pretty in the sunshine to-day. Pera is a suburb of Constantinople where the European Ambassadors and people live. It is on a hill rising suddenly from the water. Lord Raglan called on Lord Stratford on his arrival and is now staying at the Embassy. The bay is covered with innumerable caiques which are very light boats sharp at both ends and rowed by one or more men. From Scutari on the Asiatic side to Constantinople on the European about 1½ miles across they charge you one shilling. We find no news here on our arrival except that Odessa has been attacked by the Fleet and some damage done to the Mole and also that Persia has declared War against Russia and that the Russians have withdrawn from the neighbourhood of Kalafat.

I met in Malta much to my surprise as I did not know she was there Mrs Maydwell in a fair position to increase that name and looking as if she would have been much better at home which is much the best place for all officers and soldiers' wives during this business. I also met Maydwell yesterday looking not very well and thin. Eyre I saw at Gallipoli looking in very good health – he and all his staff smoking long Turkish pipes. They all enquired after you. I believe some of the troops will be sent about four miles from here and I think I shall pitch my tent as I think clean canvas is preferable to a dirty room with its attendant tenants. I made the acquaintance with my cousin Wellesley of the Guards at Gallipoli Lord Cowley's son. He has been with Omer Pacha at Shumla and seems a nice fellow. The Duke of Cambridge has not yet arrived but is to have a palace when he does. Lord Raglan has at present no house and it is complained that Lord Stratford is not of much assistance, but this may be the fault of people who expect too much and the Turks are proverbially slow. It has been very cold here and the snow lies very thick on the tops of the mountains.

Some of the officers have been very unlucky in losing their horses on board ship, the Adjutant General[110] having lost two out of three but I hope mine will arrive all right. One of the Staff Steamers broke down and had to be towed by another, however I think our activity is greater than that of the French as we have already here 17,000 Men of our contingent of 25,000 and they have only 20,000 of theirs of 50,000 and in the Naval service there is no comparison. There seems plenty of communication from here to England and this leaves to-morrow. I hope to hear from you which I have not done since we left Paris, but you no doubt waited until you heard how you were to send your letters. I am anxious to hear that Brighton agrees with you as also with Courty and Cynthy. Give my love to Mama and Hyacinthe and read what parts of this you think may interest them. I have written a few lines to Richard. Adieu my dearest Annot

Most affectionately
Yours Edward Wellesley

86

To his brother Richard

Constantinople
April 30. 1854

My dear Richard
We left the Caradoc at Malta to repair & came here on the "Queen" a very fine and fast clean steamer taken up by the Government, & which took us up the Dardanelles & anchored us in the harbour in 3 days & nights from Malta. We touched at Gallipoli where a Division of our Troops is stationed under Sir G. Brown with Eyre commanding a Brigade, & also 20000 French Troops & who are in cooperation with ourselves occupied in forming a line of intrenchments from shore to shore across the narrow isthmus, – and arrived here yesterday morning & found our Guards just landing from their vessels at Scutari where the remainder of our Men who are in number about 12,000 partly in Turkish Barracks, whereof the dirt is great & wherein the animals

are abundant, & partly in tents in a beautiful position overlooking the sea & harbour. Scutari is on the Asiatic side of the Bosphorus opposite to Stamboul distant about 1¼ across which a swift Caique will put you rowed by a stalwart Turk for the small sum of six piastres, a piastre being about twopence. The Army is not yet put into Divisions or Brigades consequently no one knows what he has got to do & there is much confusion in consequence but I suppose a few days will settle all & then I believe part of the Troops will be encamped higher up the Bosphorus. We find no news here except that Odessa has been attacked by some French and English vessels of our Fleet in the Black Sea & some damage done to the Mole but the fire of the batteries does not appear to have been silenced & the affair looks a little like buccaneering, one of our men was killed & several wounded. Lord de Ros & I & some others are still living on board here as it is not decided what we are to do, she is a very comfortable ship & I think unless they get some houses for the Staff which is talked of temporarily I shall pitch my tent as the barracks are perfectly filthy. The Euxine has not yet arrived with my horses. There are no French here as yet but I hear they are to be put in front of Constantinople when they arrive. It is said that the Russians have surrounded Kalafat & its neighbourhood. This is very beautiful although I was disappointed at the first appearance & must see more to be able to describe the harbour, we have the Seraglio point close to us with the gardens of the Harem, on our right Pera rising at once from the sea & on the opposite shore Scutari with its immense cemetery covered with Cypresses, the great peculiarity here is that the sea washes the houses, the depth being very great close to the shores, and winds about the palaces which you do not see anywhere else. One of the most beautiful views on our passage from Cape Matapan the near point of the Morea, was that of Cape Colonna on which & overlooking the sea still remains some columns of the Temple of Minerva[111] & from whence Hymettus is also seen the peaks covered with snow, - we also saw the heights of the mountains on Samothrace which are the highest of the islands of the Archipelago, except Candia, & from which the Gods, if my classics do not deceive me were supposed to overlook the encounters at Troy to do which they must have looked right over Imbros an island lying between Samothrace and the plains of Troy. I am now going to the Embassy to post this letter the French mail for Marseilles leaving this afternoon. Send the enclosed to Annot & give my best love to Mary. The women here cover their faces the eyes only being visible & it is amusing to see Mahometan niggers doing the same as if anyone wanted . . .

[rest of letter missing]

87

To his wife

Scutari
May 4. 1854.

My dearest Annot

You will be glad to hear that since I last wrote all my Horses and things arrived quite safe in the Euxine & were landed yesterday & that a note from No 1 Greson announcing that they had sailed and offering to be of any further assistance. I am now encamped with Lord de Ros & Capt Walsh his Aide de Camp in a very pretty spot near the Barracks but overlooking & close to the sea over which we have a beautiful view, we have established a mess & are going on very well as they are both very nice fellows & my Lord most amiable in every point in fact too much so I think for any one in an official position. I am attached to the Head Quarters,

As yet I have only got one servant & wish I had either of my old ones here but hope to be able to procure a good man from one of the Regiments. Lord Raglan has a house near here, but I think a Tent far preferable as the animals in all houses are most abundant & find us the most luxurious prey on all new arrivals.

A number of our Artillery Transports are hourly arriving & are stationed about 4 miles from here, the bustle & confusion attendant on all these arrivals are immense more particularly as all the staff nearly are new & there is too much discussion & too little actual work. You can imagine I have had enough to do & undo. We have had hot weather lately & the sun has brought to light the beauties of this place & it is certainly very lovely the sky & water however are the principal attractions & one ought to live on the Sea, as all illusion vanishes as soon as your foot is in a street or you enter a house whose dirt of all sorts reigns triumphant. All the men here are in excellent health & their appearance far outshines our friends at the review at Paris. We scarcely receive any news here. I do not know positively any thing about the Russians but a position in front of Constantinople is being inspected in order that if they make a sudden movement upon Constantinople the Turks may have something to fight behind. I understand there are plenty of means of communication to England but as yet have not found out the day but there is a regular post on the 5th & I believe every five days in the month. The only thing smashing amongst my luggage was a looking glass which I had packed very carefully however I must content myself by looking through a small one. I long to hear how you are going and that the children are well & no doubt Brighton has agreed with them. Adieu.

yours most affectionately
Edward Wellesley

Let me have your address at Brighton

There is a certain thin blue morning coat quite new in the Cloth box which I should like to get out if there is an opportunity. It must be consigned to Mr Hanson Barker at Constantinople a very civil man who would send it to me at the Office & the P & Oriental Company at Regent Circus would send all information about sending it.

88

To his mother

Scutari
May 4. 1854.

My dear Mama

I am now encamped here with Lord de Ros & his Aide de Camp in a very pretty spot overlooking the sea & have been attached to Head Quarters, some of the Troops including the Guards are encamped and the others are in barracks, the former being preferable as there are any number of unpleasant occupants to be found in all the houses in this part of the world. My Horses and things arrived here yesterday & we have very good stabling for the horses. Lord Raglan has a house ¼ mile from here close to the sea. There is at present much confusion in the Army as all the Staff & people are new but this is natural from the time that has elapsed since the Troops have been actively employed. Lord de Ros seems a most amiable person & we get on very well together. All the men are in great spirits but one cannot tell what they will have to do as there is not much news in this place. The scenery is very beautiful, & the sights quite delightful, & the sounds of music from the different Bands very pleasant, there is one practising every morning close to our tents & one is woken by a serenade. I trust you are all well at Brighton & you must excuse a short note this time as I have not much time to myself at present our establishment not being as yet complete.

My love to Hyacinthe

yours affectionately
Edward Wellesley

89

To his wife

Scutari
May 8. 1854.

My dearest Annot

Several Regiments have arrived here since I last wrote and I have also received a letter from you which went to Paris after I had left. I had no idea that you and the children had been so ill but was glad to see that you were getting better.

We have had plenty to do lately. I am happy to find that all the Staff Officers appointed are very active and willing although they have not had experience. Capt. Hackett[112] arrived yesterday. He had been to Spanish Place and found no one there. My groom seems a very willing man and does not mind the sort of life this is but several of the other private servants have already left their masters not liking the tents and the insects, indeed the latter are so bad that some of the people are using a powder which is sprinkled over the bed and kills the animals. The dogs in this part of the world are also a bore to people who have delicate nerves. They are innumerable and really positively rather dangerous at night. They are the scavengers of the place and not destroyed in consequence except since our arrival when they are daily and nightly shot in great numbers by the subalterns of the force.

We have no news from the seat of war but I think it probable that the Russians will not advance but content themselves with occupying the Principalities and throw upon us the onus of attacking them if we choose to do so.

My first opinion of the attack on Odessa by the Navy is confirmed and in trying to destroy the mole and forts the shot and shells set fire to the suburb of the town which was occupied and the poor people burst out and of course exasperated against us, a mode of warfare very much to be avoided as no damage is inflicted on the Emperor by burning the houses of the poor already sufficiently miserable. I have not once been over to Constantinople since I wrote and expect that I shall have to come here some day on leave after all this is over for the purpose of seeing it, but its beauties as far as natural scenery are concerned cannot be concealed and it certainly is most lovely. You can fancy how pretty a sea like the Bosphorus not more than twice the width of the Thames at Hampton and the banks lined with picturesque Mosques and quaint looking wooden houses, banks of green covered with fine cypresses and the whole lighted up by a hot sun and brilliant sky. The caiques also are most delightful little boats and the Turks who row are the only fellows except the Englishmen who have any idea of sculling. Lord de Ros his A.D.C. and I live together but at present our cuisine is indifferent as a French courier and cook of his Lordship's has given warning <u>of course</u> not understanding a tent and no blankets and a little bit of kid to eat and brown bread. We have great amusement here at the constant arrival of people of the most opposite description all clamouring for quarters. Chaplains do not comprehend being put into a fleay barrack room in company with four or five gentlemen of the same description and old Generals of which thank Heaven there are not many – think of rheumatism and sciatica and object to living in tents. This is a very wet day and we cannot disembark some of the troops in consequence.

I hope you find no difficulty in your check drawing and don't spare Mc'Grigor as I shant spend much money here.

My love to the children Mama and Hyacinthe.

yours most affectionately

Edward Wellesley

The Chain Pier is a great reviver and pray walk often on it and have a black thing done of yourself.

90

To Mrs Richard (Mary) Wellesley

Scutari

May 8. 1854.

My dear Mary

Since I have been here I have only been once on the Constantinople side of the water as our utmost energies have been taxed to put some order into a machine which like all English Armies when first employed is one of much confusion & ignorance, all our duties however are carried on in the most charming manner under Lord de Ros who independently of his great amiability is one of the most amusing people possible, & individuals who come into the Quarter Master General's Office expecting to find several grave official dignitaries solemnly writing arrive just as the last joke has been made & find the whole office in violent shouts of laughter & Soldier Clerks extremely red in the face from endeavours to conceal their appreciation of his Lordship's wit, everything is turned into a joke even the insects which infest the barracks & which are no joke at all to the people who live in them. We are obliged to cram the fresh arrivals very close & the Military Chaplains prefer a room even with the encumbrances I have put 2 of them in one room together with a

Turkish Interpreter & a Private Soldier & Clerk. We have condensed all our Doctors into a very small space & shall soon grow so large that the present ground will not hold us. Lord Raglan complains bitterly of the coffee drinking & smoking which he has to go through yesterday it was a case of five cups of coffee & five pipes with the Seraskia [?] & other Chiefs which to a man who hates smoking was intolerable enough. The Turks are inclined to give us all we ask for, but the question of billeting troops is a delicate one as a Turk can admit no Christian into his house & the ladies must not be seen, but they are very dilatory & are generally asleep at a critical moment & when something is required immediately. There was a tremendous conflagration at Constantinople the other night, but it did not seem to create any sensation the Turks taking everything very coolly. I don't expect we can move from here yet as our Cavalry only consists of Lord Lucan[113] & his Aides de Camp & the Artillery of General Cator[114] & some detonating tubes. The French openly say that they never intend to leave Gallipoli again, they are building a Chapel have occupied several houses, hoist their flag over the fort & are building all their portion of the works which are being made across the narrow tongue of land on which it stands of a stone of the most durable description & they have a line of battle ships & of other ships of war off the town, I should not wonder if at the end of the business we had to turn our friends out of their quarters as they certainly will not go of their own accord & do not conceal this; the organization of their Army is most complete (far more so than ours) which is the result of having the same in peace as in war, & the day they landed at Gallipoli their men were as if they had been on shore for months & quite ready for any ulterior operations. I think Lord Hardinge made a very good selection of Staff Officers with very few exceptions, & they are all most active which makes up for their general want of knowing what they have to do, there are a great many who were at the Cape particularly in the Commissariat. This is a lovely place & I wish I had time to see more of it, my horses landed in capital condition & Lord de Ros & I generally take a ride in the evening, a short distance from here is an Armenian village they are Christians & don't hide themselves as the Turks' the latter [their codes?] houses & everything else belonging to them are in a state of decadence. . . .

[rest of the letter missing]

91

To his wife

Scutari

May 14. 1854

My dearest Annot

Lord de Ros has gone to Varna and I am at present acting as Quarter Master General to this Army. He has gone to visit Omer Pacha at Shumla the Head Quarters of the Turkish Army and will be absent for 8 days.

We have had numerous arrivals since I last wrote and manage to land our troops quicker and carry on the business more regularly than at first. I see in the "Times"[115] many abusive articles about our Army at Gallipoli and other places most of them untrue, but in one point they are right which is that the French have more organisation than ourselves, and this of course must be the case when they keep their Army in peace the same as in War, whereas we always have to begin again whenever we take the field.

There is no news from the seat of war, the Turks are entirely apathetic and unless a cossack entered and cut their pipes in two and upset their coffee cups would remain in the same state. They are perfect fatalists and do not trouble themselves about coming events until they eventually arrive and are perhaps after all most sensible as very few of the most ably designed plans happen as their designers intended either in Military or Diplomatic affairs. The Duke of Cambridge has arrived from Vienna where he was very well received and liked and the Troops here receive him with loud cheers wherever he goes, he has a palace on the other side of the water, but generally comes here daily. He has a very fine Division consisting of 3 Regiments of the Guards and 3 Highland Regiments. I have had occasion once or twice to visit the Turkish General here one Osman Pacha to ask for several things Lord

Raglan wanted. They promise to give us anything we want but are very slow in performing and the invariable pipes and coffee take too much time and are besides disagreeable in the middle of the day. However one becomes accustomed to everything in time.

I have got a very good servant from the 77th Regiment and now only want two baggage animals to make me complete but as I have not been over to the other side since I last wrote have not been able yet to get them. We have already got some 800 men in hospital here which I hope will not increase but I fancy the country wines do not agree with the English and the promised beer and porter for the Army have not arrived. As for the climate it is fine enough very hot but not at present so much so as at the Cape, and the nights cool. I go to Lord Raglan every day at 10 with any papers there may be and then am in my office till 4 or five and then ride till dinner. My compatriot is at present Captain Hackett who is attached to Head Quarters and lives here until Lord de Ros returns. He is in his way a most invaluable man and knows all the books of regulation by heart, and is also a capital housekeeper and being an Irishman gives me Irish Stew for dinner very often. Our cuisine by the bye is not so good as when I was with old Cloete who thought of little else, but one is recommended to eat and drink moderately here and may have less means of getting food than we have at present. I think the Turks must be rather astonished at our men, their boisterous manners being so opposed to their own and they shrink from the rude grasps of the hand they receive and the loud way in which they talk as an Englishman whenever he cannot speak another language always talks his own as loud as he can and imagines he must then be understood.

I had one letter from you which went to Paris but none since. I see it takes about 12 days from England and the mail leaves here every five days.

We have no French here except St Arnaud the Commander-in-Chief. They could however advance from Gallipoli as quickly on Adrianople as he could from hence. We have news up to the 29th from England. I have pitched a marquee since my last and find it more comfortable for reading and writing than a bell tent. The houses here are however very bad. I have to go and see some to-day that the Turks wish to let us have for billets for the officers and I never saw such filthy holes in my life. I have written a note to Hyacinthe to whom and little Cynthy my best love as well as Courty and Mama

and yours always affectionately,
Edward

92

To his wife

Scutari
May 18. 1854.

My dearest Annot

I was very glad to receive two letters from you by the Post Mail from Brighton but am sorry to hear that you were going to leave it as I should have thought it would do you a great deal of good; I hope you take care of your health & drink plenty of port & porter to regain your strength. Lord de Ros returned from Varna yesterday & you will be glad to hear that Lord Raglan told him that he had been very much pleased with the way I had carried on the duties of the Department during his absence.

The whole of the Turkish Army are concentrated at Shumla with a few detachments of Cavalry in their front & Omer Pacha the Commander in Chief is very anxious that the French & ourselves should make some demonstration which he says will materially assist him. I have no doubt that the advice will be acted upon & that we shall leave this for Varna or some other place on the coast in a very short time & in fact we ought to do so as our lying idle here can be of no avail, now that the Infantry have reposed from their sea voyage our Artillery are fit for the field & the Cavalry commencing to arrive; To-day the Head Quarters of the 17th Lancers arrived & more may now be expected every day. Lord Raglan has gone this day to Varna to see Omer Pacha & will return on Sunday when I suppose we shall have some news. The Turkish Army is described as being well manned as the point of soldiers but with many bad officers.

We have been out for the last two mornings inspecting the different Divisions of the Army & nothing can exceed their fine appearance & order & their behaviour is also very good.

There is some sickness but I think this will decrease when the men become more accustomed to the Climate which is very changeable & hot Sun being suddenly followed by a cold wind & the dews at night sometimes very great. I seldom go to the other side of the Bosphorus but am occupied in this office till late, & then ride for a short time, one of my horses has turned out a capital charger being as quiet as if she had always been with Troops, this with the one I bought from the man in the Blues gives me 2 good chargers & the third horse is also a very good one though not quite as quiet as the other two with Troops. I met here George Mundy[116] with his Regiment, the 33rd, & was sorry to see in the paper of the death of the widow of Frederick Mundy as the Children must be left now without any one to look after them.

I think I forgot to tell you in my last letter that Lord de Ros insisted on my living entirely with him and was quite offended when I proposed to pay my own expenses, we have now 4 of us in his mess, Captain Hackett a most useful man having arrived from England & joined our Staff, I find all my juniors in the Department much older than myself which shows what a lottery the Army is.

My cousin William Lord Cowley's son is here & not well they do not seem a strong family & Lord de Ros himself is not a very healthy person. I heard from Seymour at the Cape & he tells me that Sir George would return about May or June & that the people were sorry enough to lose him. I wish we had him here. I hope Susan goes on well as I think she was a capital servant. I wish I had a man Susan here as new soldier servants are not so clean [clever?] as they might be, however they learn by example.

I am on the look out for a Mule or baggage animal driver so to-day an Hungarian made his appearance but as he spoke nothing but German & his own tongue I am afraid we should not get on very well. There is a most civil man Secretary to the Embassy here a certain Count Pinane who has volunteered hearing I was a relation of Lord Cowleys to send any letters I may have to the

Foreign Office & I shall send this by him this time & let me know if you received my others which were sent through the Adjutant General's Office in tolerably good time, A great number of the soldiers wives who came out here with the Army are going home again, poor things they had no place to go to not even a tent & were & are living in most miserable sorts of sheds near their regiments in the field,

I hope Courty & Cynthy are all well & that you are also improving I was not satisfied with your last account & you must remember that you should think of nothing but getting quite well, as if Austria & Prussia unite with us I don't think we shall remain here very long & I shall expect to find you perfectly well when I return. Adieu my love to Mamma & Hyacinthe. I should like to hear how poor Gerald is going on.

yours most affectionately
Edward Wellesley

93

To his brother Richard

Scutari
May 18. 1854.

My dear Richard

Lord de Ros returned from Varna yesterday having visited Omer Pasha at Shumla & inspected the Turkish Army which to the number of about 40,000 are intrenched in & about Shumla. Omer Pasha himself he says is a most clever & able man & fully understands his position, he is most anxious to have the English with him or the French as he says that a demonstration however small on our part would be most desirable for the Turks, Lord Raglan & St Arnaud go this day to Varna to see Omer Pasha & the result of his representations to them will no doubt be the march of some of the French on Adrianople. We have daily been receiving supplies of Infantry but only a Troop of the 17th Lancers have yet arrived of our Cavalry & not all of the Artillery but they are arriving every day & we send Steamers to the mouth of the

Dardanelles to tow them up Lord Raglan has inspected the Divisions here on the last few mornings & the appearance of all the Troops has been everything that could be desired, the Duke of Cambridge has a very fine Division consisting of the 3 Battalions of Guards & a Highland Brigade & the appearance of this Division on the last morning was uncommonly fine & the Guards marched past as well as if they had been in Hyde Park. I believe Lord Stratford generally not so is in perfect accord with Lord Raglan an indispensable state of things for any success of our movements. We have no French here except the Commander in Chief but they have about 40,000 men at Gallipoli & are not so particular as we are respecting appropriation of various things for themselves. There are plenty of supplies here of all kinds, but servants are very difficult to obtain I mean in the way of fellows to lead one's baggage animals without which we shall be very helpless. I am afraid our men are becoming rather sickly as we have upwards of 400 men in Hospital, the building is in very good order & the only really clean place I have seen here, and the sick Turks who share the Hospital with us seem very comfortable.

We have no news lately from the Fleet in the Black Sea but they are I believe somewhere off Sebastopol. We have plenty to do at present but the Officers are beginning to know more of their business than at first, our arrangements however for the Transport of the Soldiers tents &c are backward, horses are very difficult to obtain & there are few if any mules. I fancy the great demand for them will eventually bring more into the market particularly as very high prices are paid for them. The Turks promise us all that we ask for & I have lately been several times to a certain Osman Pacha who commands the Troops on this side of the water & he is more rapid in his movements than most Turks & you can usually dispense with the perpetual pipes & coffee which accompany all conferences. Nothing can have been worse than the arrangements at home for the Camp Equipage for the men at present we have in Barracks 3 Regiments which could not be moved as we have no Tents, – the French are better organized in this respect than we are as they always have a train of carriages for each Regiment in peace as in war & consequently can at once move from any point where they may disembark, & bringing their own horses with them have not the difficulties we have on first arriving. I heard from Annot that you had been to Robert's Marriage & that she did not expect to stop much longer at Brighton. If it was possible I should like to have had her here but as we shall most certainly move in a short time & perhaps immediately after the return of Lord Raglan it proved to be impossible & unsafe. The greatest atrocities are committed in Omer Pacha's Army by the Bashy Bazouks a species of Highland Chieftain's clans of the old time with double the ferocity, Omer Pacha has not the power of death & consequently whenever any very great crime is committed is obliged to resort to the horrible alternative of ordering a punishment equivalent to it & can order 500 strokes of a stick on the stomach which inevitably kills the unhappy sufferer in a short time. One of the blessings of civilization is that the Russians can learn all the movements of the Turks, the French & ourselves from the "Times" correspondent & also the exact numbers of all the Troops opposed to them, their position & every minute detail respecting them. I wish they were all at the bottom of the sea with only a sleepy Turk to fish them out again. Love to Mary.

affectionately yours
Edward Wellesley

94

To his wife

Scutari
May 23. 1854.

My dearest Annot

I received your letter of the 5th and was very glad to hear that you were improving in health. I hope that Hampton Court will agree with you and the children and I should much prefer your remaining at Bushy to going anywhere else until we see how things go on here, as I do not like you to be alone anywhere. I was very sorry to hear of Hyacinthe's accident and trust that she is not hurt by it. I wish by the way that we had a few cabs in the streets here as walking in them is regular treadmilling. Lord Raglan returned from Varna to-day having been at Shumla with Omer Pacha, the Russians have invested Silistria and are evidently by that advancing. We have sent some engineers to Varna to repair the jetty there and there is no doubt we shall some of us move there immediately as some commissariat officers are going there this evening and supplies are the first things we shall want. The Russians have totally destroyed the "Tiger" which vessel ran on shore in a fog near Odessa and the Captain Giffard[117] after being wounded was taken prisoner with all his men. They are well treated and have been allowed to receive their things by a flag of truce. Our Cavalry have been daily arriving since I last wrote and the 8th Hussars and 17th Lancers are nearly complete. We have moved out some of the Artillery and encamped them and their horses to make room for the former, and all the horses are in very good condition. We have a regular fleet of transports off Scutari and could now move our Army by sea at any moment but animals for baggage and tents are coming in very slowly. A Corps of Interpreters is being organised most of whom can speak English or French as well as Turkish.

In reading my letters you will find all the places upon the map. The French have shot two Russian spies at Gallipoli. They were Greeks and their papers were found upon them; Omer Pacha also caught one at Shumla and had him shot. He was a Bulgarian. I very much doubt if the feeling in that province or in Moldavia and Wallachia is so much in favour of the Turks as is represented, in fact except as a political question the mere idea of any one having any feeling for such a miserable people is absurd.

The Sultan is a wretched specimen totally enfeebled by drinking and other vices and the higher classes despicable in every way. They are going out like a candle - they have been driven out of Europe and have lost all their former great powers of endurance and Bravery, like the Greeks and Romans of old their age has passed away and we are trying to prop up a people incapable of doing it themselves. Pray give my love to Mama and Hyacinthe. I have written to no one else except you this mail.

Yours most affectionately

Edward Wellesley

May 24.

Since I commenced my letter the Light Division, some of the 8th Hussars and a Troop of Horse Artillery embark on the 26th for Varna, and the French march by land on Adrianople. The Russians have only as yet invested Silistria on one side. There are 15,000 Turks in the place and in the last campaign it held out for some months. I imagine the whole of our Army will follow to Varna during the next week but Lord Raglan like his illustrious former Chief keeps his plans very secret.

From Varna we shall move on towards Shumla Omer Pacha's Head Quarters and I trust all our Troops will be sent from Gallipoli where it was absurd ever to land them. Varna is 13 hours steam from here and the railway [sailing?] transports will be towed by the steamers by which means we can send a great number of men at a time. E.W.

95

To his brother Richard

Scutari
May 24. 1854.

My dear Richard

The Russians advancing up the right bank of the Danube have invested Silistria on that side, the investment was not completed as a man who brought the intelligence to Omer Pacha left Silistria, but by this the siege no doubt has regularly begun. Lord Raglan returned from Varna yesterday and the Light Division with all the 8th Hussars who have arrived & a Troop of Horse Artillery are ordered to embark on the 26th for Varna. The French are to march on Adrianople and I trust that the portion of Troops of ours at Gallipoli will also be withdrawn as there is no doubt that if we have anything to do we shall want every Englishman we can muster. If Silistria which has a garrison of 15,000 men holds out until the arrival of the French & ourselves at Shumla, where I suppose we shall all concentrate, of course an advance must be made to relieve the garrison. There is a rumour this morning that

Silistria has fallen which it is to be hoped is not true as if so our position at Varna would be a false one & Packiewitch who will naturally be anxious to strike an important blow for his master as speedily as he can will have advanced on Shumla only 60 miles from Silistria & perhaps have beaten Omer Pacha with his 40,000 Turks before our arrival, it is to be hoped therefore that the report about Silistria is not true as it is a most important place & upon its holding out until we all arrive depends I think the fate of the Turkish Army which I do not imagine will ever stand against the Russians commanded by Packiewitch. The capture of all the men of the "Tiger" near Odessa & blowing up of the ship is a most unhappy business & will of course create a great sensation at home. The "Trent" has just arrived with Lord Cardigan[118] & others. We had a Review this morning in honour of the Queen's Birthday, the men looked very fine & cheered enthusiastically led by Lord Raglan, they then marched past splendidly & far surpassing anything we saw in the Champs de Mars, a French Officer who is attached to the Staff of Lord Raglan said that the sight was tres important when our men all took off their Caps as they do on this & only occasion & cheered for the Queen the Colours are simultaneously dropped at the same moment to the ground & the sight was certainly magnificent. The whole of the Staff are very well mounted and the appearance of the whole Army is very great indeed. Give my love to Mary.

yours affectionately
Edward Wellesley

96

To his wife

Scutari
May 28th 1854.

My dearest Annot

I was glad to see by your last letter that you were comfortably settled at Bushy and I hope the children have entirely recovered their health. I have received all your letters and the post seems very regular here. The order for the Light Division was changed after I last wrote and none of the Troops have as yet left this place. I fancy that we only wait for St Arnaud the French Marshal to return from Gallipoli in order that we may know when the French can move in conjunction with us. The Russians we hear have made two attacks on Silistria which have been repulsed and the Turks it is also said have made a sortie and defeated a body of Russians. In the meantime our steamers and transports of which we have now a complete fleet are all moored off the shore ready to take the Troops on board and we have been constructing numerous boats for taking horses from the wharves to the shipping, and could embark the Army by Divisions in a very short time. The 79th Highlanders arrived yesterday and are a very fine body of men and have reduced the size of their bonnets and made a very good head dress for this climate, the feathers being a great protection against the sun; there is only one more Infantry Regiment to arrive and then we shall be complete in foot and the Cavalry are arriving every day. I made a fresh acquaintance with Morgan of the 17th Lancers who arrived the other day. Lord Cardigan has also arrived and his Staff. Lord Raglan has allowed the Staff to have 2 soldiers for servants and I have two very good men and have sent away my groom who complains very much of his health and looked as if he was certainly very ill. The great complaint here is about servants, the natives cannot be got and are very bad when obtained, but are absolutely essential to lead your baggage animals. On the night of the Queen's Birthday the Guards had a grand illumination and danced reels gigs &c in their Camps. There were rows of lamps about the tents and they seized hold of any Turk who might be there and made him dance and the whole scene was most extraordinary and amusing. All the men are in the highest spirits and cheer on the slightest provocation. The other day when the 55th Regiment arrived all the Rifle Brigade ran down to the shore and cheered with all their might, It is commencing to be very hot here particularly in the morning, but as soon as the sun goes down it is immediately cool and hardly any twilight. I have been once over to

Constantinople and went through the Bazaars to buy some saddlery. The makers and sellers of each article as jewellery, saddlery, pipes, and so on have a different quarter for their goods. The streets and passages are very narrow and the Turk sits composedly in his shop regarding the passers by; he always commences by asking you double the amount of what he will take for his goods by which means he finds out what the value of them is in the market. Bargaining then begins by aid of an interpreter and you stand by perfectly useless and calm until the game has ceased, when you pay, which is all you have to say to the transaction. The Turks are very good workers in leather, as yet however I have seen no silks, jewellery or the slipper department which is very good not having had the time.

At Pera where the Europeans live the shops are the same as at home and ices are also to be got by no means to be despised after a hot walk in the impracticable streets of the Capital of Islamism. I see by the papers that one of the measures in contemplation for the Army is the abolition of the rank of Major so as to assimilate the Line to the Guards, if so I presume it will be extended to the Brevets by which means I should become a Lieutenant Colonel. It will be an inexpensive arrangement for the country as no more pay will be involved and I think a very good measure.

We have been unfortunate in our Naval affairs both in the Black and Baltic seas having lost the "Tiger" and her crew in the first and the "Amphion" in the second. This I think will create some sensation in England. There is service here every Sunday in the open air and also in Lord Raglan's house for the Staff. There is a Military Chaplain in each Division, and the Bishop of Gibraltar has also been here as we are supposed to be in his diocese.

Give my love to Mama and Hyacinthe and Courty and Cynthy. How does poor Gerald go on.

Yours very affectionately

Edward Wellesley

97

To Mrs Richard (Mary) Wellesley

Scutari
June 3. 1854.

My dear Mary

We are still here but under the expectation of leaving for Varna very shortly, the Division sent there has encamped 2 miles from the town on the road to Shumla. The Russians have been repulsed from Silistria which they have never completely invested & all the news from that part of the country is very good. Lord Cardigan & some Light Cavalry have gone to Varna to-day, & also some Batteries of Artillery, the French have sent a Division to Varna & as usual they have appropriated the place to themselves. The Sultan inspected the Army the other day he arrived in a magnificent Caicque from Stamboul & then mounted a beautiful black horse superbly caparisoned, he is pale & sickly & at first gazed vacantly round & scarcely seemed to see what he was about, he rode down the Line of Troops & they afterwards defiled past him, he expressed himself very much pleased with the appearance of the men & of course had never seen anything like it before, we were kept waiting two hours for him but as the Turks slow in everything don't know the proper time this is accounted for, after seeing the Troops the Sultan went back to Stamboul; he was accompanied only by a few attendants & dressed in the ugly semi-European Osmanli costume with the red Fez cap which they all wear here. I dined the same night with Lord Stratford who was very glad to see me & there met a Mr Brodie[119] formerly in Richard's department at the F.O. now Attaché at the Embassy who offered to be of any service to me he could & said R. had been so very kind to him that he should be too happy to repay it to me.

Lord Stratford said that we should all be back in the winter, but whether he knows anything about it I cannot say, but if Austria really joins the other powers Russia can scarcely hold out against all the world. You will have heard in England of the taking by the Steam Fleet under Sir E. Lyons[120] of Redu Rabh [?] on the Mengrelion [?] Coast, it seems to be a place of more importance than was at first supposed, but I do not think that the capture of these small places will have much influence on the war, the taking of Shoreham would not have much effect on us. I am sorry to hear that Captain Giffard who was taken prisoner off Odessa is not likely to survive his wounds, the sailors have now been taken into the interior probably to St Petersburgh to gratify the people. This is the season of Ramazan during which the Turks do not eat until sunset the consequence of which is that one's boatmen are in a famished exhausted state when one pulls over the water; – at night all the mosques & minarets are illuminated & the effect is very beautiful. The Turks & others rich enough are all beginning to leave the Town for the islands in the Sea of Marmora or the banks of the Bosphorus the heat is becoming very great but the mornings & evenings are always delightful & the nights cool. Prince Napoleon's[121] Division are to be stationed on the European side of the water close to Stamboul, he is enormously fat & very much disliked by the men. St Arnaud is here, he has issued an ordre de jour to his Army full of the usual Franco inflated style & equally full of untruths as is, & was also usual in all French ordres de jour & other Military Despatches. I was sorry to hear from Annot that Augustus had been ill but I suppose by this time his marriage has taken place. I met a relation of yours in the Guards here, the Duke of Cambridge has the Guards and three Regiments of Highlanders in his Division, the bonnets of the Highlanders I think are the best head dress there is in the Army for this climate as the feathers keep off the sun & flies from the face, – the Sultan presented His Royal Highness with a white charger & magnificent horse appointments on the day of the review. I see by the "Times" of the 15th that the inactivity of the Russians is commented upon and it is strange that they have not made more vigorous efforts than they have before the French and ourselves could arrive, & perhaps when we all get in front of them they may retire altogether, their Cossacks however are far in advance of the Regular Army & some are even reported to have been seen from our Camp near Varna.

yours affectionately
Edward Wellesley

98

To his mother

Scutari

June 8. 1854.

My dear Mama

Since the last Mail left we have heard favourable news from Silistria, the Russians having been again repulsed & it is said are about to raise the siege but the Governor of the town has been killed. The Turks however have succeeded in throwing in a reinforcement of 1,800 from Shumla & a good successor for the Governor has been appointed. Our Light Division are encamped 2 miles from Varna & a French Division close to Varna, but the good news & some other cause known only to Lord Raglan have caused the rest of us not to be moved yet & we are still here. Lord Raglan has not been well & has gone to the Ambassador's on the other side for a few days, as he never goes out or is seen but is writing all day in a house near the sea where the breeze he inhales is anything but balmy from the seaweed & other unpleasantness this is not to be wondered at.

Our last Infantry Regiment the 42nd arrived last night & all the rest of the Highlanders ran down to the shore to cheer them which was returned from the ship, the men who are in the highest spirits cheer on every occasion & at intervals their hurrahs are heard all over the Camp. We have a small Mess party of four in Lord de Ros where we fare very well, we breakfast at 8 as every one gets up very early here the sun being very hot at that hour, we get no end of strawberries & also Ices of all things in the world so you will see that the camp is better supplied than I have been accustomed to and the men have been given Porter much to the delight of some Life Guardsmen we have here as Servants, as well as to all the Guards accustomed to London the latter get on even better than the Line in Camp & are always getting up some games, races &c to amuse themselves.

I was sorry to hear that Augustus had been ill & trust that he is recovered. I was in my bed in my tent the other morning when George Chetwode[122] walked in, he had just arrived with the 8th Hussars in which he had obtained his Troop, I should not have known him not having seen him for years. I have frequently seen George Mundy his Regt has now gone on to Varna his Regiment the 33rd are now called the "Duke of Wellington's Own" he having been the Colonel of them for some time. Lord Stratford whose acquaintance I made the other day said he was very glad to know me, he & Lord Raglan seem to agree very well but I doubt that he is of much assistance to the Army – our principal difficulty is in providing sufficient transport for the Army & when you hear that the Artillery alone require about 2000 Carts & 1200 Mules for the ammunition only besides which are the provisions, forage, tents &c &c you will not be surprised at the difficulty, we however have not asked the Turks to assist us in getting them but try & purchase ourselves & the operation is very slow, – we have people out in all directions at Tunis, Beyrout, besides Officers from several of the Regiments here. The French have not so much difficulty on this head as we have as they are not allowed so many horses for their Officers & are not so used to comfort as our men. We came the other day upon a Sentry who was holding an altercation with a Turk & on enquiry the reason the man said the Turk "would not give him a civil answer" rather amusing considering they neither of them could understand a word that the other said; like all Englishmen in similar cases the Soldiers think that if they only holloa loud enough in their native tongue all other nations must understand it, & consider them extremely stupid when they cannot make themselves understood. We are now continually surrounded by a crowd of Interpreters of all degrees. They are quite indispensable as our knowledge of Turkish is very limited. I hope Annot & the Children are quite well. I should prefer their remaining at Bushy as I dislike her being alone if you don't find the Children too noisy. My love to Hyacinthe

yours affectionately
Edward Wellesley

99

To his wife

Scutari
June 9. 1854.

My dear Annot

I have written by this post to Mama in which I have said that I should prefer your remaining at Bushy as I don't wish you to be alone. No more Troops have gone to Varna since I last wrote and we have heard that the Russians have been again defeated at Silistria and that they have actually raised the siege, our Light Division are encamped near Varna and 2 Regiments of Light Cavalry at a place called Devna it is reported that the cossacks have been seen near Devna the Turks have thrown a reinforcement into Silistria and are holding out very well. I have just heard that Austria has actually joined the Western Powers and the whole news is therefore very good. It is rumoured that the Duke of Cambridge's Division will go to a place called the Giants Mountain and encamp and Lord Raglan who has not been well will perhaps go and encamp himself in which case we shall all go. It is about 9 miles from here on the shores of the Bosphorus and a very pretty country I understand. We have had numerous arrivals and all the Infantry are now here, the Cavalry are coming in and also the Artillery and other implements of war. The great difficulty lies in the animals for carrying the men's Tents and spare ammunition &c which are only to be got very slowly and some of them very bad. I have bought one myself, but have scarcely time ever to go over to Constantinople as Lord de Ros relies upon one and cannot get on unless one is always near him. We have plenty to do but all the Officers attached to our Department are very active. I generally get up at 6 and ride in the morning before breakfast, the sun is very hot by 8 but we have a breeze frequently in the middle of the day. After breakfast we are in the Office or disembarking Troops &c until five or later and then I generally ride again. Some of the views about here are very beautiful but the roads and streets of the villages generally infamous. The French Cavalry about 700 in number have marched upon Adrianople (vide Map) and a Division has gone to Varna under Prince Napoleon. The whole of the rest of the French will follow the Cavalry and I trust our Army will all soon go on as we should relieve the men in Silistria as soon as we can or the people at home will have a right to say that we are very slow. Most of our difficulties lie in the commissariat; the Commissary General is a slow old gentleman[123] and not fast enough for this business. The Turks have some difficulty in getting money to carry on the War and before they were joined by the European powers could not obtain any credit, since that however they have been able to get money as the people think that the European Powers will not allow them to be cheated. The respect for European good faith is very great all over the world and particularly for English honesty. We are having these Barracks completely cleaned and a regular crusade against the fleas has commenced and they are certainly decreasing. There are not many in the Tents, but in all other places they abound, and yet the Turks are very clean and bathe perpetually so I suppose these animals are inherent in the country. I hope the children are quite well. Courty should begin to learn his letters.

Yours very affectionately
Edward Wellesley

100

To his wife

Scutari
June 13. 1854.

My dearest Annot
We have to-day embarked the 1st Division of the Army under the Duke of Cambridge in a very short space of time and much to the admiration of several French Officers who came to see how we managed these affairs, and could not understand how we got on without Men of War to assist us, they having 3 at Gallipoli for that purpose. All the men remaining behind turned out and cheered the Gordon Highlanders as they embarked. As Lord Raglan did

173

not go with the first of the Army I think we shall now remain until the last Division from here goes to Varna, and as the Steamers will not return from thence for two or three days I suppose we shall embark about the end of the week. Everything is to be sent on now to Varna. Horse, Foot and Artillery and a Depôt for sick and baggage will remain at Scutari under a Commandant whose place I do not envy. This place looks quite barren now that so many Troops have left and the Ground formerly so green is worn quite bare by the Troops. We hear by the last papers that there will be a Brevet for the Army at the end of May, and also of other extensive changes amongst which the subject of all Majors being made Lieutenant Colonels is revived and I hope will be true. I received by the same mail your letter May 26 and was glad to hear that you were getting stouter, at least that people said you were and hope you feel yourself stronger and better in every way than when I left England, when I look around and see all the English encamped here and myself included in the number what a strange revolution it appears which has brought us here and so suddenly, and what a curious thing it is that the course of events should have brought about an union of the French and English, under the nephew of the man who for fifteen years the latter fought and at last succeeded in overthrowing, and against the successor of a King who was then our firmest ally and also made greater efforts to overturn the uncle. I see that some of our Troops are to go to Athens, this will be a better quarter than some of the Home Irish Quarters Templemore for instance, the contemplation of Antiquities being more in accordance with taste than that of a turf bog, and a classic statue or temple a more elevating object to view than a Shebean house or a Hibernian Cabin. I should think that the news that Austria is pouring Troops into her provinces bordering on Wallachia is true and will have a great influence on the War. No Russians can be seen for some distance in the country between our Camps at Devna between Shumla and Varna and the Danube; an English Officer sent to reconnoitre found not even a Cossack, people who are generally some marches in front of the rest of the Army. I should not be surprised if Packiewich was meditating some desperate rush, and trust he will not carry off Lord Cardigan and the Light Troops posted in advance of our Division there, who are all quite unacquainted with the duty of outposts in the field. Thank Mama for taking so much pains about my coat. I am afraid when it does arrive I shall not be able to take [it] as I intend to leave all superfluities here when we go and take nothing but uniform.

My love to the children who I am delighted to hear are as you tell me looking so much better – the air of Hampton and the green fields to run about in must do them good. I saw the other day the old sail maker of the "Coromandel" who has taken service in one of the transports here, our . . .

[rest of letter missing]

101

To his wife

Scutari
June 18th 1854.

My dearest Annot

We are to leave here on Tuesday next 20th for Varna in the "City of London" Steamer, some of the Staff embark to-morrow in the Emperor's Steamer and Lord Raglan goes himself in the "Caradoc" Government Steamer on Tuesday also. All the troops have been sent from here with the exception of one Regiment which will embark to-morrow and the Division at Gallipoli will also go on to Varna, I believe immediately. Lord Raglan who had been to Varna for one day returned last night, and we hear from Silistria that the Russians have nearly taken an outwork of the town and that they and the Turks were firing at one another across a ditch at about 30 yards distance. Daily arrivals of Cavalry and Artillery have taken place lately, but the Cavalry come in very slowly as there are no Steamers to tow the Transports up from the Dardanelles and they frequently lie there for some days waiting for a fair wind. One of them the "Aria" with the 11th Hussars on board ran on shore there but fortunately got off without any damage. All the Naval arrangements are perfectly disgraceful and inefficient and all the statements in the "Times" and the Duke of Newcastle's statement that Admiral Boxer was a most efficient Officer and that all the transport was provided for the Army to be embarked at any time that might be necessary are not the case, as every time that any embarkations have taken place we have had to employ country boats for the troops without which we could have done nothing.

The French had a grand review yesterday before the Sultan. They have about 10,000 Men on the other side of the water and I believe about 16,000 at Varna. They have had numerous rows here with the Turks as the latter objected to the Zouaves who are dressed as Arabs and some of whom have green turbans on a distinctive sign among the Turks here of descent from the prophet and consequently not to be worn by Christians. I am sorry to say that a Turkish Sergeant was killed in a disturbance at the Cavalry Barracks near here the other day and was supposed to have been run through by a man of the 11th Hussars, the Turks have behaved very well about it and have excused the men, saying that where soldiers are there is certain to be quarrelling. I have not been over to Constantinople since I last wrote as we have had so many embarkations here lately and have been fully occupied until nearly dinner time. I was very much disgusted at Richard being obliged to do so much work, they ought to appoint some one else to his Department, in the Army if a Staff Officer goes someone else does his duty for him, and the same arrangement should be made in the Civil Service. I see that we are to have a Post Master for this Army which will be of great benefit. I shall write from Varna the passage to which is only 14 hours and your letters will be sent on regularly.

Give my love to the children who I am happy to hear are getting on so well, and also Mama and Hyacinthe.

Yours most affectionately
Edward Wellesley

102

To his brother Richard

Scutari. June 18, 1854.

My dear Richard

I was sorry to hear by the last letter that you had been suffering from your eyes the cause being no doubt the overwork that you have in the Office, I really think that if Mellish[124] is always on the sick list he should be made to resign as it is impossible for any one to continue to perform the duty of <u>two</u> for ever, and to sacrifice their health as well. In the Army a Staff Officer absent receives no Staff Pay and some one else does his duty a rule to be extended to the Civil Service with advantage.

All the Troops have left here with the exception of one regiment which embarks to-morrow and Lord de Ros and our lot go on Tuesday the 20th in the City of London, Lord Raglan leaves also on Tuesday in the Caradoc and we shall arrive at Varna, a Steam of some 16 hours, at the same time the Troops from Gallipoli are to go to Varna, and a depot only left here consisting of the sick, stores &c with a Commandant & some Doctors. The French are concentrating at Varna in great force also so that we shall soon have a tolerable Army there and in the vicinity. The Turks are holding out very well in Silistria and the Russians have not as yet made much impression, a Colonel Alexander[125] who has just been in here made the following sketch of the place which I send, he is a pudding headed old gentleman & has made the Danube flow the wrong way, by which Silistria appears on the opposite side to that on which it stands, this Department are generally slow & I recalled a certain Officer of them being told to muffle his oars on entering a river for a night attack muffled all the <u>blades</u> of them with Corn Sacks. . .

[rest of letter missing]

103

To his wife

Varna
June 24. 1854.

My dearest Annot
I just write a line to say that we arrived here in the "City of
London" on the 22nd, and are encamped near the bay about 1½
miles from the Town. Lord Raglan is in the Town and his Staff.
There are about 20,000 French here and nearly the same number
of English. The French Commander in Chief arrived to-day.
There is no particular news except that Silistria has again been
attacked and held out. Varna is a small town with a bay and the
weather is not so hot as at Constantinople. I imagine we shall move
forward in about 10 days, but the Commissariat are as usual very
slow in procuring transport for the Army. Adieu the post is going
and I have no table to write on. Our office is in an empty house
and all our tables were left behind of course.

Yours affectionately
Edward Wellesley
Love to the children and to Mama and Hyacinthe

[This is the last letter to her that has survived]

104

To his brother Richard

Varna. July 15. 1854.

My dear Richard
The last Mail brings the news by the "Times" that Russia has
concentrated to evacuate the Principalities a fact which will give a
total change to the features of the War, and of course to our own
position. Russia under the plea of great respect for the Court of
Austria has been able to withdraw from a contest in which she had
been worsted & has substituted political reasons for those which
were no doubt Military namely the reverses before Silistria & the

demonstration of the Western Armies in Bulgaria. I think Austria has in these events assumed a fine & high position; - regardless of any figure for former injuries by England, and also of personal gratitude & friendship for Russia, she has acted as most conducive to the peace of the world. I conclude an armistice must follow the evacuation of the Principalities & that diplomacy will take the place of Arms, for we shall scarcely now follow the Russians to the Pruth to attack them on the other side, neither shall we I imagine attack the Crimea or any other part of Russia until further demands have been made on the part of France & England for the security of Turkey, which demands if not complied with may lead to an attack on Russia, but in that case without the aid of Austria or Prussia who will consider I suppose their portion of the engagement fulfilled when the Russians cross the Pruth, & at liberty to even engage with Russia against us if we attack her. We had Omer Pacha here a few days ago, after raising the siege of Silistria, and the French Army about 27,000 has remained by him. St Arnaud who has not forgotten his dramatic days is followed upon these occasions by a Trooper carrying a silken Tricolor, an effect very good on the stage but not common with Commanders in Chief of the present day, he rode down the line of Troops accompanied by Lord Raglan, on a white horse given him by Omer Pacha, & by the latter on his left hand, Omer Pacha is about 48 but looks older as the novels say, he has simple but dignified manners & a favorable contrast between him & the Marshal might be seen; an immense Staff followed these Chiefs including every costume under the sun Spahis from Africa act as a sort of Body Guard to the Marshal, they have the red cloaks & burnous of the Arab a certain Beatson[126] appeared in the dress of the Irregular Cavalry of India, Dundas[127] & Lyons on two small ponies suitable for the fat & untenable seats of the Navy, French & English, Turks of all degrees came after. The Troops defiled past which occupied two or three hours shouting as usual Vive L'Empereur et les Anglais but the cheers were rather faint as the dust was very great by far the finest body of men are the Zouaves & their Regiments have very good Bands. After the review we adjourned to the French Officers tent who made us drink a horrible liquid called absinthe a sort of inferior anisette. The French Cavalry are daily arriving from Adrianople from whence they have been marched under the command of General Bosquet[128] a very good Officer, he & General Canrobert[129] are considered very good Officers as also Truchet[130] who is a species of Commissary & Quarter Master General combined & day nurse to St Arnaud it is said. We hear of divisions in their Army & that the Marshal is not liked. Lord Cardigan & some squadrons of Light Cavalry have patrolled the banks of the Danube but with this exception our army has not moved beyond Devna 18 miles from here & I suppose now will not do so at all, his Lordship [Cardigan] knocked up half his horses & had to shoot several, the weight is very great that a Dragoon Horse has to carry & I do not think that they will be able to do any work in this country unless it is reduced. The Duke of Cambridge is encamped with his Division at Aladyn 9 miles from here on the road to Devna the Officers & Men have been rather sickly & in fact the general lull & want of excitement for the Soldiers will most have this effect throughout the Army. The 2nd Division under Sir de Lacy Evans[131] have a beautiful wooded Camp 13 miles from here & nearer Devna than the Guards, & the 3rd Division are encamped outside Varna as well as some of the Cavalry, the remainder being at Devna. A lamentable accident happened to the 6th Dragoons an account of which you will have seen in the papers Colonel Moore[132] behaved very well & nobly the crew infamously having seized a boat which would have held 30 for 3 men & refused to put back; one great merit of caution frequently the case in Transports is that of not seeing daily that the boats are ready for launching at a moment's notice, it is no use having boats in ships if they are not ready for instant use. Perhaps it is fortunate that the Army has not been obliged to move as the Commissary General is totally inefficient & we should certainly starve, any one but Lord Raglan would have sent him home long ago, the greatest irregularity prevails in the issue of Food & Forage seen here which would be fatal if we had to move, I don't speak personally upon this point as we get Omelettes for breakfast every morning, but if we marched those luxuries would vanish & we should have to depend upon the Commissariat for our Beef &

Bread as at the Cape. Talking of the Cape I was very glad for the sake of our men in that War to see that Medals are to be given for it, no Soldiers more deservedly earned this reward than those employed there & the Duke of Newcastle is entitled to their gratitude for this early acknowledgement of merits not recognized by his predecessors, & he has commenced his career as War Minister in a manner that will cause his name to be remembered by the Army. My love to Mary.

yours affectionately
Edward Wellesley

105

To his brother Richard

Varna. July 30. 1854.

My dear Richard

Since I last wrote to you I have paid a visit to Silistria & Schumla, the former renowned as having stood the late siege & the latter as the Head Quarters of Omer Pacha & where had Silistria fallen the Russians would have met their next enemy & probably have fared as badly as at Silistria, Schumla being fortified & possessing also a number of outworks forming an intrenched Camp where a large Army could have been assembled & have defended well as the Turks are very effective behind Walls. We rode the first day 28 miles with our English horses & halted at a village called Pravadi where we were put into a Bulgarian peasant's house for the night & all I can say of this place is that if Trajan when he established his Colonies here found as many inhabitants to contend against in every house as I did in this one it speaks greatly to his credit having conquered the country. Not consequently much refreshed by the night's repose we started the next morning & after a long ride reached Schumla in the evening & were kindly installed by the Governor in a very good house where we left our Horses & servants & taking post horses or rather ponies left the following morning at daylight taking with us merely a Zaptier or guide an Interpreter & a hair brush. We thought that we could ride fast to Silistria as we had little time but found that the Turkish hour which one reads of in "Murray" & imagines a Tatar at full speed flying across the plains means the shuffle of a Turkish pony or pace of 4 miles an hour when fresh & 2½ when tired. Upon attempting to put our horses to full speed our Zaptier remonstrated, but we threatened him with immediate punishment if he did not come on so leaving his gun behind, for he was by way of being a guard as well as a guide he cantered on evidently in much panic. We reached the village half way between Schumla & Silistria & were there to get fresh horses but none were to be had so after waiting we proceeded with our tired horses much to the disgust of the Zaptier who at first positively refused to move but changed his mind when he saw that we were determined. After three more hours we arrived at a small hamlet called Karalar & bivouacked for the night under a hedge a much more acceptable place than most rooms in Turkey, – the Turks were very civil & hospitable providing us with dinner & had been ordered they said to be very careful of all English Officers who passed. At daylight we rode on to Silistria which we reached at 10 having had a first view of the Danube some time previously here a muddy turbid stream some 1200 yards across. The Town of Silistria was not so much injured as I had imagined but the northern side is tolerably knocked about & the roof of the Mosque as also the minaret riddled with shot. The townspeople behaved with much courage during the siege although they were obliged to live in the Cellars & 150 of the women & children were killed. No attack took place against the town itself, but the Russian approaches were made against a detached fort to the North East against which all the efforts were made as the possessing it would have given them the command of the Town and the other outworks defending Silistria would have been rendered useless. This fort is a complete ruin & has certainly witnessed some hard & very close fighting, the last parallel established by the Russians was close on the parapet & they must have fought hand to hand, the ground is covered with fragments of Shells. Mining was also attempted against this fort but the Russians seem to have failed in this as no damage was done & in one instance a mine exploded back killing the miners. The ground about the fort is much in favour of the besiegers being broken up into ravines & gullies which could be made use of as cover for their troops, & in point of fact they seem to have made too much of the post as I am convinced our men would have run[?] into the ground where they had after incredible labour & fighting established their third parallel on the first day & on the second have taken the place by assault. The Russians however after hammering away for 40 days & losing many of their best Generals, in one night evacuated the place & recrossed the Danube across which they had a bridge below Silistria & it is a curious fact in Turkish indolence that no effort was made to impede their retreat or harass them in the passage of the river which might have been done so easily, both parties were perhaps glad that the affair was over & more particularly no doubt the Russians who we were credibly informed were in a famishing condition & begged for bread where [when?] they were pushed up to the assault & received it from the Turks on the point of the bayonet. The Turks destroyed all the works of the Russians upon their evacuating the place, but the Russians still remain on the opposite bank & we could perceive their videttes as also some Camps in the neighbourhood of Kalarasch a village opposite Silistria. I pitied their position the Wallachian bank being low & swampy & torrents of rain fell the night we were there which must have made their ground a perfect marsh. A large Camp of Turks is pitched near Silistria & the soldiers appear elated with their victory & the Egyptians are fine looking men, the Arnouts however appear to have behaved best in the fort & the English Officers named Butler & Nasmyth[133] materially aided in the defence the former was killed & the Turks at the suggestion of Omer Pacha are going to erect a monument to him in the fort which he so gallantly assisted to defend. We returned to the half way village & reached Schumla in 2 days & then rode from thence in one day 53 miles to Varna, we took another Zaptier from Schumla to shew us the shortest road but after vainly endeavouring to keep pace with the trot of an English horse packed up & the last we saw of him was this excellent guide far astern looking also at us in dismay from the top of a hill.

When I returned to Varna I found a great change during the week I had been absent Lord de Ros very ill & unable to speak to me, the Divisions all moved & the Cholera having broken out, many Officers having also various complaints. You must not mention so that it may come to the ears of his immediate family as a slight report has been made of it, – but Lord de Ros has been very ill & being of a weakly constitution is now only slowly recovering his attack seems to have been fever accompanied with severe headache, to-day we have got him on board a ship in the bay & I trust that he will soon amend & in the meantime I am doing his duty. The Men have been in the habit of eating the fruit now becoming quite ripe & drinking large quantities of it, & we have lost by Cholera about 50 Men, the Light Division at Devna have suffered most, the Light Cavalry least, all the Camps have been moved & there are no cases to-day & I hope a sudden change in the weather we have had yesterday from excessive heat to rain & a cool temperature may drive it away. The people in the town I am told are dying at the rate of 40 a day, and as they have no doctors or medicines their condition is truly pitiable. A ship as an Hospital has been established in the bay & I think we have certainly a clever man as Principal Medical Officer[134] & the attention of all Officers is drawn to the arresting of this disease; it is kept as secret as possible but Lord Raglan's attention is I believe always devoted to little else. This Country at this season is I believe always more or less unhealthy, and the French have suffered more than ourselves having lost as it is reported 3 or 400. . .

[rest of letter missing]

106

To Mrs Richard (Mary) Wellesley

Head Quarters. Varna.
August 25. 1854.

My dear Mary

I send you 2 specimens of Photography more as showing that the science [?] of the Quarter Master General's Department is not neglected in this part of the world than as flattering likeness of the subject for I have had an attack of fever & other unpleasant symptoms since I last wrote to Richard & was <u>taken</u> by our Artist immediately after my recovery. Every one here has been more or less ill & the whole of our Officers laid up one after the other, Lord de Ros & W. Wellesley have been obliged to go to Therapia & I am afraid will not be able to return here. I was laid up for a week but then shook it off & am now quite well again & acting in Lord de R's place for the second time since I came out. The Troops have suffered very much from Fever & Cholera & the French Army most dreadfully, we have lost many Officers & Soldiers and the Fleet has also suffered materially, there has also been much sickness in this town, but I am happy to say that it is now gradually subsiding and our men recovering & scarcely any deaths. There is no doubt this is a most unhealthy place at this season of the year, in fact the Russians lost half their Army when they besieged the town in 1828, & we are fortunate in escaping as we have. In the meantime great preparations are making for embarkation & next week I think we shall be off. Sevastopol is openly talked of & the "Times" newspaper has held out for some time hints for the Russians to place it in a good state of defence. Some of our Artillery are now going on board, & the Cavalry & Infantry follow. This small Bay is now so full that the ships are creeping out to sea, for we have French & English Men of War, French & English Transports, Steamers of all descriptions and country Boats of all shapes. The Wharves are so crowded that it is difficult to move and all is excitement & haste, and I do not think there is a single combatant in this or the French Army who will regret to leave this place. A general gloom has been cast over it by the numerous deaths which have occurred.

I am glad to see that Sir G. Cathcart has left England for this Army & also that he has brought some more Regiments with him, our friends the French with all their bravado will not be able to bring many more Infantry into the field than we can & if we have anything to do we shall require all the Englishmen that can be collected. The temperature here has become sensibly cooler during the last fortnight, I have been living on board a Transport in this Bay until yesterday & found the sea air very reviving. I am now encamped upon a hill overlooking the sea, all the lovely valleys have been abandoned & people all fly to the hills where illness is supposed to be blown away by the sea breeze.

I trust Richard has been relieved from his overwork by this time. I see the F.O. is again expected to fall, but I should think it will outlive the present Ministry.

yours affectionately
Edward Wellesley

107

To his brother Richard

Transport "Ganges"
Balzik Bay
September 7. 1854.
12. noon

My dear Richard

We are at this moment streaming out of Balzik Bay, the Fleet consisting of 10 sail of line, & 12 Steamers and Transports in all 129 English Ships, each Steamer has 2 sailing transports in tow and the whole are very fine ships none under 700 tons. The French Fleet & Transports are lying ahead of us & we shall then all proceed I suppose in Company. We did not leave Varna until the 5th & remained at anchor here yesterday. Balzik is a small village & the place has been selected for a watering place by the Fleet the water being obtainable here more easily than any other Bay upon the Coast. The weather is very fine and as the distance is not more than 240 miles to the Coast of the Crimea we should be off it in 60 hours. I trust when we do get there there is no hesitation or want of decision may prevail but I do not think that Admiral Dundas is very much in favour of these operations and I would not implicitly trust any French men in these days & do not think that St Arnaud is any more to be trusted than his Master if his own interests were concerned in not acting up to what he has stated.

In these operations everything will depend upon Combination as the Forces divided are not strong enough to meet the Russians said to be in the Crimea, the French having as usual much exaggerated the numbers they would send out here, and having also lost 7000 men by disease. However I do not doubt we shall be successful in any thing we attempt, politics have nowadays so much to do in war that perhaps we are not destined to go to the Crimea or to land there after all.

We have left a Depôt of Horses & the Brigade of Heavy Cavalry at Varna which will gradually be sent on after us & in a short time when our connection with that place will for ever end I trust & no one will regret it.

The French have embarked about 25,000 Infantry 68 Guns Artillery 200 Cavalry we have about the same number of Infantry – 54 Guns – 1200 Cavalry. The latter the Light Cavalry Brigade under Lord Cardigan he himself is a good soldier & bears all the incident hardships of this life without grumbling I cannot say the same for many of our Generals & as for the Guards & their Officers they are the worst grumblers in the world not being accustomed to the ordinary hardships of the Soldiers of the Line they are not prepared to submit to those necessarily attendant upon this service, the old Officers of the Guards with their Peninsular experience were very good, the present equally bad & unsoldierlike.

I had a slight return of my fever the other day also accompanied with shiverings What I was rather inclined to think might be ague but I threw it off & am now quite well again, it seems quite absurd to write about being ill as I never have been so until this moment, but every one here is a Doctor & Quinine is continually handed about, My servant disappears every day from 9 to 5. having had his ague & fever fit, he told me the other morning that he was all right until after Breakfast when he is taken with the "Most awfullest shakings" that can be conceived. It is quite laughable all this; but no doubt this voyage will make every one quite well.

Lord Raglan has appointed General Airey to the Quarter Master General during the absence of Lord de R who has now positively gone home, Airey was Military Secretary to Lord Hardinge, he is a gentlemanly man & a man of business & I have no doubt we shall go on very well, I knew little of him personally except that he met me at Lord Raglan's house & told me to come & see Lord Hardinge & introduced me when I got my appointment. Lord Raglan expresses himself to me much pleased and satisfied

[with] me, and thanked me for the manner in which I had carried on the duties as Head of the Q.M. General's Office during Lord de Ros's illness. I saw him daily during this time sometimes three or four times a day, he is very well which I attribute to his constant business detaining him so much in his house that he cannot be exposed to the sun & the pestilential air of the Bulgarian plain & lake.

Tell Mary I received her letter of the 18 August & with regard to my late servant Ballinger I have not seen him lately but believe he is quite well, he got better after he had left me & Charteris Lord Lucan's Aide de Camp took him, if I chance to meet him I will speak to him about his wife.

I was truly glad to hear that Gerald's state was improving I trust he will eventually be restored to calm & that the clouds which oppressed his brain will pass away.

I received a notice from Coutts that the Interest to 22 April had been received & I suppose as I had directed them it has been paid to Mama, if not I should like to know, & also inform me of the exact amount which was divided to be transferred to my name from Gerald's as I was never that I was aware of informed of it, the whole was I know divided between you & me but I should wish to have a note of what the half was in order that I may know if the interest is sent correctly.

September 9. 11 a.m. We have just arrived at the rendezvous ordered 40 miles W. of Cape Tarkan and are now lying to waiting for further orders, the sea as far as one can perceive is covered with sails, and if the Russians imagine we crowd our Ships as I suppose they do their own, they must suppose an immense force is coming against them.

September 10. Still at anchor in the middle of the sea rather a curious position, Lord Raglan is absent in the "Caradoc" reconnoitring the coast, and has not yet returned. It is reported that St Arnaud is very ill, he has heart complaint it is said which may at any moment finish his career, it is also said that Canrobert another French General and a very able man has the commission of Marshal in his pocket if the other dies.

September 11. Lord Raglan returned at 6 this morning having run along the coast from Sevastopol to Eupatoria, a Steamer came out of the harbour but quickly retreated when she saw the "Agamemnon". At 12 the whole fleet weighed again and we are now standing in for the land where I fancy we shall arrive in the night and land to-morrow morning, the exact point is not yet ascertained, but will probably be about 30 miles from Sevastopol. The weather is most propitious & rather cold. I am sorry to say there is still some sickness amongst the men several of them having died since we left Varna.

September 12. Last night we had squally weather & several of the ships had to cast off their towing ropes, this morning consequently the Fleet was much scattered and the French a long distance behind us. We sighted Cape Tarkan in the morning and are now 6 P.M. 10 miles from the shore near Eupatoria, we shall lie to to-night and I suppose land to-morrow morning. It is to be hoped the Russian Fleet will not manage to get out of Sevastopol as they might do a vast amount of damage if they escaped whilst all the Fleet are here. We have very cold Autumn weather. The land we now see is low and with no appearance of wood, a few cottages can be seen.

September 13. We stood in to the land this morning & sent in a Steamer to Eupatoria a small town which you will see marked on the map. The French are much scattered and much behind us. We anchored near the shore in the afternoon.

September 14. 9 a.m. We are just on the point of landing some of the French actually on shore, it is a fine calm morning with no wind which is fortunate for our purpose. The point selected for landing is about 15 miles from Eupatoria towards Sevastopol.

My love to Mary.

yours affectionately
Edward Wellesley

108

Mrs Richard (Mary) Wellesley to Edward Wellesley

Wednesday. Sept 27/54.
Torcross Devonshire

My dearest Eddy – You will like a short resumé of our past & present proceedings Richard's holidays began at last ten days ago.

We spent the first few days with my family at Putney, from whence he attended to divers private affairs which had been obliged to manage themselves for the last twelve months. We then went to Brighton for a night to see your Mother & Hyacinthe. The latter was very flourishing yr Mother not very well. We went from Brighton to Portsmouth & from there by sea to Torquay which is about 20 miles from the small retired fishing village where we are at present established very comfortably & quietly in a small cottage on the top of a Cliff, where Richard has the advantage of beautiful air & scenery, perfect quiet & the latest bathing England can afford. I am happy to say his health has not suffered apparently from his hard work. Mellish has returned most unwillingly to work where I hope he will remain at least for the next three months, when if he chooses to retire in Richard's favour he may be allowed to do so. My future plans are as yet undecided excepting that we propose travelling in France, but whereabouts there we have not yet settled. We staid [sic] a week at Hampton Court not long ago, where we had an opportunity of making acquaintance with Augustus's wife & liked her exceptionally. He has been unwell again & applied last week for yet another sick leave from the Ordnance, which was granted to him, on the condition of finding a substitute to do his work & he & Clare started on Saturday for Paris, where I believe they propose to spend their leave & I suppose yr Mother will now return to Bushy. We are anxiously awaiting the next account from the East, & open the newspapers in fear & trembling for the success of the expedition to Sevastopol. Where are you likely to spend the winter? Is there any given point of the Coast where we might be likely to meet each other. It wd be very pleasant if you cd join us anywhere – between this & Xmas when we return to England. I see Ld de Ros has arrived, & that Col. Airey is your new Chief.

Goodbye & God bless you, dearest Eddy.

We still have very good accounts of poor Gerald so much so that his doctor thinks he may shortly see yr Mother, he seems far more restored than we had ever expected, perfectly sober & happy & without the least inclination to leave Balliford [?], where he is most kindly & carefully taken care of. I will write by the next Mail & tell you my further arrangements. Ever your Most affectionate Mary Wellesley

109

From *The Times* of October 16. 1854.

DEATHS

Immediately after the battle of the Alma, at which he was present, of cholera, aged 31, Major Edward Wellesley, 73rd Regiment, Assistant Quartermaster-General and Acting Deputy Quartermaster-General during the illness of Major-General Lord De Ros, leaving a widow and two children.

110

Captain Woodford to Richard Wellesley

Nov 18 [1854]

My dear Wellesley – I have received both your letters by post & Burghersh[135] & I have tried to carry out your wishes as far as possible – Yesterday poor Edward's things were sold & the proceeds will be paid into the Commissariat Chest here – which will be payable by the Lords of the Treasury on his proper representatives making themselves known to them – By this Mail I send you a Commissariat acknowledgment for 136£, 4 shillings & 5 pence – partly pay, & partly the proceeds of the formal sale of horses & horse furniture which Mr Filder, Commissary General, says will be paid by the Treasury as I have already said - General Airey sent home a cheque for £50 by the last Mail. I am sorry to say that his keys are no where to be found – his watch & a few pocket books, despatch box & folio writing case, & dressing case I shall send home to you by the first opportunity also the Sword & sabretache – I also kept back at the sale, red coat & epaulettes as they would never have fetched here anything like their value – We are unable to find any more private papers than pocket books, & but a small sum of money £4. 13. 6. and I have left the despatch box untouched that it may be opened only in England - you must understand that at the time he went on board ship, poor fellow, we were on the march[136] & it has been impossible to collect the things from different ships until now, owing in the first place to my being unable to give my attention to the matter & things having been shipped & reshipped & transferred again & partly from our being 5 miles from the sea & the little communication we had had with the ships – As to the other part of your letter, relating to his last moments, I am afraid I can tell you but little for his servant – a soldier, 44th could not go on board with him in consequence of his having been left with the baggage – I have written to the Captain of the Danube (In the meantime we have had a hurricane on the 14th & the Danube is a Wreck) who took him on board his small steamer to convey him to the proper ship, & I shall make a point of getting an answer from the Captain & you shall hear what he has to say – Up to the last time I saw Edward I took leave of him after putting him into the Araba[137] to take him down to the beach on the 20th he was sensible perfectly, but almost unable to articulate, altho' poor fellow he thanked me for arranging his pillow & making him as comfortable as the Araba would allow. Pray understand that I require no thanks for anything I have done about his things – I feel deeply & sincerely for your grief, knowing what it is so well myself to lose Brother & Sister – & I had known him for the last three years & we had seen a great deal of each other. I will let you know by what ship the box may be going, & I hope that I have done all that you wished

Believe me
sincerely yrs
Charlie Woodford

All his private papers are probably in his Despatch Box

III

List of effects of the late Major Wellesley 73rd Regiment sold by Auction at Alma, on the 22nd Sept. 1854, & at the Head Quarters before Sebastopol on the 17th November 1854

No.	Articles	Amount £ S. D.
1	Bay Horse	50.
1	Black Do.	50.
1	Bay Mare	51.

No.	Articles	Amount £	S.	D.
2	Bat Horses	4.	5.	
2	English Saddles & 1 Bridle	4.	10.	
1.	Pair of Holsters	5.		
1.	" Boots [Bags?]	10.		
1	Bed [?] & Straps		5.	
1	Regimental Bridle Complete	1.	-.	-.
1	Pair of Saddle Shoe Pockets with Shoes & nails		5.	
1	Pack Saddle complete	2.	16.	
1	Pair of girths [?]		6.	
2	Race Caps		5.	6
1	Horse Brush [?] & 2 Rollers	2.	-.	-.
6	Pairs of Cloth Boots		9.	-.
2	Hoods	2.	8.	
2	prs Hobbles & Chiffrey Bit		5.	6.
	[Illegible]		10.	
	[Illegible]		1.	
4	girths [?] & hood [?]		6	
1	Horseman's Tent	1.	-.	–
3	Blue Coats & Scales	4.	9.	
1	Riding Coat		17.	
1.	Shell Jacket	2.	-.	-.
1	Pr Gold Lace Trousers	1.	3.	-.
2	Pr Cloth Do	3.	14.	-.
2	Forage Caps & Covers	2.	2.	-.
1	Silk Coat & Waistcoat		3.	-.
4	Prs White Trousers		14.	6.
1	Pr Braces		7.	-.
15	Shirts	1.	18.	-.
1	Blue Jacket & Trousers	1.	1.	-.
1	Red Waistcoat	1.	-.	-.
1	Handkerchief		3.	6.
11	Pocket Do.		11.	-.
13	Pairs of Socks		5.	6.
9	Towels		13.	-.

193. 9. 6

No.	Articles	£	S.	D.
		\multicolumn{3}{l}{Amount}		

No.	Articles	£	S.	D.
3	pr Boots	3.	17.	
2	Pillow Cases		2.	6.
1	Sheet		6.	–
3	Stocks		3.	6.
10	Prs Gloves	1.	1.	–.
2	India Rubber Buckets		2.	6.
1	Do. Do. Tub	2.	6.	–.
2	Sponges & Comb	1.	6.	0.
2	Red Hackles [lashes?]		14.	0.
1	Shoe Horn		1.	0.
1	Swimming Belt		4.	0.
1	Washboard Stand	2.	15.	0.
4	prs Spurs	1.	7.	0.
1	Cocked Hat & [erased]		5.	–
5	prs Straps		3.	–
1	pr Saddle Bags	2.	10.	
1	Lantern	\multicolumn{3}{l}{[torn]}		
1	Tin Box		10.	?
1	Candlestick		14.	?
1	Camp Kettle		6.	–
1	Box of Cigars	1.	4.	–
1	Tin [illegible]		3.	–
1	Canteen Complete	2.	14.	–
	Plates & spoons &c		7.	–
	Mustard, Salt & Pepper		10.	7.
1	Waterproof Apron		16.	0
2½	Bottles of Eau de Cologne		17.	6.
1	lb Powder		5.	–
1	Gold Hand Brush		7.	–
1	pr Boot Hooks		2.	–
1	Riding Cane		1.	6.
1	Whip		10.	–
2	Hair Brushes & Case		17.	–

No.	Articles	Amount £	S.	D.
I	Looking Glass		8.	-
I	Pair of Candlesticks		11.	6.
		222.	15.	1.
I	Pistol Belt & Case	2.	7.	-
3	Cases of Pistol Bullets		3.	-
I	set of [?] Hooks		17.	-.
I	--- Bed Irons	2.	6.	-
4	Pieces of Soap		9.	-
I	Felt Hat	[torn]		
I	Table Cover	3.	7.	-
I	Chair & Do.	1.	12.	-
I	Bag		6.	6.
I	Staff Band & Belt	2.	.-	.-
2	Candles		1.	2.
I	Pot of Bear's Grease		9.	-
2½	Dozen Penny Stamps		2.	6.
I	Head Stall		3.	6.
2	Bed Straps		2.	6.
I	Sponge		1.	-
2	[?] for Caps		2.	-
I	Box & 1 pr Boot Trees. 1 pr Shoe Trees		12.	-
6	Brushes		11.	6.
		244.	5.	3.

Robt Blane A.A.G
Major [?] President
Members { Charlie Woodford Captn DAQMG
{ John Hackett Capt DAQMG

Headquarters before Sevastopol. Nov 27. 1854

112

A. Rodney[116] at Calais to Mrs Richard (Jane) Wellesley at Bushey Cottage, Hampton Court Green

Dec 22nd [1854]

My dearest Jane

I wish to inquire how you, & my dear cousin Hyacinthe are, I hope well. I was, & I am truly concerned for your affliction, your sad loss, & bereavement of such an excellent son, brave courageous to the last, he merited to live to be rewarded, but who can hope to escape such Climate, poor Mrs Edward how I do feel for her, so devoted Wife, her happiness is gone.

It is a sad War.

I rejoiced that my Nephew was lucky at the battle of The Alma, his Regt the 33rd suffered more than any other, he wrote to his Mother the day after the Battle, a most interesting account "How Blake & self ever escaped I know not, it was the Almighty that preserved us" "Where our Colours had to stand 4 officers were shot holding them, my Charger was shot under me I have lost everything, but I care not, but thank God that he spared me."

I rejoice he is rewarded George is made "Brevet Lt Colonel for distinguished service in the field how pleased he will be at this. My poor nephew George Rodney[137] is quartered on the Heights of Balaklava 4 times poor fellow his tent has been blown down. The Hardships our troops have are dreadful.

I hope you have good Weather for the Season. The wind here is awful, especially on Thursday night; I have not closed my Eyes this last Week, it was impossible in such gales.

I think of the poor sailors

Pray let me hear from you, Pray accept my best wishes, I wish you comfort, health, & happiness, the same to my dear Hyacinthe, & believe me to be

My dearest Jane,
Your attached Aunt
A.Rodney

Notes

1   Frontispiece. In a letter to his daughters, dated 11 November 1853, Sir George Cathcart wrote: 'My excellent and faithful friend & compagnon d'armes Major Wellesley started this morning going home with his wife and daughter whom he is to pick up at Cape Town where they have been all the time of the war. He is the bearer of a sketch in oils done by Captain Goodrich of the Cape Mounted Rifles. He is really a very clever artist and the likeness of both men and horses is very good indeed. The same party has ridden with me some 2000 miles much in the same manner and the scene is exactly like the Orange river desert about sunset. The tone of the colouring is perfect and my old horse Rifleman trotting twelve miles an hour, and keeping all the others at a gallop is a perfect likeness.' (*Correspondence*, p. 353). The frontispiece is reproduced from an engraving in the possession of the editor. The original picture belongs to The Earl Cathcart.

2   William Wellesley-Pole, who became the 4th Earl of Mornington, married the heiress Catherine Tylney-Long in 1812 and added her surname to his. Three years after her death in 1825, he married his mistress Helena, widow of Captain Bligh of the Coldstream Guards, and led a very dissipated life. In 1831 he abducted one of his own children, having been deprived of their custody by the Court of Chancery, for which he was committed to prison, although a MP. He died in 1857, having been supported financially for many years by the 1st Duke of Wellington.

3   Edward John Littleton (1791–1863). MP for Staffordshire from 1812 until created Baron Hatherton in 1835. When his first wife, Hyacinthe Wellesley, Edward's aunt, died in 1849, he married again in 1852.

4   Lord Fitzroy Somerset (1788–1855), later Lord Raglan, youngest son of the 5th Duke of Beaufort. Commissioned at the age of 15 into the 4th Light Dragoons. Joined Wellington as an ADC in 1807 and remained with him throughout the Peninsular War, becoming his Military Secretary in 1811, being wounded at Waterloo, where he lost his right arm. He remained at Wellington's side when the latter became Master-General of the Ordnance in 1818 and combined that post with that of Commander-in-Chief at the Horse Guards on the death of the Duke of York in 1827. When Wellington became Prime Minister in 1828, he remained Military Secretary with Lord Hill and when Wellington returned to the Horse Guards in 1842. When the Duke died in 1852, he had hoped to succeed

him, but Lord Hardinge was appointed and Lord Fitzroy became MGO, being created Baron Raglan. In 1854 he was appointed to command the Army sent to Turkey, and died in the Crimea in 1855.

5   Sir Henry George Wakelyn Smith (1788–1860). Commissioned into the 95th Regiment at the age of 17 in 1805 and first saw action in the disastrous River Plate expedition in 1807. He then joined the Light Division in the Peninsular War, where he met his Spanish wife, and fought in almost every action. He returned from service in America to take part in the Battle of Waterloo as a brevet lieutenant-colonel. In 1828 he went to the Cape of Good Hope as Deputy Quartermaster General on the staff of Lieutenant-General Sir Galbraith Lowry-Cole, continuing there with his successor Lieutenant-General Sir Benjamin d'Urban. His subsequent career in South Africa is described in Part I. He went to India in 1840 as Adjutant-General and took part in the Gwalior campaign. On the outbreak of the Sikh War in 1845, he was given command of a division, with the honorary rank of major-general and gained fame from his victories at Aliwal on 28 January and Sobraon on 10 February 1846, which brought the war to an end. These exploits were followed by his appointment as Governor and Commander-in-Chief of the Cape Colony in 1847, where he served until his replacement by Lieutenant-General the Hon. Sir George Cathcart in 1852. Thereafter he was appointed commander of, first, the Western and then the Northern Military District in England, an appointment he held until 1860, having been promoted Lieutenant-General in 1854.

6   The Hon. Sir George Cathcart (1794–1854), third son of the 1st Earl Cathcart. Commissioned into the 2nd Life Guards in 1810. Promoted in 1811 to lieutenant in the 6th Dragoon Guards and ADC to his father, Ambassador to Russia, accompanying Tsar Nicholas I in the field against Napoleon 1813–14. ADC to Wellington at Waterloo. Thereafter served in various regiments on successive promotions until becoming Deputy Lieutenant of the Tower of London in 1846. Major-General 1848. Governor and C-in-C of the Cape Colony April 1852–March 1854, when he was appointed Adjutant-General. In July 1854 he assumed command of the 4th Division under Lord Raglan in Bulgaria. Killed at the Battle of Inkerman 5 November 1854.

7   Iris Butler, *The Eldest Brother*, London (Hodder & Stoughton) 1973.

8   Sir Benjamin d'Urban (1777–1849). Commissioned into the 2nd Dragoons 1793. Served in the Netherlands and West Indies 1794–7 and Peninsular War 1808–14. Major-General 1819. Governor of Antigua 1820, Demarara 1824, British Guiana 1831, Cape Colony 1833–7, Lieutenant-General 1837, Commander-in-Chief Canada 1847–9.

9   Burgher was the term used for settlers and for volunteer forces raised from their ranks.

10   Henry Somerset (1784–1862), eldest son of Lord Charles, who was

Governor of the Cape 1814–27 and an elder brother of Lord Fitzroy Somerset. Served with the 10th Hussars in the Peninsular War, ADC to his uncle, Lord Robert Somerset at Waterloo and then to his father at the Cape. In 1823 he assumed command of the Cape Corps, which became the Cape Mounted Rifles. Served continuously there until 1854. Local Major-General 1851. Later Lieutenant-General and Commander-in-Chief Bombay.

11 Charles Grant (1778–1866). MP for Inverness. President of Board of Trade and Treasurer of the Navy 1827–8. President of Board of Control (India) 1830–4. Secretary for War and Colonies 1835–9.

12 Sir George Napier (1784–1855). Commissioned into the 24th Light Dragoons in 1800. Transferred into the 52nd Light Infantry and served with them in the Peninsular War, losing his right arm in the assault on Ciudad Rodrigo 19 January 1812. Lieutenant-Colonel of the 71st at the end of that war, transferring to 3rd (Scots) Guards until 1821, when he went on half-pay. Brevet Lieutenant-Colonel 1825, Major-General 1837, Lieutenant-General 1846, General 1854.

13 Lieutenant-General Sir Peregrine Maitland. 17th Regiment. Major-General 1809. Lieutenant-General 1830.

14 1,000 foot of the 27th and 91st, 350 horse of the 7th Dragoon Guards, a few gunners and sappers and 400 Cape Mounted Rifles.

15 Sir Henry Pottinger (1789–1856). Joined the East India Company's marine service at the age of 12, transferring a year later to their army. Served in several campaigns before retiring in 1840 on health grounds and granted a baronetcy. British representative to China from 1841 and first Governor of Hong Kong 1843–4. Governor of Cape Colony 1846–7 and of Madras 1847–54.

16 Sir George Berkeley. 35th Regiment. Major-General 1837. Lieutenant-General 1846.

17 Major Henry D. Warden. Ensign in Cape Corps 1820. Lieutenant Cape Mounted Rifles 1825. Captain 1839. Major 1846. Retired 1849. Dismissed from his post in the Orange River Sovereignty by Sir Harry Smith with no pension. Died in poverty. Claimed to have been an illegitimate grandchild of Bonnie Prince Charlie.

18 The 3rd Earl Grey (1802–1894). Succeeded his father July 1845 and was Secretary for War and the Colonies 1846–52. He never served in another Cabinet and was a strong critic of the Crimean War.

19 Lieutenant-Colonel William Eyre. Commanding Officer of the 73rd Regiment. Promoted Major-General 1853. Commanded a brigade and later a division in the Crimea.

20 Lieutenant-Colonel George Mackinnon, Commandant of Kaffraria.

21 During the governorship of Sir Galbraith Lowry-Cole, 3,000 vagrant Hottentots were settled on the Kat River on land from which the Gaikas had been expelled. Hermanus was half Gaika and half Hottentot, and had been an interpreter for Harry Smith in his first campaign.

22   Sir Theophilus Shepstone (1817–1893), son of a missionary, the Reverend
      William Shepstone, who emigrated to the Cape in 1820. Gained fluency
      in native languages at his father's mission schools and became interpreter
      in Kaffir languages to the Governor of the Cape. In 1838 accompanied the
      expedition to Natal, where he became agent for the native tribes. In 1854
      he was appointed Secretary for Native Affairs, thereafter playing a
      prominent part in the affairs of Natal and relations with the Zulus. In
      1877 he led a small body of police into the Transvaal, declaring it British
      territory and being appointed its administrator. On the death of Cetewayo
      in 1884, he was declared Chief of the Zulus.

23   William King, *Campaigning in Kaffirland*, London 1855. Quoted in
      Fortescue, *History of the British Army*, Vol. XII p. 545.

24   Lieutenant-Colonel Courtenay Chambers, Edward Wellesley's uncle.

25   Sir George Napier's brothers were:
      Sir Charles Napier (1782–1863). Commissioned at the age of 12 into the
      33rd Regiment. In 1809 commanded the 50th at Corunna, receiving five
      wounds. Wounded again at Busaco in 1810, but does not appear to have
      lost an arm. Gained fame in India as the conqueror of Sind 1842–6.
      Sir William Napier (1785–1860). Commissioned at the age of 15 into the
      Royal Irish Artillery. After several changes of regiment, joined his
      brother George in the 52nd. Survived Corunna and several subsequent
      battles in the Peninsula until wounded in the head at Casal Novo in
      1811. Back in action with the 43rd, he was wounded again as Wellington
      crossed the Pyrenees in 1814. Best known for his *History of the
      Peninsular War*. Colonel 1830, Major-General 1841, Lieutenant-General
      1851.
      Captain Henry Napier, Royal Navy (1759–1853). Better known for his 26-
      volume history of Florence than for his naval career, in which he took part
      in the bombardment of Copenhagen.
      The Napiers, like the Wellesleys, were a family of the Protestant
      Ascendancy in Ireland. In the 1798 rebellion, their father, Colonel
      George, rallied his sons to help defend their house near Dublin.

26   Lady Emily Wellesley was the wife of the Reverend Gerald Wellesley,
      fourth of the Wellesley brothers. Born Lady Emily Cadogan, daughter of
      the 3rd Earl Cadogan, she ran away from her husband with one of her
      daughter's boy friends, the 21-year old Lord Walscourt. The fact that her
      husband did not take legal action for divorce was said to be the reason
      why, in spite of pressure from his two influential brothers, the Marquess
      and the Duke, Lord Liverpool refused to give him even an Irish bishopric.
      Her sister, the first wife of the youngest Wellesley brother, Henry, later
      Lord Cowley, ran away from him with Lord Henry Paget, later Marquess
      of Anglesey, Wellesley obtaining £24,000 in damages.

27   A writership usually referred to the appointment at the lowest level of an
      official in the service of the East India Company; but it was also used to

refer to the position of clerk in certain government departments. In this case, it was probably the former.

28 Lord R. and Lady W. probably refer to his grandfather the Marquess, who died in 1842, and his second wife. The Duke, of course, is the Duke of Wellington.

29 Montagu Chambers, his uncle. Another brother, Newton Chambers, was ADC to Lieutenant-General Sir Thomas Picton at Waterloo, where both he and the general were killed.

30 Lieutenant-Colonel Charles Jowett Vander Meulen, Commanding Officer of the 73rd Regiment.

31 Their eldest son, Arthur, a major in the 50th Regiment, was killed at the battle of Ferozeshah in India in December 1845, serving under Harry Smith's command.

32 Sir George Brown (1790–1865). Commissioned into the 43rd Regiment at the age of 16. Served at Copenhagen and in the Peninsula with them and in the 85th, with whom he also served under General Ross in America. Joined the staff of the Horse Guards as Assistant Adjutant-General in 1828 and served there continuously until 1853, promoted to Colonel in 1841 and appointed Adjutant-General by the Duke of Wellington in 1850. Lieutenant-General 1851. He resigned in December 1853, Lord Hardinge having become Commander-in-Chief after the Duke's death, a post Brown himself coveted. Commanded the Light Division in the Crimea, being wounded at Kertch and invalided home on the day that Lord Raglan died, 28 June 1855, being promoted General that year. Commander-in-Chief in Ireland 1860–5.

33 The Army List of the time gives the seniority of captains in the 73rd as:
W.R. Faunce 31 May 44
W.B.J. O'Connell 23 Sep 45
R.P. Campbell 24 Oct 45
P.B. Bicknell 3 Oct 47
E. Wellesley 26 May 48
H. Austen 17 Nov 48
W.E. Bewes 3 Aug 49
G. Renny 28 Dec 49
C. Harison 21 Mar 51
G.F. Burne 18 Apr 51

34 William Henry Colley Wellesley (1834–95), eldest son of the 2nd Lord Cowley (later 1st Earl Cowley). Coldstream Guards. Lieutenant 1852. Captain 1854. Succeeded his father as 2nd Earl Cowley 1884. See also letters 74, 85, 92 and 106.

35 Actually Lieutenant-General Sir John Macdonald. Adjutant General 1830-50.

36 The former Juana Maria de Los Dolores de Leon. At the siege of Badajoz in 1812, when she was 14, her elder sister, having rescued her from her

convent school, approached some British officers, one of whom was Harry Smith, and asked for their protection. Smith fell in love with her on the spot and obtained permission from the Duke of Wellington to marry her. She accompanied him in the field for the rest of the Peninsular War and ever thereafter.

37 Lieutenant Patrick Fletcher.

38 Major Frederick George Augustus Pinckney.

39 Major Robert Parker Campbell. Price-King does not appear among the officers of the 73rd in the Army List.

40 Her husband was the Regimental Paymaster.

41 Henry Robert Eardley-Wilmot, Royal Artillery. Commanded the guns supporting the 73rd.

42 Henry Laurence Maydwell, 41st Regiment.

43 Abraham Josias Cloëte (1794–1886). Son of a member of the Colony's Council. Commissioned into the 15th Hussars at the age of 13, transferring to the 21st Light Dragoons at the Cape in the same year. ADC to the Governor, Lord Charles Somerset. Having served with his regiment in India, he returned to the Cape in 1820 as Deputy Assistant Adjutant and Quartermaster General, responsible for supervising the occupation of the eastern district by settlers in that year. In 1840 he became DQMG, in reality Chief of Staff, and remained in that post until 1854, when he was knighted and promoted major-general. Commanded the troops in the West Indies 1855–61. Retired 1871 as a general.

44 Lieutenant Frederick Reeve.

45 2nd (Queen's) Regiment and 60th Rifles from England and the reserve battalion of the 12th from Mauritius.

46 Dr Bickersteth does not appear in the Army List as one of the military surgeons. He must have been a civilian medical practitioner.

47 The Reverend Dacre does not appear in the Army List as a chaplain.

48 Fingoes were former native inhabitants of Natal who were driven out by the Zulus and took refuge in the area of the River Kei, where the Xhosa called them 'dogs' and treated them as such. D'Urban declared them to be British subjects and planned to settle 17,000 of them west of the Kei.

49 Major William Hogg. Commissioned into the 7th Dragoon Guards 1837. Captain 1845. Major in the regiment 1845 and in the army 1848, when he changed his name to Hogge. Retired 1850.

50 Captain H. Wood Parish.

51 Hyacinthe. She was born on 5 October 1851. In later life she married William Dalby, who was knighted for his services as an ear, nose and throat surgeon. They had five children.

52 Lieutenant-Colonel William Bates Ingleby, Commander Royal Artillery in Cape Colony. Colonel 1854. Major-General 1860.

53 If, as it appears, this refers to the Eyres, it is a surprising comment. Elsewhere he often expresses his admiration for Colonel Eyre and his

gratitude for his kindness, quoting Eyre's favourable remarks about himself.

54   This could have been money inherited by their aunt, Lady Charles Bentinck, from her father the Marquess Wellesley, when he died in 1842, and which might have been left to their father, if he had not died in 1831. The Montagu referred to is presumably the solicitor.

55   Charles Fulke Greville (1794–1865), a cousin of the Bentincks. Clerk to the Privy Council 1821–59. Close friend of major political figures. Well known for his political diary, published after his death. The son was Lieutenant A.G. Greville, 60th Rifles.

56   The house was The Lodge, West Molesey. By 1854 his mother and sister were living at Bush(e)y Cottage, Hampton Court Green, which was not a Grace and Favour residence, but was probably under the jurisdiction of the Queen's equerry.

57   Lieutenant-Colonel George William Fordyce.

58   The *Birkenhead*, carrying drafts for nearly every regiment from Simonstown to Port Elizabeth, struck a rock off Danger Point and broke in two. Almost all in the fore part were drowned. Women and children were taken off in boats from the stern half before it sank, while the men stood calmly on deck. Five officers and 109 men survived by swimming ashore or clinging to driftwood; 14 officers and 349 men were drowned.

59   Lieutenant-Colonel Charles Francis Seymour, Scots Fusilier Guards. Accompanied General Cathcart in the same capacity to the Crimea, where he was killed beside him at the Battle of Inkerman.

60   Captain The Hon. Michael Curzon, Grenadier Guards.

61   Formed in February 1852, headed by the Earl of Derby, with Sir J. Pakington as Secretary for War and the Colonies. It only lasted until December, when it was replaced by one headed by the Earl of Aberdeen, in which Sir James Graham was First Lord of the Admiralty and the Duke of Newcastle Secretary for War and the Colonies.

62   Lieutenant-Colonel John Michel, 6th Regiment. Captain 1826. Major 1840. Lieutenant-Colonel 1842. Colonel 1854. Major-General 1856. Lieutenant-General 1866. General 1874. Commander Forces in Ireland 1875–80.

63   Captain Charles Woodford, The Rifle Brigade. Was to serve under Edward Wellesley as DAQMG on Lord Raglan's staff in 1854. See letters 60 and 110.

64   Cathcart's book was *Comments on the War in Russia and Germany in 1812 and 1813*, published in 1850.

65   Captain Richard Tylden (1819–55). Commissioned into the Royal Engineers 1837. 2nd Captain 1846. Major 1853. Brevet Lieutenant-Colonel 1854. Colonel 1855. Posted to the Cape 1848. Sent to survey the Amatolas with command of North Victoria district, where he raised a local force of burghers and Fingoes, which defeated Sandili. Brigade-Major to

his father, Brigadier-General W.B.Tylden, Commander Royal Engineers under Lord Raglan in Crimea. Severely wounded in command of the engineers in the attack on the Redan July 1855 and died on arrival in Malta in August.

66 Sir John Fortescue, in his *History of the British Army*, took a different view. He wrote (Vol. XII, p. 555): 'Most honourable to him of all, perhaps, was the fact that he accepted an invitation to dinner from Lord Grey himself, who had been driven from office at the fall of Lord John Russell's administration in February 1852. Harry Smith gave the Minister credit for having acted towards him from a sense of public duty only, and feeling no personal resentment against him, saw no ground for a quarrel. Lord Grey was far too great a gentleman not to appreciate what he justly styled "most handsome and honourable conduct", and the two men met as friends and parted with increase of mutual esteem. Of all Harry Smith's actions this, perhaps, is best worth remembering both by soldiers and statesmen.'

67 John Montagu. Colonial Secretary at the Cape, having previously held the same post in Tasmania.

68 Lord Charles Somerset, 2nd son of the 5th Duke of Beaufort and therefore an elder brother of Lord Fitzroy Somerset. Governor of Cape Colony 1814–27. Father of Major-General Henry Somerset.

69 The Reverend Cassalis of the Paris Evangelical Missionary Society was a close adviser to Moshesh.

70 The Duke died, aged 83, on 14 September 1852. Lord Wellesley had died, aged 82, ten years earlier.

71 His uncle, Colonel Courtenay Chambers, appears to have died some time between 1846 (see letter 6) and 1851 (see letter 17).

72 The half-caste Griqua were also known as Bastaards (sic).

73 The Doppers were a sect of Dutch Baptists with a strong following among the Boers.

74 Henry Hardinge, 1st Viscount Hardinge of Lahore (1785–1856). Commissioned into the Queen's Rangers of Canada at the age of 13. Purchased lieutenancy in the 4th Regiment 1802. Wounded under Wellington at Vimeiro and took part in the retreat to Corunna under Sir John Moore. Served on the staff of the Portuguese army under General Beresford in the Peninsula, thereafter transferring to the Grenadier Guards. British military commissioner with Field Marshal Blücher in the Waterloo campaign, losing his left hand at Ligny. Clerk to the Ordnance when Wellington was Master-General 1823–7. Secretary at War 1828–30 and 1841–4. Governor-General in India 1844–8. Thereafter Master-General of the Ordnance until the death of Wellington.

75 In January 1852 the Sand River Convention recognized that the Boers beyond the Vaal had the full right 'to manage their own affairs and to govern themselves' on condition that they did not allow slavery within

their territory. The Bloemfontein Convention two years later applied the same formula to the area between the Orange river and the Vaal, freeing them from allegiance to the British Crown.

76 Exeter Hall, in the Strand in London, a meeting place for Church of England groups, described as 'being popular with a certain form of enthusiastic Evangelicals.'

77 Included in Cathcart's despatch to the Duke of Newcastle, Secretary for War and Colonies, of 13 January 1853, reproduced in his *Correspondence* (p. 232).

78 Captain Walter Beresford Faunce, senior captain of the 73rd Regiment.

79 The war in Burma broke out in February 1852 and ended in December with the cession by the Court of Ava of the southern province of Pegu. 5,700 men of the Bengal and Madras armies, under Major-General Godwin, captured Rangoon in April and advanced almost unopposed up the Irawaddy to Prome. The campaign was followed by the so-called Subalterns' War (one of them being Lieutenant Garnet Wolseley of the 80th) against Burmese ex-soldiers known as *dacoits* under Myat Toon.

80 Sir Robert Peel (1822–95). Eldest son of the more famous Sir Robert. Succeeded his father on his death in 1850 as MP for Tamworth. Shipwrecked off Genoa in April 1854 and swam ashore. Chief Secretary in Ireland 1861–5, but did not hold office again.

81 Henry Pelham Clinton, 5th Duke of Newcastle (1811–64). MP for South Nottinghamshire 1832–46. Succeeded his father as Duke 1851. Secretary for War and Colonies from December 1852, remaining responsible for the former when control of the War Office was separated from that of the Colonial Office on 12 June 1854. Resigned 1855. Returned to the Colonial Office 1859–64.

82 Stratford Canning (1786–1880). Joined the Foreign Service in 1807, when his cousin, George Canning, was Foreign Secretary. Made his first visit to Turkey in 1808 as First Secretary to Sir Robert Adam's mission to establish peace between that country and Russia. He stayed there, becoming Minister Plenipotentiary 1810–12, when he moved to the same post in Switzerland. He returned to Turkey in 1824 and was thereafter initially concerned with negotiations arising out of the Greek struggle for independence until 1832. In 1841 he returned to Constantinople as Ambassador, remaining there until 1858, having been created Viscount Stratford de Redcliffe in 1852.

83 The Treaty of Kutchuk Kainardji was signed in 1774 between Russia and Turkey. In Article VII the Sublime Porte 'promises to protect the Christian religion and its churches' and 'also allows the Russian minister to make representations in regard to the new church at Constantinople'.

84 Omar Pasha (1806–71). Commander-in-Chief of the Turkish army in Bulgaria and the Crimea. A Croat, his original name was Michael Lattas. He deserted the Austrian army and became a Muslim on entering the

Ottoman service. Fought in Albania in 1843, Kurdistan in 1846 and Bosnia 1850–2. He was removed after his failure to relieve Kars in 1855, but re-employed in Montenegro in 1861 and Crete 1866–8, becoming Commander-in-Chief of the whole Turkish army in 1867.

85 A.W. Kinglake, *The Invasion of the Crimea*, London 1863. Vol. II, p. 107.

86 Armand Jacques Leroy de Saint Arnaud (1801–54). The son of a *préfet* of the First Empire. Enlisted in the *gardes du corps* of Louis XVIII in 1817, but left the army to fight in the Greek War of Independence 1827–31. In 1836 his debts forced him to join the Foreign Legion in Algeria under Bugeaud, where he gained fame fighting Abd el Krim. As Minister for War in 1852 he was instrumental in suppressing resistance to the *coup d'état* which elevated Louis Napoleon from President to Emperor, for which he was rewarded with a Marshal's baton. Died of cholera after the Battle of the Alma in the Crimea at the end of September 1854.

87 Field Marshal Prince Paskevich (1782–1856). Known as Erivanski, from his conquest of the province of Erivan in the Russo–Persian War of 1827.

88 Kinglake II, p. 108.

89 Ibid. pp. 120, 121.

90 Sir George Augustus Wetherall (1788–1868). Commissioned into the 7th Regiment as a Lieutenant at the age of 7 and joined the Nova Scotia Fencibles at the age of 15. He served on his father's staff at the Cape in 1809 and in Java in 1811. He filled various staff appointments in ascending ranks in India and Canada. Deputy Adjutant-General at the Horse Guards from 1850, promoted Major-General 1851, he became Adjutant-General on 1 December 1854. Lieutenant-General 1857. General 1863. Governor of the Military College at Sandhurst 1866 until his death at the age of 80 two years later.

91 Arthur Cavendish Bentinck, son of Lady Charles (see Note 94). Then a major in the 7th Dragoon Guards. Lieutenant-Colonel 1854. Colonel 1858. Major-General 1868. Father by his first wife, Elizabeth Hawkins-Whitshed, of the 6th Duke of Portland, and, by his second wife, Elizabeth Baroness Bolsover, of Lady Ottoline Morrell.

92 Richard Airey, later Lord Airey (1803–1881). Commissioned into the 84th Regiment at the age of 18. Purchasing his promotion step by step, he commanded his regiment in 1838 and shortly afterwards joined the staff of the Horse Guards as Deputy Adjutant-General, then Deputy Quartermaster-General and finally Military Secretary to Lord Hardinge, when he became Commander-in-Chief in 1852. Resigning that post in order to command a brigade in Bulgaria in 1854, he was appointed on arrival to replace Lord de Ros as Lord Raglan's Quartermaster-General [107]. When conditions in the Crimea came under severe criticism in 1855, Lord Raglan resisted strong press and political pressure to dismiss him; and he was retained by Raglan's successor, General Sir John Simpson. Quartermaster-General at the Horse Guards 1855–65.

Governor of Gibraltar 1865–70. Adjutant-General 1870–6. Major-General 1854. Lieutenant-General 1862. General 1871.

93   William Lennox Lascelles FitzGerald (1797–1891). Son of Lord Edward FitzGerald and Charlotte Baroness de Ros. Commissioned into the 1st Life Guards 1819. Lieutenant-Colonel 1831. Major-General 20 June 1854. Captain of the Yeoman of the Guard 1852 and Quartermaster-General of the Army in Turkey 1854. Deputy Lieutenant of the Tower of London 1860. Lieutenant-General 1861. General 1868.

94   Lady Charles Bentinck (1788–1878), formerly Anne Wellesley, daughter of The Marquess. Ran away from her first husband, Sir William Abdy, with Lord Charles Bentinck, third son of the 3rd Duke of Portland, whom she married as his second wife in 1816.

95   George William Frederick Charles, 2nd Duke of Cambridge (1819–1904). Only son of the first Duke, who was the youngest son of George III. He was therefore a first cousin of Queen Victoria. Came to England from Hanover when she ascended the throne in 1837 and was made a brevet colonel in the British army, attached to the 33rd Regiment and then the 12th Lancers. Commanded the troops in Corfu as a Colonel 1843–5. Promoted Major-General in that year and appointed Commander Dublin District 1847–52. Thereafter he was Inspector-General of Cavalry until being appointed to command the 1st Division under Raglan, being promoted Lieutenant-General on 19 June 1854. Invalided home in December 1854 and replaced Lord Hardinge as Commander-in-Chief at the Horse Guards, being promoted General, on 15 July 1855. He held the post for 40 years, reluctantly handing it over to Lord Wolseley in 1895. Field Marshal 1862.

96   Lord Grey proposed that the separation between the Horse Guards and the Ordnance should be brought to an end, and that the administration of the army should be united under the control of the War Office. Lord Raglan, as Master-General of the Ordnance, strongly opposed it.

97   Lady Cowley (Olivia Cecilia) was the sister of Lord de Ros. Lord Cowley (1804–84), the eldest son of Henry Wellesley, 1st Lord Cowley, started his diplomatic career as attaché to his father, the Ambassador at Vienna. After a number of diplomatic appointments, in 1852 he became Ambassador in Paris, a post held by his father 1841–6. He remained in the post until 1867, having been created Earl Cowley in 1857.

98   The Grand Duchess, widow of Charles Louis Frederick, Grand Duke of Baden, was formerly Stephanie de Beauharnais, daughter of Count Claude de Beauharnais, whose first cousin, Vicomte Alexandre de Beauharnais, was the first husband of the Empress Josephine and father, by her, of Hortense, wife of Louis Bonaparte, King of Holland, and mother of Napoleon III.

99   The Duchess of Hamilton, Princess Marie Amélie of Baden, was the daughter of the Grand Duchess.

100 A Galignani appears to have been some sort of newsletter.

101 Anne Cavendish Bentinck, daughter of Lady Charles (Note 94). She never married.

102 Arthur Richard Wellesley, 2nd Duke. The Duchess was formerly Lady Elizabeth Hay, daughter of the 8th Marquess of Tweeddale. They had no children.

103 William Alexander Anthony Archibald Douglas, 11th Duke of Hamilton (1811–63). Succeeded his father in 1852. Married Princess Marie of Baden in 1843 and lived thereafter principally in Paris and Baden.

104 Viscount Wellesley, son of 'Wicked William' (See Note 2), 4th Earl of Mornington. He became the 5th Earl on the death of his father in 1857 and died unmarried in Paris in 1863.

105 Henry Wellesley. See Note 34.

106 James Howard Harris, 3rd Earl of Malmesbury (1807–89). When travelling in Italy in 1827, made the acquaintance of Queen Hortense and her son, the future Napoleon III, with whom he formed a lasting friendship. Succeeded his father as Earl in 1841. Foreign Secretary in Lord Derby's two Cabinets from February to December 1852 and February 1858 to February 1859. Lord Privy Seal 1866–76. He was therefore out of office on this occasion.

107 The Right Hon. Edmund Hammond. Foreign Office Clerk from 1824. Attached to Sir Stratford Canning's Special Mission to Turkey 1831. Under-Secretary of State for Foreign Affairs 1854. Retired 1873. Created Baron Hammond 1874. Died 1890.

108 John Bidwell. Foreign Office Clerk from 1798. Superintendent of the Consular Service 1821–51. Died 31 October 1853. There is no record of Cunningham.

109 Edward Boxer (1784–1855). Entered Royal Navy as an able seaman 1798 and soon promoted to midshipman. Saw service in various ships 1801–15. Captain 1823. Inspecting Commander in the Coast Guard 1824. Flag Captain Halifax 1827–30. Commanded HMS *Pique 36* 1837–41. Harbour-Master Quebec 1843–53. Rear-Admiral March 1853. Admiral Superintendent Bosphorus 7 April 1854 and Balaclava 18 December 1854 until his death of cholera on board HMS *Jason* 4 June 1855.

110 James Bucknall Bucknall Estcourt (1803–55). Commissioned into the 44th Regiment 1820. Transferred to 43rd as lieutenant 1824. Captain 1825. 2nd in Command to Colonel Chesney in the Euphrates expedition 1836, when promoted Major. Brevet Lieutenant-Colonel 1839. Half-pay 1843–54 and MP for Denbigh. The Crimea was his first experience of active operations. Brigadier-General February 1854. Major-General 12 December 1854. He came under the same criticism in 1855 as did Major-General Airey. Died of cholera 24 June 1855, a few days before Lord Raglan.

111 Better known to-day as the temple of Poseidon at Sounion.

112 John Hackett, 77th Regiment.

113 George Charles Bingham, 3rd Earl of Lucan (1800–88). Commissioned into the 6th Regiment 1816. Transferred to several other regiments and spent some time on half-pay before commanding the 17th Lancers 1826–37, after which he devoted himself mainly to his Irish estates. Colonel 1841. Major-General 1851. Applied for a brigade in Raglan's force, but was given command of the Cavalry Division. Famous for his altercation at Balaclava with Lord Cardigan, his brother-in-law. Not further employed after he left the Crimea in March 1855, but promoted Lieutenant-General 1858. General 1865. Field Marshal 1887.

114 Major-General William Cator (1785–1866). Commissioned into the Royal Artillery 1803. Served with the Royal Horse Artillery as 2nd Captain in the Walcheran expedition 1809, where he formed a close friendship with Lord Fitzroy Somerset. In Peninsular War was wounded at Barosa and took part in various battles in the later stages of the campaign. 1st Captain 1825 in command of the Chestnut Troop. Brevet Lieutenant-Colonel 1830. Colonel 1846. Director-General of Artillery 1852, which post he retained when appointed to command the Royal Artillery of the Army in Turkey with the rank of Brigadier-General. His health gave way at Varna in August 1854, when he returned to his post of Director-General, from which he retired in 1858. Major-General 1854. Lieutenant-General 1859. General 1866.

115 *The Times* correspondent was the famous William Howard Russell, who was to prove a very sharp thorn in Lord Raglan's side.

116 Brevet Major George Mundy appears to have been a relation of Edward Wellesley's mother. In the letter of condolence [112] to her from her aunt Miss Rodney, he is referred to as the aunt's nephew. It is perhaps more likely that he was her great-nephew and therefore a first cousin of Edward's mother.

117 Captain Henry Wells Giffard. Born 1810, joined Royal Navy 1824. Midshipman at Battle of Navarino 1827. Commander 1838. Captain 1841, when commanding HMS *Cruiser* on China station. 1852 assumed command of HMS *Tiger*, a paddle-wheel frigate. On 11 May 1854, in company with two other steamers, *Tiger* was detached from the main fleet to cover Odessa. She ran aground in fog close under a cliff, from which Russian artillery, to which she could not reply, poured shot and shell into her, setting the ship on fire. Captain Giffard, severely wounded, having lost a leg, ordered surrender. He and his crew were well treated by the Russians, but Giffard died on 1 June, and was buried at Odessa with full honours. A barometer from the ship is still in the naval museum there and one of its guns stands at the top of the great flight of steps, leading up from the harbour, which features in the famous film *Battleship Potemkin*.

118 James Thomas Brudenell, 7th Earl of Cardigan (1797–1868). Purchased a cornetcy in the 8th Hussars 1824 and further promotion to Lieutenant-

Colonel by 1830, transferring to command the 15th Hussars 1832 and the 11th Hussars 1836, gaining notoriety for a number of incidents involving his relations with his subordinates. Major-General 1847. Famous for his part in the charge of the Light Brigade at Balaclava. Inspector of Cavalry 1855–60. Lieutenant-General 1861.

119 William Brodie. Attaché Stockholm 1853, Constantinople 1853–9, Washington 1860, Rio de Janeiro 1862. 2nd Secretary 1862–3.

120 Rear-Admiral Sir Edmund Lyons (1790–1858). Entered the Royal Navy and saw service in various ships throughout the Napoleonic wars. Commander 1812. Captain 1814, but did not go to sea again until 1828, when he was involved in the actions connected with the Greek War of Independence. Minister Plenipotentiary at Athens 1835–49, and subsequently to Switzerland and Sweden. Rear-Admiral 1850. 2nd in Command of the Mediterranean Fleet 1853, succeeding Admiral Dundas as Commander-in-Chief January 1855. Created Baron Lyons 1856.

121 Prince Napoleon (1822–91). Second Son of Prince Jerome Bonaparte, nicknamed Plon-Plon and well known for his support of popular democratic ideas. Elected representative for Corsica after the 1848 revolution. On the establishment of the Second Empire, he was nominated successor to Napoleon III, as the latter had no children. When the latter's son, the Prince Imperial, was killed serving with the British in the Zulu War in 1879, he resumed his position as claimant to the Napoleonic succession.

122 George Chetwode. Lieutenant 8th (King's Royal Irish) Light Dragoons 1847. Captain 1854. Major 1856. Retired by sale of his rank of Lieutenant-Colonel 1861.

123 William Filder, CB.

124 Richard Charles Mellish. Joined the Foreign Office 1824. At the embassy in Constantinople 1828–30. Gentleman Usher to Queen Adelaide 1834–49. Retired 1 January 1855.

125 Lieutenant-Colonel Charles Carson Alexander (1793–1854). Commissioned into the Royal Engineers 1813. 2nd Captain 1831. Captain 1840. Major 1846. Lieutenant-Colonel 1848. Exhumed Napoleon's body at St Helena 1842. Succeeded Brigadier-General W.B. Tylden (see note 65) as Commander Royal Engineers in the Crimea when the latter died 22 September 1854, dying himself a month later.

126 Major (local Colonel) Theodore Francis Broughton Beatson. Major in Her Majesty's Indian Forces 20 June 1854. Raised a force of 4,000 irregular Turkish cavalry in spite of the opposition of Lord Raglan, which was overridden by the Duke of Newcastle. Retired 1860.

127 Vice-Admiral Sir James Whitley Dundas (1785–1862). Entered the Royal Navy 1799. Commander 1806. Changed his surname from Deans to Dundas 1808 on marrying his cousin Jane, only child and heiress of Charles Dundas, Lord Amesbury. Captain of HMS *Tagus* 1815–19. Rear-

Admiral 1841. Commander-in-Chief Mediterranean 1852–5. Vice-Admiral 1852. Admiral 1857.

128 Pierre Joseph François Bosquet (1810–61). Served under Generals Bugeaud and St Arnaud in Algeria. Commanded the French 2nd Division in the Crimea and was severely wounded at the Malakov June 1855. Best known for his comment on the charge of the Light Brigade at Balaclava: 'C'est magnifique, mais ce n'est pas la guerre'. Marshal 1856.

129 François Certain Canrobert (1809–95). Made his name in Algeria. ADC to Louis Napoleon 1850. Succeeded St Arnaud in command of the French in the Crimea and promoted Marshal. Resigned May 1855 as the result of a disagreement with Lord Raglan, handing over to General Pelissier.

130 Actually Colonel Louis Jules Trochu. Officially St Arnaud's senior ADC, but appears to have acted as Military Assistant or *Chef du Cabinet*. Later commanded a brigade in the Crimea. As a General commanded a division in the Franco–Austrian War of 1859. Forced to retire on publication of a book in 1867 revealing weaknesses in the French army. Headed Government of National Defence in besieged Paris after defeat at Sedan in 1870, resigning when Prussians opened bombardment of Paris January 1871.

131 Lieutenant-General Sir George de Lacy Evans (1787–1870). Commissioned into the 22nd Regiment in India 1806 and took part in the capture of Mauritius. Transferred to the 3rd Dragoons and joined them in the Peninsula 1812. Served under General Ross in America, returning to join General Picton's staff at Waterloo, gaining brevet promotion to Major and Lieutenant-Colonel. On half-pay as Captain 1818–31 while a MP. 1835–7 commanded the British Legion fighting for the Queen of Spain against the Carlists, later returning to Parliament. Major-General 1846. Promoted to Lieutenant-General and appointed to command of the 2nd Division in the army sent to Turkey 1854. Severely wounded at the Battle of The Alma. Returned to England after Inkerman, resuming his parliamentary career.

132 Lieutenant-Colonel Willoughby Moore. Commissioned into 3rd Light Dragoons, transferring to 6th Inniskilling Dragoons as Captain 1828. Major 1840. Lieutenant-Colonel 1843. Embarked with the headquarters of his regiment in the *Europa* May 1854. On the night of 31 May, 200 miles out of Plymouth, the ship caught fire. Moore remained on board seeing to the safety of his men, but was driven by the fire into the mizzen chains, where he perished. Veterinary Surgeon Kelly, 4 Sergeants, 12 men and 1 woman also died, as did all the horses.

133 Captain Butler was from the Ceylon Rifles and Captain Nasmyth from the Indian Artillery. They had formed part of a locally raised force, led by British officers, under General Cannon.

134 The Inspector-General of the Medical Services in Raglan's command was

Dr John Hall, but he may have been left at Scutari. The Principal Medical Officer at Varna may have been Dr Duncan Menzies, Surgeon 1st Class.

135 Major Francis Fane, Viscount Burghersh, was one of Raglan's ADCs and his nephew. His mother, the Countess of Westmorland, was a sister of Lady Raglan. Burghersh was therefore a second cousin of Edward Wellesley. Shown in the Army List as unattached.

136 After the Battle of The Alma, north of Sebastopol, the Franco-British force marched right round to the south of the fortress, the British then basing themselves on the small harbour of Balaclava.

137 An araba was a local form of wheeled carriage.

138 There is no George Rodney shown in the 33rd Regiment in the Army List. The previous references seem to be to George Mundy (see note 116). Either she has written 'Rodney' for 'Mundy' by mistake or she had another nephew of that name in the Crimea.

Bibliography

(books published in London unless noted otherwise)

Butler, Iris, *The Eldest Brother*, (Hodder & Stoughton, 1973).

Cathcart, Sir George, *Correspondence*, (Murray, 1857).

Fortescue, Sir John, *A History of the British Army*, Vols XII (1927) and XIII (1930), (Macmillan).

Godlonton, R. and Irving, Edward, *Narrative of the Kaffir War 1850–51*, Grahamstown & London (Pelham Richards, 1851).

King, William, *Campaigning in Kaffirland*, (1855).

Kinglake, A.W., *The Invasion of the Crimea*, Vols. I & II, Edinburgh & London (Blackwood, 1863).

Lehmann, Joseph., *Remember You Are An Englishman*, (Jonathan Cape, 1977).

Oatts, L.B., *Proud Heritage: The Story of the Highland Infantry*, Vol. II, (Nelson, 1959).

Russell, W.H.E., *The British Expedition to the Crimea*, (Routledge, 1858).

Smithers, A.J., *The Kaffir Wars 1779–1877*, (Leo Cooper, 1973).

Stewart, P.F., *History of the 12th Lancers*, Oxford (Oxford University Press, 1950).

Sweetman, John, *Raglan*, (Arms & Armour, 1993).

Woodward, Sir Llewellyn, *The Age of Reform 1815–1870*, Oxford (Clarendon, 1962).

Index

ARMY RECORDS SOCIETY
(FOUNDED 1984)

Members of the Society are entitled to purchase back
volumes at reduced prices.
Orders should be sent to the Hon. Treasurer, Army Records Society,
c/o National Army Museum,
Royal Hospital Road,
London SW3 4HT

The Society has already issued:

Vol. I:
The Military Correspondence of
Field Marshal Sir Henry Wilson 1918–1922
Edited by Dr Keith Jeffery

Vol. II:
The Army and the
Curragh Incident, 1914
Edited by Dr Ian F.W. Beckett

Vol. III:
The Napoleonic War Journal of
Captain Thomas Henry Browne, 1807–1816
Edited by Roger Norman Buckley

Vol. IV.
An Eighteenth-Century Secretary at War
The Papers of William, Viscount Barrington
Edited by Dr Tony Hayter

Vol. V:
The Military Correspondence of
Field Marshal Sir William Robertson 1915–1918
Edited by David R. Woodward

Vol. VI:
Colonel Samuel Bagshawe and the
Army of George II, 1731–1762
Edited by Dr Alan J. Guy